The Feminine Monarchy: Or The History Of Bees

Charles Butler

In the interest of creating a more extensive selection of rare historical book reprints, we have chosen to reproduce this title even though it may possibly have occasional imperfections such as missing and blurred pages, missing text, poor pictures, markings, dark backgrounds and other reproduction issues beyond our control. Because this work is culturally important, we have made it available as a part of our commitment to protecting, preserving and promoting the world's literature. Thank you for your understanding.

THE
Feminine Monarchie:
OR
THE HISTORIE OF BEES.

SHEWING

Their admirable Nature, and Properties,
Their Generation, and Colonies,
Their Gouernment, Loyaltie, Art, Industrie,
Enemies, Warres, Magnanimitie, &c.

TOGETHER
With the right ordering of them from time to
time: And the *sweet* profit arising thereof.

Written out of Experience
By
CHARLES BVTLER. *Magd:*

Plaut: in Trucul: Act: 2. Sc. 6.
Pluris est oculatus testis unus, quam auriti decem.

LONDON,
Printed by IOHN HAVILAND for Roger Iackson,
and are to be sold at his Shop in Fleetstreet, ouer
against the Conduit. 1 6 2 3.

THE PREFACE
TO THE Reader.

HE great Naturalist, to expresse the excellency of the nature of Bees, saith thus, *Inter omnia insecta principatus Apibus, & iure præcipua admiratio; solis ex eo genere hominum causa genitis.* Of all *insecta* the Bees are chiefe, and worthily to be most admired; being the only things of that kinde, which are bred for the behoofe of men. The later part of which saying, although the delicate Silk-worme haue in some hoter Climates disproued; (for in the colder countries, such as is our Iland of *Britaine*, I doubt mee shee will neuer quit cost: and therefore is here to be entertained only of them, that doe more respect their pleasure, than their profit; and doe content themselues with the beholding of their queint worke, not expecting any further recompence for their expence and paines;) yet must she needs confesse the former, and wheresoeuer she meet the ingenious and laborious Bee, yeeld the precedence to her, as to hir Better. For the fruit of the Silk-worme serueth only to couer the body; but the fruit of the Bees to nourish and cure it: that is to be applied outwardly, this to be inwardly receiued: that for comlinesse and conueniency, this for health and necessity. But, to omit comparison, the worke and fruit of the little Bee is so great and wonderfull, so comely for order and

Plin. Nat. hist. l. 11, c. 4. 5.

¶ 3   beauty,

The Preface to the Reader.

beauty, so excellent for Art and wisdome, & so full of pleasure and profit; that the contemplation thereof may well beseeme an ingenious nature. And therefore (not without cause) are the Bees called the Muses Birds: *Apes cum causa Musarum esse dicuntur volucres.* [Var.l.3.c.15.]

The loue of which did so rauish *Aristomachus* and *Philiscus*, that, as *Plinie* reporteth, they were pleased to spend most of their time in this pleasing businesse. *Ne quis* (saith he) *miretur amore earum captos Aristomachum Solensem duodesexaginta annis nihil aliud egisse; Philiscum vero Thasium in desertis apes colentem Agrium cognominatum: qui ambo scripsere de his.* [Nat.Hist. l.11.c.9.] *Aristotle* thought his *Historia animalium* vnperfect, vnlesse he had inserted a Tract of the Nature of Bees: of which he discourseth more at large, than he doth of any other liuing creature. *Plinie* likewise, in his *Naturalis historia*, is very copious in this argument. Besides whom, diuers other haue written thereof: as *Columella*, *Varro*, *Palladius*, *Averroes*. Yea the learned & graue Fathers of the Church, *S. Ambrose*, and *Isidore* haue thought it a subiect fit for their penns. Vnto which I may adde infinite others of later times, both in Latine and English.

But the many yeeres experiments & obseruations, which those great Bee-masters *Aristom.* and *Philiscus* had leaft in writing to posterity; Time, ah iniurious Time, hath buried in obliuion. And for the rest that are extant, they seeme vnto me to rely more vpon the relation of others, than any certaine knowledge of their owne. Notwithstanding there are scattered in them, specially in *Aristotle* & *Plinie*, among many false and friuolous conceits, some true and profitable notes: which being found agreeable to experience, I haue here and there in this Treatise, as the matter requireth, for ornament and authoritie inserted. But the later Writers, imitating the ancient where they thought good, chusing some of their directions, and refusing o-

The Preface to the Reader.

thers, doe, for the most part, vnluckily light vpon the worse: so that, being compared, they are no way matchable vnto them; whom by the aduantage of time they might haue surpassed. Among which *Georgius Pictorius* a learned Physician deserueth best, as hauing taken most paines in perusing the ancient Authors, and gathering their matter into his method. Whom one *T. H.* of *London* translating word for word into English, as well as he could, concealing the Authors name, aduentured to publish in his owne name. These and the like when a Scholar hath throughly read, hee thinketh himselfe throughly instructed in these mysteries: but when he commeth abroad to put his reading in practise, euery silly woman is ready to deride his learned ignorance.

Wherefore considering how great the vertue and efficacie of the fruit of Bees is, both for the preseruing, and restoring of mans health, I thought it not amisse to spend some by-time for my recreation, in searching out their nature and properties, their helpes and hinderances, that I might know how to doe good vnto them, which are so good for vs, and what is the due and right ordering of these delightfull, profitable, and necessary creatures. And hauing to my contentment, though to my cost, in some sort obtained my desire, I was incited, euen by the rule of charitie, to communicate that to my neighbours and country-men, which I haue since found so beneficiall to my selfe: so that the Reader may now freely reape the fruit of that, which the Author hath deerely sowen vnto him. *V.c.10,p.3.*

The Philosopher intreating of the breeding of Bees, professeth himselfe vncertaine of their sex: and therefore, willing in this vncertaintie to grace so worthy a creature with the worthier title, he euery where calleth their gouernour *Βασιλεὺς, Rex*. As many as followed him, searching no farther than he did, were content to say as he said. So that I am inforced *De generat. an.l.3.c.10.*

The Preface to the Reader.

forced (vnlesse I will chuse rather to offend in *rebus*, than in *vocibus*) by their leaue and thine (learned Reader) to straine the ordinarie signification of the word *Rex*, and, in such places, to translate it *Queene*, (sith the males heere beare no sway at all, this being an *Amazonian* or *feminine* kingdome. *v.*

V.c.4.n.11.

In distinguishing the times of the yeere, I vse the Astronomicall months, as most naturall and fitting to my purpose. *v.* Where note that by the name of each moneth, is commonly vnderstood the first day of the same moneth, (namely, wheresoeuer this preposition *At*, is set before it) except onely where it followeth, *In*, or *After*, or otherwise the sense doth plainly shew that it is spoken of the whole Moneth.

V.c.3.n.36.

When you haue once, for your satisfaction, perused this Booke, you need not afterward seeke farre for any thing therein, whereof you doubt: the *Index* of the Chapters or Contents of the Booke; and of the Marginall notes, or Contents of the Chapters will readily direct you. For example, if you would know the Spleeting of Hiues, or the manner of Hiuing Bees; looking into the *Index* of the Chapters, you shall perceiue the one to appertaine to the Third, and the other to the Fifth; and running ouer the Contents of either Chapter, you shall finde the first to be the Tenth note, and the other the 53. Then turning to these Marginall Notes in the said Chapters, you haue in the Text ouer against them your desire.

Note also, that whereas you haue in the Margin, with these Marginall Notes, certaine References vnto other places of the Booke, for further explanation of those places against which they stand; *V.* signifieth *vide*, or *See*, *C.* with his number the Chapter, and *N.* with his number the Marginall Note. But if *N.* follow *V.* without *C*; then doth it note some Note of the same Chapter.

I am

The Preface to the Reader.

I am out of doubt that this Booke of *Bees* will in his Infancie lie hidden in obscuritie, as the Booke of *Tropes* and *Figures* did for a while goe vnregarded, without friends or acquaintance: but as that did by little and little insinuate it selfe into the loue and liking of many Schooles, yea of the Vniuersitie it selfe, where it hath beene both priuately and publikely read; (a fauour, which this Mother doth seldome afford to hir owne Children, left haply she should seeme too fond ouer them:) so this will in time trauell into the most remote parts of this great kingdome of Great *Britaine*, and be entertained of all sorts both learned and vnlearned: although the *Muses Birds* are fittest for the *Muses*, and the knowledge of their long-hidden secrets was chiefly published for the *Muses* friends. *Quibus me, quicquid sum, & studia mea dico. Wotton. May* 30. 1623.

CHAR: BVTLER.

A   Ad

Ad Authorem.

Va natura Apibus, quæ membra, scientia, sensus,
  Virtutes, ætas, ingenium, pietas,
 Quæ statio, & sedes, soboles, examina, tecta,
  His hæc tradendi prompta ubiq; modus;
Quæ princeps, populus, regimen, respublica, mores,
  Qua sint arma, hostes, prælia, castra, duces,
Quam celeri campos gressu, sylvasq; peragrant,
  Qua cellas fingunt arte, labore replent,
Quam prosint hominum generi cœlestia dona,
  Utque magis prosint quo moderanda modo;
Per te miranda hæc levium spectacula rerum
  Mystica tot seclis clausa reclusa patent.

Aut a consilijs Apibus, Butlere, fuisti,
Aut a consilijs est Apis ipsa tuis.

WHen I had view'd this Common-wealth of *Bees,*
  Obseru'd their *Liues,* their *Art,* and their *Degrees*:
As ; how, beside their painefull *Vulgar ones,*
They haue their *Prince,* their *Captaines,* and their *Drones* :
How they *Agree* ; how temp'ratly they *Feed* ;
How curiously they *Build* ; how chastly *Breed*;
How seriously their *Bus'nesse* they intend ;
How stoutly they their *Common-good* defend ;

                                         How.

How timely their *Prouisions* are prouided;
How orderly their *Labors* are diuided;
What *Vertues* patterns, and what grounds of *Art*,
What *Pleasures*, and what *Profits* they impart:
When these, with all those other things I minde
Which in this *Booke*, concerning *Bees*, I finde:
Me thinkes, there is not halfe that worth in *Mee*,
Which I haue apprehended in a *Bee*;
And that the *Pismere*, and these *Hony-flies*,
Instruct vs better to Philosophize,
Than all those tedious *Volumes*, which, as yet,
Are leaft vnto vs by meere *Humane-wit*.
For, whereas those but only *Rules* doe giue;
These by *Examples* teach vs how to liue.

 Great *God Almighty*! in thy pretty *Bee*,
Mine Eie (as written in small letters) sees
An *Abstract* of that Wisdome, Power, and Loue,
Which is imprinted on the *Heau'ns* about
In larger *Volumes*, for their eies to see,
That in such *little prints* behold not Thee.
And in this Workmanship (oh Lord) of thine,
I praise thy *wisdome*, and thy *Power* diuine.

 And *Praise* deserues this *Author*; who hath chose
So well his Times of Leisure to dispose;
And in that *Recreation* to delight,
Which honour *God*, and vs aduantage might.
For, since our humane weakenesse doth require,
That in our serioust *Labours* we retire;
(Because vnlesse the String be sometime slacke
The strongest Bow will haue the feeblest backe)
What *Recreation* better can befit
Our graue *Diuines*; than (when the *Holy writ*
Is laid aside) in *Gods* great booke of *Creatures*
To reade his *Wisdome*, and their vsefull *Natures*?

 Thus doth our *Author*. And, not only thus;
But, like his *Bees*, makes hony too for vs.
And is contented that, to helpe vs thriue,
We should partake the profit of his *Hiue*.

A 2   For

For which (*my sbath*) I thanke him : and for those,
The *Muses-Birds*; whose nature here he showes,
And mauger such as will his *Paines* contemne,
The *Muses* thus, by me, doe honour them.

GEORGE WITHER.

Ad Carolum Butler.

Ante melè chartis promisisti, ut Rhetor, apinum,
   At nunc mellitè promis, ut Histor, apes.
Incipis ex apibus, sed & in mel desinis ipsum :
   Suaviter incœptum suavius exit opus.

WARNERVS SOVTH.

The Chapters, or the Contents of *this* BOOKE.

MY Booke of Bees I divide into ten Chapters.
1 The first, of the nature and properties of Bees, and of their Queen.
2 The second, of the Bee-garden, and Seats for the Hiues.
3 The third, of the Hiues, and the Dressing of them.
4 The fourth, of the Breeding of Bees, and of the Drone.
5 The fift, of their Swarming, and the Hiuing of them.
6 The sixt, of their Worke.
7 The seuenth, of their Enemies.
8 The eighth, of Feeding them.
9 The ninth, of Remouing them.
10 The tenth, of the Fruit and Profit of them.

The Notes or the Contents of the first Chapter, concerning the nature and properties of Bees.

1 BEes yeeld great profit with small cost.
2 Euery country fit for Bees.
3 Bees abhorre idlenesse.
4 Bees haue a Common-wealth.
5 Their working, watching, fighting, dwelling, diet, wealth, and young ones are all in common.
6 Bees alwaies loyall to their Soueraigne.
7 Bees endure no gouernment, but a Monarchie.
8 A memorable experiment.
9 The description of the Queene-Bee.
10 Bees haue also inferiour Gouernours or Captaines.
11 Which are knowne by peculiar markes.
12 Two sorts of Bees.
13 The parts of a Bee.
14 Hir hornes.
15 Hir eyes.
16 Hir fangs.
17 Hir tongue, with the parts of it.
18 Hir foure wings.
19 Hir feet.
20 Hir two weapons.
21 Hir fangs commonly vsed against insecta.
22 Hir speere sometime.
23 Stinging present death to Bees.
24 The speares commonly vsed against other creatures.
25 Haire and feathers cause the Bees to sting.
26 Wooll and woollen do not offend them.
27 Fustian, Leather, and Veluet naught among Bees.
28 The Bees in their anger aime at the head.
29 When any is stung, the company must be gone.
30 The Bees haue the worst, when they sting.
31 They lose their sting and entrals, and consequently their liues.
32 The speere, of it selfe, pierceth deepe when

when the Bee is gone.
33 How to prevent the paine & swelling.
34 Nothing but Time can cure their stinging.
35 What things the Bee-master must avoid.
36 The six properties of a Bee-master.
37 Safer to walke then to stand among Bees.
38 The fittest time to stirre about Bees.
39 In the heat of the day they are most angry.
40 How to be armed when the Bees are angry.
41 Bees dangerous to Cattell.
42 The Bees Senses.
43 Their sight dimme.
44 Their smelling very quicke.
45 Hearing and feeling.
46 Tasting.
47 Their Vertues.
48 Fortitude.
49 Prudence and knowledge.
50 A strange tale concerning the knowledge and devotion of Bees.
51 Temperance.
52 Iustice.
53 Chastity.
54 Cleanlinesse.
55 The age of Bees.
56 The difference betweene the young Bees and old.
57 The office of the young Bees.
58 And of the old.
59 Bees want eftsoones to play.
60 They are soone kild with cold.
61 How to revive them.
62 The Bees excellencies.
63 Bees a chiefe exemplar of the divine power and wisdome.

The Contents of the second Chapter, concerning the Beegarden, with Seats for the hiues.

1 Of fiue things requisite in a Bee-garden, the first is, that it be nigh at hand.
2 That it be safely fenced from cattell and winds.
3 The north & east fences should be high.
4 The South and West fence must be also good, but not so high as to hide the Sunne from the Hiues.
5 In rough winds the Bees need a skreene.
6 That it be sweet.
7 Neither very cold in winter, nor hot in Summer.
8 A grassie ground is best, but kept notte and dry.
9 Beset with trees and bushes.
10 Two sorts of Seats.
11 The benches not so good as single stooles
12 Swarmes may be set on Benches.
13 Woodden Stooles better than they of stone.
14 The size of stooles.
15 Which way the stooles should be set.
16 How neere to each other.
17 How neere to the fences.
18 Annus climactericus.
19 The Bees Register.
20 The stooles height.
21 How to be footed.

The Contents of the third Chapter, concerning the Hiues, and the Dressing of them, both before and after Hiuing.

1 Two sorts of Hiues.
2 Strawne Hiues with their inconueniencies and remedies.
3 Wicker Hiues with their inconueniencies and remedies.
4 Strawne Hiues best.
5 The fashion of Hiues.
6 The size of Hiues.
7 When Hiues are to be made & provided.
8 How Hiues are to be dressed before they receive the swarmes.
9 The pitching of Hiues.
10 The spraying or sleeting of them.
11 The making of the Cop, and of the Spleets.
12 The seasoning of them.
13 The seasoning of an old Hiue.
14 How Hiues are to be ordered when the Bees are in them.

15 The

15 The Hiues alwaies well hackled.
16 How to make a Hackle.
17 The Cap of two sorts.
18 The wreathed Cap.
19 The platted Cap.
20 The bignesse of the Hackle.
21 The length of it.
22 The Belt or garth.
23 The hackle never then to be taken off.
24 The Hiues alwaies close cloomed.
25 Then seldome to be moued.
26 How a Hiue lifted vp is to bee set downe againe.
27 The Hiue-doore.
28 The Gate or Summer-doore.
29 Of the doore posts and the vse of them.
30 The Winter-doore, or Wisket.
31 The vse of it.
32 The Barre.
33 The vse of it.
34 The Settle.
35 How to order the Bee-hiues throughout the yeere.
36 The Moneths and Quarters of the Melissa-an yeere.
37 SVMMER.
38 In GEMINI set the Doores wide open.
39 CANCER.
40 To make the Bees swarme.
41 To keepe them from swarming.
42 LEO.
43 How and when to kill the Drones.
44 HARVEST.
45 VIRGO.
46 To keepe the weaker Hiues from robbing.
47 Set vp the Winter-doores.
48 And keepe them shut till they offer to goe abroad.
49 The reared stalls now to be set downe againe.
50 In Virgo try whether the Bees will liue.
51 Now take the Combes.
52 LIBRA.
53 Try them againe in Libra also.
54 Now set vp the Wickets to the best, &

keepe the rest shut till the Bees offer to goe abroad.
55 SCORPIO.
56 Continue the shutting and opening of the Wickets this moneth also.
57 How to dresse the Hiues for Winter.
58 WINTER.
59 SAGIT. CAPRIC. AQVAR. three still moneths.
60 How the Bees spend their time in them.
61 The first sharpe weather in Capr. shut the Bees in.
62 And in pleasant weather let them loose, if it may be, once a fortnight.
63 The SPRING.
64 PISCES.
65 The first faire day in Pisces, set the Bees at liberty.
66 New dresse their Troughs.
67 Cleanse the Stools.
68 And feed or driue light stalls.
69 ARIES.
70 The second chiefe robbing-time.
71 In TAVRVS, remoue the Barres.
72 In GEMINI, the Winter-doores.

The Contents of the fourth Chapter, concerning the Breeding of Bees, and concerning the Drone.

1 The Drone no labourer.
2 Diuers opinions of the Drones originall.
3 The Drone is the Male-Bee.
4 Diuers reasons prouing the Drone to be the Male.
The first reason is, that they are suffered in breeding-time onely.
5 The second reason is, that the Drones being taken away in breeding-time, the Bees breed no more.
6 The third reason is, that they are bred by the Bees.
7 The fourth reason is, that the Waspes and Dorres haue drones, which are their males.
8 The breeding of Waspes by Drones.

9 The

9 The breeding of Dorres by Drones.
10 The fift reason is the apparent signes of their Sex.
11 Aristotles obiections answered.
12 When the Bees begin to breed.
13 The chiefe time of breeding.
14 The first breed are females.
15 The manner of their breeding.
16 The Bee-seed is first turned into a Worme.
17 The Worme being dead groweth to the shape of a Bee, and then liueth againe.
18 The breeding of the Lady-Bees.
19 When the Drones are bred.
20 When they come abroad.
21 Two vses of the Drones.
22 Where they lie.
23 The male-Bees are subiect to the females.
24 When the Bees leaue breeding, and beat away their Drones.
25 The Bees compared to the Amazons.
26 They rid not their Drones all at once.
27 When forward stalls begin.
28 When the backward.
29 When full stocks that haue not swarmed.
30 When those that are ouer-swarmed.
31 Sometime the Bees cast out euen the white Cephens.
32 Timely ridding of Drones a good signe.
33 Sometime they rid their Drones in the Spring.
34 And afterward breed new againe.
35 Sometime it is good to helpe the Bees in this worke.

The Contents of the fifth Chapter, concerning the Swarming of Bees, and the Hiuing of them.

1 The parts of a swarme.
2 When you may see the Queen-Bee.
3 The swarme no younger then the stocke.
4 Many Drones in a swarm a good signe.
5 A kinde spring for swarmes.
6 Swarming weather.
7 The swarming-houres.
8 The two swarming moneths.
9 Rathe swarmes.
10 Late swarmes.
11 Black-berie swarmes are seldom to be kept.
12 A prime swarm & an after swarme.
13 A stall may cast foure times.
14 Diuers causes of breaking the prime swarme.
15 One prime swarme worth two after-swarmes.
16 The vulgar Bees appoint the rising of the fore-swarmes, and that vpon foure grounds.
17 Fiue signes of the first swarming.
18 The signes of present swarming.
19 To lie forth continually is a signe they will not swarme.
20 The causes of their lying forth.
21 The remedy and meanes to make them swarme.
22 What is to be done to those that by no meanes will swarme.
23 How to replenish an ouer-swarmer.
24 How to double a stall.
25 How to driue all the Bees into the new hiue, and so to take the old.
26 The signes of after-swarmes.
27 The rising of the after-swarmes is appointed by the Rulers.
28 The Bees Musicke.
29 The Princes part.
30 The Queenes part.
31 The other Ladies parts.
32 In the Bees song are the grounds of musicke.
33 Before swarming the voices come downe to the stoole.
34 The manner of their swarming.
35 The prime swarme being broken, the next may call and swarme within the eighth day.
36 All the swarmes of one hiue come within a fortnight.
37 What vse there is of tinging the swarme.
38 What to doe if the swarme bee way-ward.

39 Some swarmes prouide them houses aforehand.
40 And then they flie away directly to the place.
41 Vacua aluearia stent semper parata in Apuario.
42 The hiuing of Bees.
43 When they are to be hiued.
44 The token of their flying away after they bee setled.
45 How to fit the Hiues to the swarmes.
46 Better to vnder-hiue a stall then to ouer-hiue him.
47 Three things requisite to hiuing.
48 The Mantle.
49 The single Rest.
50 The double rest.
51 The brush.
52 What the Hiuer must doe.
53 The manner of Hiuing.
54 Foure meanes of hiuing a Swarme.
55 How to hiue a Swarme that lighteth vpon a bough.
56 Either high.
57 Or low.
58 How if it light vpon a high tree.
59 How if vpon the body of a tree.
60 How if it light vpon the top of any thing.
61 How if it light in the middle of a dead hedge.
62 How if it light on some hollow side of a stub or tree.
63 How if it flie into a hollow tree.
64 How if it light vpon another Hiue.
65 The swarme is alwaies to be kept together, lest the Bees kill one an other.
66 The swarme to be set neere the lighting-place.
67 What to doe if a swarme part.
68 Vniting of swarmes is profitable.
69 The manner of vniting.
70 Another way.
71 Two speciall inconueniences to bee auoided in this worke.
72 1. Superfluous multitude.
73 2. Ciuill Warre.
74 To preuent the first.
75 To preuent the second.
76 When most danger is.
77 A storie of a deadly feud.
78 The causes of a swarmes going home againe.
79 How to stay them.
80 How to keepe them from other Hiues.

81 Set not a swarme neere an others hiuing-place.
82 What to doe when the swarme is new hiued.
83 How to remoue it in the euening.
84 How to set it on his seat.
85 How to vse it in the morning.
86 Foule weather the first day doth much discourage a swarme.
87 Foule weather continuing doth make it droupe and die.
88 A swarme may liue six daies without Honie.
89 How to preuent the drouping and death of a swarme.
90 How to cure a a drouping Swarme.

The Contents of the sixt Chapter, concerning the Bees worke.

1 Bees most industrious creatures.
2 In three monaths they cannot worke.
3 All the yeere after they lose no time.
4 Three fruits of Bees labour.
5 The first and ground of all is Wax.
6 How Wax is gathered and wrought.
7 How you may see the working of the combs.
8 How much wax they bring at once.
9 The admirable Architecture of their combs and cells.
10 The Drone-combe.
11 The Queenes cells are built single in diuers places.
12 In fashion round.
13 The common error anent these cells.
14 The combes doe often change their hue.
15 Wax is gathered only in foure months.
16 Honey the second fruit is gathered in 9. moneths.
17 Two sorts of Hony.
18 How Ambrosia or grosse honie is gathered.
19 Ambrosia is the Schadons food, as water their drinke.
20 Being kept, it is soone corrupted.
21 And then becommeth most vnsauory stopping.
22 Much stopping maketh the Bees forsake their hiues.
23 This Ambrosia is commonly taken for wax.
24 Which errour is disproued by sense.
25 And reason.
26 And by authority.

27 How the pure Nectar is gathered.
28 Two sorts of Nectar.
29 Liue-hony of two sorts.
30 The finest ordinary is a kinde of Virgin-hony.
31 All hony courser or finer, according to the soile.
32 The first cells they close with waxe.
33 Nectar and Ambrosia made of many simples, whereof each moneth yeeldeth varietie.
34 Dandelion continueth longest.
35 What Pisces yeeldeth.
36 What Aries.
37 Taurus.
38 Gemini.
39 Cancer.
40 Of Honie-dewes.
41 The Bees worke most earnestly in a Hony-Moon.
42 What the Honie-dew is.
43 When the Honie-dewes are most frequent.
44 The time when they fall.
45 What Leo yeeldeth.
46 Virgo.
47 Libra.
48 Scorpio.
49 The Bees gather but of one kind of flower in one voyage.
50 They gather honie out of poison.
51 What store of Honie a stall may haue.
52 Bees haue necessary vse of water.
53 Chiefly for their breed.
54 The making of the watring-place.
55 How to finde wilde Bees.
56 Bee-troughs in Gardens profitable.
57 The forme and size of a Bee-trough.
58 The trough couer, and the vse of it.
59 The seasoning and ordering of the Bee-trough.
60 Bee-troughs of stone.
61 Sometime they water in the streets.
62 And after a showre, all about the garden.

The Contents of the seuenth Chapter concerning the Bees enemies.

1 The Bees enemies are many.
2 1. The Mouse.
3 Remedies against the Mouse.
4 2. The Wood-pecker.
5 3. The Titmouse.
6 The subtill practise of the Titmouse.
7 4. The Swallow.
8 Remedie against the Titmouse and Swallow.
9 5. The Hornet.
10 The Hornets sting is dangerous.
11 6. The Waspe.
12 When she feedeth vpon Bees.
13 When she stealeth honie.
14 When they sweare away.
15 In what yeere the Waspes are few.
16 In what yeere they abound.
17 Remedies against the Waspes.
18 7. The Moth.
19 8. The Snaile.
20 What harme the Moth doth.
21 9. The Emet.
22 10. The Spider.
23 11. The Toad.
24 12. The Frog.
25 13. The Bee the Bees greatest enemie.
26 Robbing or fighting of Bees in winter and summer but litle.
27 In the spring more earnest.
28 The most spoile is made in Harvest.
29 What Stalls are most subiect to robbing.
30 What Bees are the robbers.
31 How they begin the fray.
32 Theeues of diuers Hiues agree together in robbing.
33 The description of the Bees battell.
34 In the battell is heard a sound like a drum and a flute.
35 The assault of the enemy.
36 The defence of the besieged.
37 Neither side willing to yeeld.
38 The exercise of the defendants when the enemy retireth.
39 The Waspes like Vultures.
40 The battell ended they bury their dead.
41 The second assault of the enemy.
42 When the true Bees yeeld, they goe with the Conquerours.
43 Remedies.
44 To preuent robbing.
45 And to stay it, if you finde it in time.
46 When it is too late, and what is then to be done.
47 Robbing hurtfull also to the Theeues.
48 In what yeeres robbing is most rife.
49 Bees kill poore swarms that wander in the spring.
50 To

50 To preuent the death of poore swarmes.
51 Many killed in swarming.
52 14. The Weather.
53 In Summer heat hurteth the Bees.
54 In Winter the Sun-shine in frost and snow.
55 The Remedy.
56 Also the Easterne winds and great frosts.
57 And the cold continued maketh them sicke.
58 The raine rotteth the Hiues.
59 The Remedy.
60 The greatest losse by weather is in the springs, for then infinite multitudes are beaten downe, laden and weary, with stormes and wind.
61 At the rising of a Cloud they post home.
62 Yet will they goe a field in the midst of a warme showre.
63 How to restore Bees to life.
64 The wind causeth many to be drowned.
65 The Remedie.
66 The last and most enemy of all.

The Contents of the eighth Chapter, concerning the Feeding of Bees.

1 In seuen moneths the Bees spend of their stocke.
2 Three sorts of swarmes diuersly prouided.
3 The first sort.
4 The second.
5 The third onely are to be fed.
6 Stockes out of proofe neuer to be fed.
7 Try your swarmes in Virgo.
8 What quantity of Honie is requisite.
9 Try againe in Pisces or Aries.
10 The Bees food.
11 Priuate feeding.
12 Carelesse feeding is staruing.
13 Publike feeding.
14 The first time of feeding.
15 The second time of feeding.
16 The third time of feeding.

The Contents of the ninth Chapter, concerning the Remouing of Bees.

1 Fiue things to be auoided in remouing Bees.
2 Remoue alwaies in faire weather.
3 Not in Winter.
4 Nor in Summer.

5 The Autumne & Spring are fit times for remouing.
6 Libra the best moneth in all the yeere.
7 When to remoue a swarme.
8 The time of the day, and manner of remouing.
9 The vsuall manner of remouing.
10 Which is fit for poore stalls.
11 How a good stall is to be carried.
12 How a bad.
13 What to doe when they are brought home.
14 And what when they are seated.

The Contents of the tenth Chapter.
Part. 1. concerning the taking of the Combs.

1 The first kinde of Vindemiation.
2 The best time for killing Bees.
3 What stalls are to be taken.
4 The manner of killing Bees.
5 Sundry meanes to kill Bees.
6 The Bees being dead, house the Hiue.
7 The second kinde of Vindemiation.
8 The time and manner of Driuing Bees.
9 This Driuing of Bees vnprofitable.
10 The Honie taken is little and naught.
11 And the Bees driuen, few and poore.
12 Another kinde of driuing.
13 At two times.
14 Driuing in Virgo.
15 The manner of driuing in Virgo.
16 How to helpe those driuen Bees that want.
17 Driuing in Pisces.
18 How to reuiue those that are chilled in driuing.
19 A third kinde of Vindemiation.
20 Exsection vsed at two times.
21 What part to be exsected is vncertaine.
22 Exsection ancient, but not profitable.
23 Neither first.
24 Nor second.
25 Specially for our Country.

Part 2. concerning the trying of Honie and Wax, and the making of Meade.

1 The Combes to be diuided into three parts.
2 Necessary Instruments being first prouided.
3 The dressing of the first part for Honie in two shoots.

4. The

4 The first shoot for fine ordinary Honie.
5 Or for Virgin-Honie, which is most fine.
6 Two sorts of Virgin-honie.
7 Corne-Honie got out by water or fire.
8 The second shoot for course Honie.
9 The dressing of the first part in one shoot.
10 The vulgar Honie grosly handled.
11 The working of Honie, and how to helpe it.
12 Diuers Countries yeeld diuers kinds of Honie.
13 How to know good Honie.
14 Good Honie with standing waxeth hard and white.
15 The best of the Honie is in the bottome.
16 The dressing of the second part for Meth.
17 How to make the Meth-liquor in two shoots.
18 Two sorts of Hydromel, Mede and Methæglen.
19 When the liquor is strong enough for Mede.
20 What proportions of water to Honie.
21 How and how long the Must must be boiled.
22 The receit of Spices.
23 How the Must is to be used when it is boiled.
24 The making of Methæglen.
25 The Queenes Methæglen.
26 The dressing of the third part for Wax.
27 First boile it with water.
28 Then straine it by pressing.
29 Next make the Wax into Balls.
30 Last of all melt it and cast it in a mould.
31 And keepe the cake from cracking.
32 How to know good Wax.

Part 3. concerning the vertues of Honie, Meth, and Wax.

1 The properties and vertues of Honie.
2 Against both outward and inward griefes.
3 For whom Honie is best.
4 English Honie.

5 Too much honie unholsome.
6 The different operations of raw and boiled Hony.
7 Two waies to clarifie honey.
8 The quintessence of Hony.
9 The vertues of it.
10 The making of it.
11 The vertue of Honie in Confections.
12 Marmalade made of honie.
13 Marchpane.
14 Preserues.
15 Conserues.
16 Syrups.
17 Honie to be preferred before Sugar.
18 Hony good in outward Medicines.
19 A salue for an old sore.
20 An other.
21 The properties and vertues of Mede and Methæglen.
22 Meth much used of the ancient Britaines.
23 Whence Meth and Methæglen haue their name.
24 The properties and vertues of naturall Wax.
25 Artificiall Wax.
26 To make white Wax.
27 To make red Wax.
28 To make greene Wax.
29 Oile of Wax.
30 The vertues of it.
31 The making of Oile of Wax.
32 The vertue of Wax in compound medicines.
33 A Cerecloth.
34 A Cerecloth to refresh the Sinewes and Muscles.
35 A Cerecloth to comfort the stomacke.
36 A Cerecloth for the Wormes.
37 A Salue for a greene wound.
38 An other.

THE

THE FEMININE MONARCHIE,

Or

The Historie of BEES.

CHAP. I.

Of the Nature and properties of Bees, and of their Queene.

Mong all the Creatures which our bountifull God hath made for the vse and seruice of man, in respect of great profit with smal cost, of their vbiquitie or being in all Countries, and of their continuall labour and comly order, the Bees are most to be admired.

For first with the prouision of a Hiue and some little care and attendance, which need be no hindrance to other businesse, but rather a delightfull recreation amid the same; they bring in store of sweet delicates, most holesome both for meat and medicine, *Fructus apum ab omnibus desideratur & quæritur: nec pro personarum diuersitate discernitur, sed indiscreta sui gratia regibus pariter ac mediocribus æquali suauitate dulcescit: nes solùm voluptati, sed etiam saluti est.* And an other saith, *Mille ad usus vitæ laborem tolerant & opera conficiunt*: as they well know, who know the rare vertues of Honie and Waxe: a taste whereof I will giue you in the last chapter.

Bees yeeld great profit with small cost.

Ambrosius Hexamer. l.5. cap.21.

Plin. nat. hist. l.11.c.5.

Secondly,

C. 1. *Of the Nature and properties of Bees,*

2.
Euery Countrey fit for Bees.

Secondly, whereas *non omnis fert omnia tellus,* some Countrey yeeldeth one fruit, some an other; some beareth one graine, some an other; some breedeth one kinde of Cattle, some an other; there is no ground (of what nature soeuer it be, whether it be hot or cold, wet or dry, hill or dale, woodland or champian, meddow, pasture, or arable: in a word, whether it be battle or barren) which yeeldeth not matter for the Bee to worke vpon.

And thirdly, in their labour and order at home and abroad they are so admirable, that they may be a patterne vnto men, both of the one and of the other. For vnlesse they be let by weather, weaknesse, or want of matter to worke on, their labour neuer ceaseth. In admiration whereof, one saith, *Quos efficacia industriaq̃, tantæ comparemus nervos? Quas vires? Quas ratione medius fidius viros?* And for their order, it is such, that they may well bee said to haue a Common-wealth, since all that they doe is in common, without any priuate respect. *Nihil norunt nisi commune:* They worke for all, they watch for all, they fight for all. In their priuate quarrels, when they are from the Hiue or common treasury, howsoeuer you vse them, they will not resist, if by any meanes they can get away. *Cum ruri sint, nec sibi invicem, nec ullis alijs nocent; at vero apud suos alueos pugnant acerrimè.* Their dwelling and dyet are common to all alike: they haue like common care both of their wealth and young ones. *Sola in omni genere animantium communem omnibus sobolem habent, unam omnes incolunt mansionem, unius patriæ clauduntur limine, in commune omnibus labor, communis cibus, communis operatio, communis usus, & fructus est.* And all this vnder the gouernment of one Monarch, of whom aboue all things they haue a principall care and respect, louing, reuerencing, and obeying her *v:* in all things.

Prætereà regem non sic Ægyptus & ingens
Lydia, nec populi Parthorum aut Medus Hydaspes
Observant: rege incolumi mens omnibus una est:
Amisso rupere fidem; constructaq̃ mella
Diripuere ipsa, v: & crates soluere fauorum:
Ille operum custos, illum admirantur; & omnes

3.
Bees abhorre idlenesse.

Plin. nat. hist. l.11.c.5.

4.
Bees haue a Common-wealth.

Nat. hist. li. 11. c. 5.

5.
Their working, watching, fighting, dwelling, dyet, wealth, and young ones are all in common.

Arist. hist. anim. lib. 9. cap. 40.
Ambr. Hex. lib. 5. cap. 21. & Basil. Hexam. Homil. 8.

6.
Bees alwaies loyall to their Soueraigne.

V. Præfat.
Virg. Georg.
V. c. 7. n. 27. & 42.

Circumstant

*Circumstant fremitu denso, stipantq́, frequentes,
Et sæpe attollunt humeris, & corpora bello
Objectant, pulchramq́, petunt per vulnera mortem.*

If she goe forth to solace her selfe, (as sometime she will) many of them attend her, guarding hir person before and behinde; they which come forth before her, euer now and then returning, and looking backe, and making withall an extraordinarie noise, as if they spake the language of the Knight Marshals men, and so away they flye together, and anone in like manner they attend her backe againe. This I may say, because I haue seene it: although the Philosopher be of another minde: *Reges,* saith he, *nunquam foris visuntur, nisi cum migratur.* If by hir voyce she bid them goe, they swarme: if being abroad she dislike the weather, or lighting-place, they quickly returne home againe: while she cheereth them to battaile they fight, *v*: while she is well, they are cheerefull about their worke; if she droope and dye, they will neuer after enioy their home, but either languish there till they be dead too, or yeelding to the Robbers, *v*: fly away with them *v*: *Rege mortuo mæret plebs ignava, non cibos convehit, non procedit, tristi tantùm murmure glomeratur circa corpus ejus.*

But if they haue many Princes, as when two flye away with one swarme, or when two swarmes are hiued together; they will not be quiet till one of thē be cassiered: which somtime they bring downe that euening to the mantle, *v.* where you may finde her couered with a little heape of Bees: otherwise the next day they carie her forth either dead or deadly wounded. Concerning which matter, I will here relate one memorable experiment. Two swarmes being put together, the Bees on both sides, as their manner is, made a murmuring noise, as being discontented with the suddain congresse of Strangers: but knowing wel that the more the merrier, the safer, the warmer, yea, and the better prouided; they were quickly made friends. And hauing agreed which Queene should reigne, and which should die, three or foure Bees brought one of them downe betweene them, pulling and haling her as if they were leading her to execution: which I by chance perceiuing, got hold of her by the wings, and with much adoe tooke

Hist. an. l. 9. cap. 40.

Vid. c. 7. n. 35.

V. c. 7. n. 27.
V. c. 7. n. 42.
Nat. hist. li. 11.
c. 17.

7.
Bees endure no gouernment, but a Monarchie.
V. c. 5. n. 46. & 47.

8.
A memorable experiment.

"tooke her from them. After a while (to see what would
"come of it) I put her into the Hiue againe: no sooner was she
"among them, but the tumult began afresh, greater then be-
"fore, and presently they fell together by the eares, fiercely
"fighting and killing one another, for the space of more then
"an houre together: and by no meanes would cease, vntill the
"poore condemned Queene was brought forth slaine and
"laid before the doore. Which done, the strife presently en-
"ded, and the Bees agreed well together.

Somtime when one swarme is put to another, though they do not fight, yet will they not agree of their choice in two or three daies, keeping their Queenes close on both sides. But then all this while they neuer be at quiet day nor night, nor once offer to work, vntill one of them being deposed, they be vnited in the other. *Vide plura super hac re c.5.n.74.75.76.*

Likewise if the old Queene bring forth many Princes (as she may haue six or seuen, yea sometime halfe a score or more, which superfluitie nature affoordeth for more suretie, in case some miscarrie) then, lest the multitude of Rulers should distract the vnstable Commons into factions, within two daies after the last swarme, yea sometime (when vnkinde weather keepeth him in ouer long) euen before he come forth, you shall finde the superfluous Princes dead before the Hiue: I haue taken eight of them vp together brought out of one hiue, when two were alreadie gone forth with their swarmes. For the Bees abhorre as well Polyarchie, as Anarchie, God hauing shewed in them vnto men, an expresse patterne of A PERFECT MONARCHIE, THE MOST NATVRAL AND ABSOLVTE FORME OF GOVERNMENT.

Hom. Il. α. 9.

Οὐκ ἀγαθὸν πολυκοιρανίη, εἷς κοίρανος ἔστω.

The description of the Queene-Bee.

The Queene is a faire and stately Bee, differing from the vulgar both in shape and colour: hir backe is all ouer of a brighter browne: hir belly euen from the top of hir fangs, to the tip of hir traine, is of a sad yellow, somewhat deeper then the richest gold. Shee is longer then a hony-Bee, by one third part, that is, almost an inch long: shee is also bigger then a hony-Bee, but not so bigge as a Drone, although somewhat longer: hir head proportionable, but that

that it is more round then the little Bees, by reason hir fangs be shorter: hir tongue not halfe so long as theirs: for whereas they gather with the one Nectar, with the other Ambrosia; *v.* shee hath no need to vse either, being to be maintained, as other Princes, by the labour of hir subiects: hir wings of the same size with a small Bee, and therefore in respect of hir long body, they seeme very short, resembling rather a cloake then a gowne; for they reach but to the middle of hir traine or nether part: hir legges proportionable, and of the colour of hir belly, but her two hind-legges more yellow: hir nether part so long, and halfe so long as hir vpper part, more picked then a small Bees, hauing in it foure ioynts or partitions, and in each ioynt a golden barre, in stead of those three whitish rings which other Bees haue at their three partitions. The speere she hath is but little, and not halfe so long as the other Bees: which, like a Kings sword, is borne rather for shew and authority, then for any other vse. For it belongeth to hir subiects as well to fight for her, as to prouide for her. *Plinie* writeth thus doubtingly of it: *Non constat inter authores Rex nullumne solus habeat aculeum, majestate tantum armatus, an dederit eum quidem natura, sed usum ejus illi tantum negaverit: illud constat imperatorem aculeo non uti.* But *Aristotle* doth truly approue the later opinion, as certaine: *Reges aculeos habent, sed non utuntur. Quocirca carere eos aculeis nonnulli existimant. Plinie* describeth them thus, *Omnibus forma semper egregia, & duplo quam cæteris major, pennæ breviores, crura recta, ingressus celsior, in fronte macula quodam diademate candicans: Multum etiam nitore à vulgo differunt.* If you desire to see this stately Prince, read *cap.* 5. *n.* 34. The breeding of her you may see *c.* 4. *n.* 18.

 Besides their Soueraigne, the Bees haue also subordinate Gouernours and Leaders, not vnfitly resembling Captaines and Coronels of Souldiors: For difference from the rest they beare for their crest a tuft or tossell, in some coloured yellow, in some murrey, in manner of a plume; whereof some turne downeward like an Ostrich-feather, others stand vpright like a Hearn-top. And of both sorts some are greater

V. c. 6. *n.* 17.

Nat. hist. l. 11. cap. 17.

Hist. an. l. 5. cap. 21.

Nat. hist. l. 11. c. 16.

10. *Bees haue also inferiour Gouernours or Captains.*

11. *Which are known by peculiar markes.*

and some lesse, as if there were degrees of those dignities among them. In all other respects they are like to the vulgar. These I thinke are they that *Plinie* meaneth, where he saith, *Circa regem satellites quidam, lictoresque assidui custodes authoritatis.* In lesse then a quarter of an houre you may see three or foure of them come forth of a good stall; but chiefly in *Gemini*, before their continuall labour haue worne these ornaments. So that he might well say, *Rempublicam habent, consilia, ac duces.* All which hee that seriously considereth, must with admiration acknowledge that singular wisdome, order, and gouernment in them, which in no other creature, man onely excepted, (if yet to be excepted) is to be found: whence some haue inferred a farther matter,

His equidem signis atque haec exempla sequuti,
Esse apibus partem divinae mentis, & haustus
Æthereos dixere—

12. *Aristotle* maketh two sorts of Bees, the one (which is best) short, diuers coloured, and round; the other long, like vnto waspes. *Optimum genus apum quae breves, variae, & in rotunditatem compactiles; secunda quae longa & vespis similes.* And in another place he putteth a difference betweene wilde and tame: saying, *Differunt inter se apes parentibus natae urbanis, & quae rustico montanoque victu educatae prodierint: sunt enim hae sylvestres horridiores aspectu, & iracundiores, & minores; sed opere & labore praestantiores.* Whom *Plinie* followeth almost *verbatim:* saying, *Apes sunt etiam rusticae sylvestresq́, horridae aspectu, multo iracundiores; sed opere ac labore praestantiores. Urbanarum duo genera: optimae breves, variae, & in rotunditatem compactiles; deteriores longa, & quibus similitudo vesparum, etiamnum deterrimae ex iis pilosa.* But these differences my experience hath not found: neither doe I see how they can be; seeing the swarmes of tame Bees doe often flie into trees, and so become wilde; and the swarmes of wilde Bees are not seldome found, and put into hiues. Indeed the wilde are more angry then the tame: but that is because they are lesse vsed to the company of men. Moreouer, there is some difference in the bignesse of Bees: For they that are loaded seeme greater and longer then those that

and of their Queene.

that are leere: also the Nymphs, *v.* when they come first abroad, are not growne to their full bignesse which afterward they haue, and the old ones doe wither, and become little againe. *v.* Likewise in these three ages their colours also do varie: for in their middle age they are browne, whereas before they are more pale, *v.* and at the last they turne whitish againe. *v.* But these are differences of Bees in the same stall, and not of one stall from an other, since these diuers sorts are in euery stall.

The seuerall parts of a Bee haue their seuerall vses.

Hir horns growing in the middle of hir forehead, with two ioyncts, one close to the head, the other towards the middle, so that she can put them forth at full length when shee will, and draw them in againe close to hir head; are the proper *organum* of the sense of feeling; by which, with the least touch, the Bee sodainely senteth any tangible obiect: and therefore they serue to giue warning in the darke, and when she is busie, of any obuious thing quicke or dead that might offend her.

Hir two cheekes being transparent, like Lanthorne, doe serue, though immoueable, in stead of Eyes: through which the species of things visible are conueied to the cómon Sense.

For gathering hir prouision, shee hath two instruments, hir fangs and hir tongue: hir fangs in fashion of a paire of pincers hang not, as the iawes of other things, one ouer an other, but side-way one against the other, as is most conuenient for hir vses.

Hir tongue is of that length, that hir mouth cannot hold it: but being doubled between hir fangs vnder hir chinne, it reacheth to the necke. It is diuided into three parts: whereof the two outmost serue as a case to couer the third, which being the chiefe, the Bee in hir worke putteth forth beyond the other, and draweth in againe as shee will. And this third part is likewise parted into three, so that there are fiue in all.

To set these instruments on worke, Nature hath furnished her with 4. wings, which swifter then the East-winde, carry her into all the foure coasts of the world, and thence with

V.c.4.n.20.

v.n.56.

V.c.4.n.17.
V.n.56.

13.
The parts of a Bee.

14.
Hir hornes.

15.
Hir eyes.

16.
Hir fangs.

17.
Hir tongue, with the parts of it.

18.
Hir foure wings.

with hir precious lading beare her backe againe, vntill hir inceſſant labour hath worne them out. *v. n.* 56.

19.
Hir feete.

Hir rough and dew-clawed feet apt to take hold at the firſt touch are in number ſixe, that ſhee may ſtand faſt vpon foure, while ſhe vſeth the other two to wipe hir eyes, hir wings, hir tongue, or any other part, and to conuay the gathering of hir fangs to hir thighes. *v. c.* 6. *n.* 18.

20.
Hir two weapons

21.
Hir fangs commonly vſed againſt inſecta.

For hir defence ſhe is doubly weaponed. Hir fangs ſhee vſeth when ſhe is not much angry, againſt all *inſecta*, as other Bees, Drones, Waſpes, &c. therewith pinching and holding them commonly by the legs or wings, and ſometime by the hornes: but this is rather a chiding, then a fighting, and a warning, rather then a puniſhment; though withall ſometime ſhe bend her ſpeere againſt them, as if ſhee would kill and ſlay.

22.
Hir ſpeere ſometime.

Hir ſpeere ſhe is very loth to vſe, if by any other meanes ſhe can ſhift hir enemy, as knowing how dangerous it is to hir ſelfe: for if ſhe chance therewith to ſtrike any hard part, as the breſt or ſhoulder, ſhee is enforced to leaue hir ſpeere behinde her, and ſo ſhe killeth and is killed *v.* with the ſame ſtroke. Yet when the Bees are very angry; as namely when they are aſſaulted with a multitude of robbers at once, *v.* or when in the ſpring a hungry ſtall forſaking his owne home preſſeth into their hiue, *v.* they fall ſodainly vpon them with their poyſoned ſpeeres (*Apibus natura cuſpides dedit, & quidem venenatas*) but then they make ſhort worke. For by that time they haue put vp their weapons, ſome die preſently: others loſing the vſe of their wings tumble on the ground like mad things, vntill in a while they loſe their liues too: others when they are wounded, runne away in great haſte (as hauing their errand) either drawing on the ground one or moe of their legs, or doubling their nether part toward the ground, or turning the ſame awry to the one ſide or the other: but as many as are ſtricken, within an houre after will not bee able to wag out of the place, and within two or three at the moſt, they will be quite dead. I haue looked on, while thus they quickly cut off a whole ſtall, and among the reſt, making then no difference, they ſpared not the

*V.n.*31.

*V.c.*7.*n.*36.

*V.c.*7.*n.*49.

Nat.hiſt.li.21. c.13.

23.
Stinging preſent death to Bees.

the Queene her selfe. After this manner doe they deale with the Drones at the time of the yeere, when they will not otherwise be beaten away. *v.c.4.n.24.*

But their speares or stings they vse chiefely against things of other sort, as men, beasts, and fowles: which haue outwardly some offensiue excrement, as haire or feathers, the touch whereof prouoketh them to sting: although such stinging be alwaies mortall to themselues (as anone is shewed. *v.*) For the skinne hauing receiued the sting, holdeth it so fast, that when they would be gone, they leaue both it and part of their entrals which are fastned to it. *Aculeum apibus natura dedit ventri consertum.* If they light vpon Poultry, although their desire bee to the quicke, if they can quickly come at it; yet will they put forth their speares as soone as they touch the feather: and if they chance to hit the hard part thereof, the sting sticketh fast, as in the skinne; and therefore Goose-wings are naught to be vsed in the hiuing of Bees.

Likewise, if they light vpon the haire of your head or beard, (saue onely when they come home loaden, or the weather is cold) they will sting, if they can reach the skinne; although Wooll and Woollen doe not offend them: and if being otherwise angered, they strike their speares in Woollen, they can easily pull them out againe. But the nap of new Fustian displeaseth them, because it seemeth hairy; and the stuffe is so fast, that it holdeth the sting. Wherefore such apparell is not fit among Bees: as also Leather in Gloues or otherwise, for assoone as they touch it they will strike, if they be any whit mooued, and their speares they cannot recouer againe. Veluet in facing of hats or else-where, doth anger them as much as any thing, making them strike assoone as they touch it: but it hath not power to hold their speare.

When they are angry, their aime is most commonly at the head, and chiefely about the eies, as knowing that there they may do most harme, for that part swelleth most and longest: and yet I neuer heard that any euer stung the verie eye, as if they were forbidden to touch that render part. But the bare hand

---

24. *The speares commonly vsed against other creatures.*

25. *Haire and feathers cause the Bees to sting.* V. n. 31. Nat.hist. l.11. c.18.

26. *Wooll and woollen doe not offend them.*

27. *Fustian, Leather, and Veluet naught among Bees.*

28. *The Bees in their anger aime at the head.*

Of the Nature and properties of Bees,

hand that is not very hairie, they will seldome or neuer sting, vnlesse they be much offended.

29.
Whē any is stung, the company must be gone.

When you are stung, or any in the company, yea though a Bee haue striken but your clothes, specially in hot weather, you were best be packing as fast as you can: for the other Bees smelling the rancke sauour of the poyson cast out with the sting, will come about you as thicke as haile: so that fitly and liuely did he expresse the multitude and fiercenesse of his enemies, that said, *They came about me like Bees.* Then is there no way to appease them but flight: the more you resist, the fiercer they are. They are like vnto incorrigible shrewes: there is no dealing with them but by patience: though when they sting they are sure to haue the worst. For

30.
The Bees haue the worst when they sting.

the wound endangereth neither life nor limb: two nights sleep will take away the swelling, and two minutes the paine, (vnlesse it be in very rheumaticke or humorous bodies: of which sort I haue knowne some so swollen and disfigured with that little stroke, that you could scarce know them by their fauour in fiue or sixe daies after.) But on the other side,

31.
They lose their sting and entrals, and consequently their liues.
Virg. Georg.
Hist. an. l 9.
c. 40.

whereas the Waspe, Hornet, and Dorre, doe sting often without any hurt to themselues; the Bee neuer stingeth but once, and then she leaueth hir speere and entrals, more or lesse behinde her, *Animamq̃, in vulnere ponit.* (*Intereunt qua percusserint, quoniam sine intestini eruptione aculeus eximi non potest.*) For within foure and twentie houres after, or, if much of hir entrals come forth with the sting, within halfe that

32.
The speere of it selfe pierceth deeper when the Bee is gone.

time, she dieth. But the speere reteining life when the Bee is gone, if it be not presently pulled out, will worke it selfe into the flesh vp to the hard end, and so cause the paine and swelling to be both greater and longer. Therefore when you

33.
How to preuent the paine and swelling.

are stung, instantly wipe off the Bee, sting and all, and wash the place with your spittle: so shall you preuent both paine and swelling, which otherwise nothing but time can cure:

34.
Nothing but time can cure their stinging.

for the poison is so subtill, that it quickly pierceth the flesh, and the wound so little, that no Antidote can follow after: and yet I haue heard commended for a remedie, the iuyce of Housleeke, of Rue, of Mallowes, of Iuie, of a Marigold leafe,

leafe, of Holyhock and Vineger, of Salt and Vineger, and diuers other things.

Id malua peculiare est, ut imposita ictibus vesparum & apum dolores leuet. Fern. Meth. l. 6. cap. 4. *Stercus vaccinum vesparum ictus sanat, & indito aceto tumores digeris.* Fern. Meth. l. 5. cap. 27 Rue drunken with Wine, *or rather with Hydromel,* or the leaues stamped with Honie and Salt, and laid to the wound, is good against stinging of Bees, Waspes, Hornets, and Scorpions; *Dodoeus, l. 2. c. 83.*

Verum hoc mihi præ cæteris probatur remedium. Vt primùm se quis ictum senserit, aculeum adhuc epidermidi inhærentem cum ipsa ape instanter abstergat (nam si paulisper sinatur, dum verò cutem penetrauerit; vehementior inde, diuturnior, & sanatu difficilior euadet tum dolor tum tumor) dein, quam mox reddi potest, propriâ vulnus urinâ maluæ folia sæpiuscule proluant, dum subsequens hoc comparetur emplastrum. R. Cardui Benedicti virentis contriti M. I. Oui albumen quasi in oleum coagitatum: misce, fiat emplastrum, quod lini retrimentis impositum, vulneri linteo alligetur: ubi aruerit, recens repone: sed vulnus nequaquam fricetur.

But if thou wilt haue the fauour of thy Bees that they sting thee not, thou must auoid such things as offend them: thou must not be (1) vnchaste or (2) vncleanely: for impuritie and sluttishnesse (themselues being most chaste and neat,) they vtterly abhorre: thou must not come among them (3) smelling of sweat, or hauing a stinking breath, caused either through eating of Leekes, Onions, Garleeke, and the like; or by any other meanes: the noisomnesse whereof is corrected with a cup of Beere: and therefore it is not good to come among them before you haue drunke: thou must not be giuen to (4) surfeiting and drunkennesse: thou must not come (5) puffing and blowing vnto them, neither hastily stirre among them, nor * violently defend thy selfe when they seeme to threaten thee; but softly mouing thy hand before thy face, gently put them by: and lastly,

35.
What things the Bee-master must auoid.

* Which not onely increaseth their anger, (specially in hot weather, v. n. 38.) but inciteth others to take their parts: and if by striuing and striking you chance to kill one, the Bees presently perceiuing it by the strong smell of the humour (for she smelleth then as if she had stung, v. n. 29.) will be so eager vpon reuenge, that by no meanes can they be pacified, vntill they haue the field.

thou

C. 1.   *Of the Nature and properties of Bees,*

36.
The six properties of a Bee-master.

37.
Safer to walke, then to stand among Bees.

38.
The fittest time to stirre about Bees.

39.
In the heat of the day they are most angry.

40.
How to be armed when the Bees are angry.

thou must be (6) no Stranger vnto them. In a word, thou must be chaste, cleanly, sweet, sober, quiet, and familiar: so will they loue thee, and know thee from all other.

At any time, when nothing hath angred them, one may boldly walke along by them: but if hee stand still before them within the space of a pearch in the heat of the day, it is maruell but one or other spying him from the Hiue, will haue a cast at him.

If you haue any thing to doe about your hiues, the fittest time is in the morning, when the Bees are new gone abroad; and in the euening before they be come in: for then the weather being coole, and the company few at home, they are not so apt to be quarrelling, vnlesse they be much prouoked. Likewise at other times of the day, when the weather is cold, wet, or windie, they are patient enough.

But about noone in hot weather, and specially when they haue tasted of the Hony-dewes, they are soone angry, and very eager.

But whensoeuer you haue occasion to trouble their patience, or to come among them being troubled, it is better to stand vpon your guard, then to trust to their gentlenesse. For the safeguard of your face (which they haue most mind vnto) prouide a purs-hood made of course boultering, to be drawn and knit about your collar: which, for more safetie, is to bee lined against the eminent parts with Woollen-cloth. First, cut a peece about an inch and a halfe broad, and halfe a yard long, to reach round by the temples and fore-head from one eare to the other: which being sowed in his place, ioyne vnto it two short peeces of the same bredth vnder the eyes, for the balls of the cheekes: and then set another peece about the bredth of a shilling against the top of the nose. In stead of this, you may vse a Cypres Band or a Boulter, hauing a Handkerchiefe betweene your fore-head and it, to beare it out from the skinne, and your hat on your head to hold it fast. And if they be so earnest that you feare stinging your hands, put on a paire of woollen cuffes or gloues. When you haue on this Helmet and Gantlets, as a man armed at all points, you may boldly deale with them, being out of
the

the danger of their poysoned speares. At other times when they are not angried, a little peece halfe a quarter broad to couer the eyes and parts about them, may serue: for then, though it be in the heat of the day, vnlesse they may strike about the eyes, they care not to strike at all.

Vnto Cattel which haue not the reason by flight or otherwise to saue themselues, they are more dangerous. A Horse in the heat of the day looking ouer a hedge, on the other side whereof was a stall of Bees, while hee stood nodding with his head, as his manner is, because of the Flies, the Bees fell vpon him and killed him. Likewise, I heard of a Teeme that stretching against a hedge, ouerthrew a stall on the other side, and so two of the Horses were stung to death. I doubt not but through negligence many such mischances haue happened else-where. For this thing hath beene long since obserued by that great Philosopher. *Necant* (saith he) *vel maxima animalia ictu sui aculei: jam equus occisus ab apibus est.*

41
Bees dangerous to Cattell.

Arist. hist. an l. 9 c. 40.

ANd such are the sorts of Bees, with their integrall parts. Among which, though there do not appear those outward *Organa* of senting which other *Animals* haue, nor is seene in the head that inward principall * part, which is the fountaine and seat of all Senses, Phantasie, and Memorie; yet haue they the Senses themselues, both outward and inward: which their subtill and actiue spirits doe excite and quicken, for the works of their curious Art and singular Vertues. *Quamvis non sint membra quæ, velut carina, sensus invehant; esse tamen his auditum, olfactum, gustatum, eximia prætereà naturæ dona, solertiam, animum, artem quis facile crediderit. Creat Deus minima corpore acuta sensu animantia: ut majori attentione stupeamus agilitatem muscæ volantis, quàm magnitudinem jumenti gradientis.*

42
The Bees senses.

* *Cerebrum commune sentiendi principium.* Fer. Phil. 5. c. 14.

Nat. hist. l. 11. c. 4.

Augustin. de Genesi ad literam. lib. 3.

Of all the fiue Senses their sight seemeth to be weakest: & weaker when they come home loaded, then when they are feere: and being loaded weaker on foot, then when they are flying. If, when they come home loaded, they light beside the doore, they will goe vp and downe seeking for it, as if they were in the darke: and vnlesse by chance they hit vpon it,

43.
Their sight dim.

Of the Nature and properties of Bees,

it, they must flye againe before they can finde it. As many as fall beside the ftoole when it waxeth darke, ten to one they lye abroad all night: yea, if at fuch time being troubled by any thing they come forth from the ftoole, though then they be fresh and luftie, they will leape vp and downe, runne and flie to and fro, till they be wearie; but by no meanes can they finde the way in againe. And therefore it is that when they flie abroad, they take fuch paines at the doore in rubbing and wiping their glazen eies, that they may the better difcerne their way forth and backe.

44. Their smelling very quicke.

But their fmelling is excellent, whereby when they flie a-loft in the aire, they will quickly perceiue any thing vnder them that they like, as Honie, Rozin, or Tarre, though it be couered. As fooneas the Honie-dew is fallen, they prefently winde it, though the Oakes that receiue it *v.* be a farre off: which the Poet, fpeaking of the excellencie of fome creatures in this fenfe before others, doth thus expreffe,

V.c.6.n.41.

Lucret.l.4.

——————*Ideoq̃, per auras Mellis apes, quamvis longè, ducuntur odore.*

And by this fenfe they finde out any ftrange Bee, which is not otherwife to be knowne from their owne company, and that in the darke Hiue: where, when they are difpofed, they will by the fame meanes cull out the Drones, yea and pull out the Cephens *v.* that are fhut vp in the cells, not medling with any of their owne Sex.

V.c.4.n.30.

45. Hearing and feeling.
Hist. an. l.9. cap. 40.

Their hearing and feeling are verie quicke. If you touch their Hiue but lightly, or the ftoole, or the ground neere it, they prefently perceiuing it, make a generall noife: although *Ariftotle* doubt whether they heare, or not. *Quanquam incertum eft an audiant.* But if they did not heare, to what purpofe is that muficke made in the Hiues, before the fwarming? *v. c. 5. n. 28.* and in the battaile, *vid: c.7. n.34.* or his tinging of fwarmes to make them come downe, *v:* ☞ in *c.5. n.37.*

46. Tafting.

And of their fift fenfe I make no queftion, fithens they are vfed to things of fo different taftes: although here may feeme the leffe vfe of it, becaufe their fmelling is fo perfect.

And

and of their Queene.   C. I.

And such are their outward senses. The inward qualities | 47.
of their minds are farre more excellent. Their curious art | *Their vertues*
and workmanship to be admired rather then imitated of
men, See *cap.* 6.

Their singular vertues are no lesse admirable. | 48.
In valour and magnanimitie they surpasse all creatures: | *Fortitude:*
there is nothing so huge and mightie that they feare to set vpon, and when they haue once begunne, they are inuincible:
for nothing can make them yeeld but death: so great hearts | *V. c.* 7. *n.* 37.
doe they carrie in so little bodies *v.* In priuate wrongs and
iniuries done to their persons (for which cause men will soonest quarrell) they are very patient: but in defence of their
Prince and Common-wealth they doe most readily enter
the field, ———— *Et corpora bello* | Virg.
Obiectant, pulchramq, petunt per vulnera mortem. v. | *V. n.* 5.

Whereby appeareth their singular fortitude, no lesse | 49.
then their prudence doth in the gouernment of their | *Prudence and*
Common-weale *v.* beside which, their wisedome and | *knowledge.*
knowledge in other matters is verie much: as of their ene- | *V. c.* 1 *n.* 4. 5. 6.
mies, of their fellowes and friends, of the Drones, when | *& 7.*
they haue too many, and when they neede them not at all,
also of the times and seasons of the yeare. Their wit and
dexteritie, as well in gathering as in working their sweetes,
is inimitable. *v.* Moreouer, as skilful Astronomers, they haue | *V. c.* 6.
fore-knowledge of the weather. *Prædiuinant enim ventos* | Nat. hist. l. 11.
imbresq, & tunc se pleraq, continent tectis. Item, *Præsagiunt* | c. 10.
apes & hyemem & imbres, v. And in stormy and windie | Hist. an. l. 9.
weather, it is a wonder to see what cunning those that are | c. 40.
abroad doe vse to shift the wind when they come home loa- | *V. c.* 7. *n.* 61.
den: how they flie alow by the ground, among the bushes,
in the lanes, and lee-sides of the hedges. *Iuxta terram vo-* | Nat. hist. li. 11.
lant in aduerso flatu vepribus hebetato. But aboue all, one | c. 10.
excellent skill they haue, which the most excellent femals,
though much they desire it, must yeeld themselues to want:
for they know certainly when they breed a male, and when
a female: which thing appeareth by this, that they lay their | *V. c.* 6. *n.* 10. *&*
Cephen-seeds in a wide combe by themselues, *v.* and the | *c.* 4. *n.* 19.
Nymph-seedes in the rest, which are of a smaller size. *v.* So | *V. c.* 6. *n.* 19.
that

that what wanteth in the sight of their eies, is fully supplied in the sight of their minde. *Cùm sit infirma robore apis, valida est vigore sapientiæ & amore virtutis.*

Ambr. Hex. l.5. c. 21.

And yet I haue read of a greater knowledge then all this: How there were Bees so wise and skilfull, as not onely to descrie a certaine little God a mightie, though he came among them in likenesse of a Wafer-cake; but also to build him an artificiall Chappell. If I should relate the Storie, all men, I know, would not beleeue it: notwithstanding, because euery man may make some vse of it, you shall haue it.

50.
A strange tale concerning the knowledge and deuotion of Bees.

A certaine simple woman hauing some stals of Bees which yeelded not vnto her hir desired profit, but did consume and die of the murraine; made hir mone to an other Woman more simple then hir selfe: who gaue her counsell to get a consecrated Host, and put it among them. According to whose aduice she went to the Priest to receiue the Host: which when she had done, she kept it in her mouth, and being come home againe she tooke it out, and put it into one of hir Hiues. Whereupon the murraine ceased, and the Honie abounded. The Woman therefore lifting vp the Hiue at the due time to take out the Honie, saw there (most strange to be seene) a Chappell built by the Bees, with an altar in it, the wals adorned by maruellous skill of Architecture, with windowes conueniently set in their places: also a doore and a steeple with bells. And the Host being laid vpon the altar, the Bees making a sweet noise, flew round about it.

But whether this doe more argue the supernaturall knowledge and skill of the Bees, or the miraculous power of the Host, or the spirituall craftinesse of him, whose comming is by the working of Satan with all power and signes and lying wonders, some scrupulous *Skeptick may make a question: and presuming to examine euery particular circumstance ouer narrowly, will make obiections against the truth of the Storie: which, by their leaues, in the behalfe of my Authour, I must not spare to answer. First, it may be they will obiect that the Host being held so long in the Womans mouth, could not choose in that space but melt and marre.

*A Gellius, l. 11. c. 5.

Indeed,

and of their Queene.

Indeed, if it did remaine, as it was, a Wafer-cake, this were likely enough: but being turned into flesh, the case is altered. If they shall say that because it was now Honie-haruest, at which time good stals, such as this was, are full of Wax and Honie, that therefore there could not be roome enough for a Chappell with a steeple and bells in it; I answer, that this is as weake and simple as the former. For seeing it is knowne that a Blacke-smith of *London* did make a Locke and a Key so little that a flye could draw it; why should not the little Smith of *Nottingham*, which doth the worke that no man can, frame a little Chappell in a little roome? But then perhaps they will reply, if wee grant you this, yet how could the Bees flie about the altar in that little Chappell, seeing they are scarce able to flie in so narrow a close roome as the emptie hiue? As for that, it may be a mistaking of a word: haply the woman said they did but crawle. If they shall aske how the woman could see the altar with the Host standing in the Chancell, and the Bells hanging in the steeple, seeing the waxen walls were not transparent; they may easily thinke that the Bees would giue their dame leaue to looke in at the windowes. And if they shall say that those bells being made of such metall would giue but a weake sound, when they were rung to Mattins; they must consider the Parishioners dwelt not farre off. And so I thinke these captious Criticks will hold themselues satisfied.

Vnto this Storie my Author immediatly addeth an other, like vnto it, and as likely: how certaine Theeues hauing stollen the Siluer Box wherein the Wafer-Gods vse to lye, and finding one of them there, being loth, belike, that hee should lye abroad all night, did not cast him away, but laid him vnder a Hiue: whom the Bees acknowledging, aduanced to an high roome in the Hiue, and there in stead of his siluer boxe, made him another of the whitest Waxe: and when they had so done, in worship of him, at set houres they sung most sweetly beyond all measure about it: yea the owner tooke them at it at midnight, with a light and all. Wherewith the Bishop being made acquainted, came thither with many others: and lifting vp the Hiue, hee saw there neere the top a most fine boxe, wherein the Host was laid, and the Quires of Bees singing about it, and keeping watch in the night, as Monkes doe in their Cloisters. The Bishop therefore taking the Host, carried it with the greatest honour into the Church: whither many resorting, were cured of innumerable diseases.

I doubt not, but some incredulous people will quarrell this Storie as well as the former: making question, since the combs in the top of the Hiue, are not past halfe an inch one from an other, how there could be roome for a boxe of that bredth that would containe the Host; and then being there, how it might be seene by the Bishop, seeing those spaces are alwaies filled with Bees, and the Storie saith, that they were then singing about it: and therefore perhaps they will suspect the whole Narration, supposing it rather to be an vnaduised deuice of some idle Monke, which, if he had consulted with them that haue skill among Bees, might haue made his tale more probable. Alledging moreouer, that therefore there is no mention made of any particular person, time, or place, lest the circumstances should disproue the matter it selfe. All which obiections I could as easily answer as the former, if I thought it needfull; But now because some may be as ready to mistrust my relation, as others are to obiect against the truth of the Stories; I will here in mine owne behalfe for their satisfaction, set them downe in my Authors owne words.

Nam miranda canunt, sed non credenda Poetæ.

Cum mulier quædam simplicis ingenij nonnulla apum aluearia possideret, neq; illa redderent expetitum fructum, sed lue quadam tabescentes morerentur; de consilio alterius fœminæ simplicioris, accessit ad sacerdotem perceptura Eucharistiam: quam sumptam tamen ore continuit, domumq; reuersa extractam collocauit in uno ex alueariis. Lues cessauit, mella affluebant. Itaq; suo tempore mulier, apertis, ut mel educeret, alueariis, vidit (miranda res) exædificatum ab apibus sacellum, constructum altare, parietes miro Architecturæ artificio suis fenestris appositè suis locis ornatos, ostium, turrim, cum suis tintinabulis, Eucharistiam vero in altari repositam circumuolabant suaui susurro perstrepentes apes.

The other he reporteth thus. *Quidam fures, ut argenteum vasculum in quo condita erat Eucharistia auferrent, & illam secum rapuerunt: sacratissimum vero C. corpus sub alveari projecerunt. Post aliquot dies Dominus alvearis videt apes certis horis sæpius, dimissis operis ad cibos conuehendos, totos esse in quodam mellifluo concentu edendo. Cumq; fortè de media nocte exsurrexisset, conspicatur supra alveare illustrissimam lucem, suauissimeq; præter omnem modum modulantes apes. Rei nouitate inusitatâ, & prorsus admirandâ perculsus, Deiq; monitu intimo agitatus rem defert ad Episcopum. Is plurimis secum assumptis eo se conferens, aperto alveari videt Vasculum elegantissimum effectum è candidissima cera prope alvearis fastigium, in quo reposita erat Eucharistia, circa illud choros apum circumsonantes, & excubias agentes. Acceptum igitur Episcopus sacramentum maximo cum honore in templum reportavit: quo multi accedentes ab innumeris sunt morbis curati.* Tho: Bozius de signis Ecclesiæ, Lib. 14. c. 3.

In which Storie wee may note, besides the wonderfull knowledge and deuotion of the Bees, an incredible power and vertue also. For this God which they kept and compassed, is said to haue the gift of healing, which others, though of as good a making, we know doe want. The conclusion, which my Author necessarily inferreth hereupon, is better then all the rest. *Ex his necesse est dicamus in Eucharistia verum C. corpus esse.* But if thou wilt grant me that hereby is proued the incredible knowledge and skill of the Bees, for my part I will vrge thee no farther.

In the pleasures of their life, the Bees are so moderate, that perfect temperance seemeth to rest onely in them.

Also, in their owne Common-wealth, they are most iust, not the least wrong or iniurie is offered among them. But indeed I cannot much commend their Iustice towards strangers: for all that they can catch is their owne: vnlesse they may be excused in this respect, that the Bees of diuers hiues are at deadly feud, or rather as Kingdomes, that are at defiance one with an other. *v. c. 7. n. 25.*

Their Chastitie is to be admired. *Integritas corporis virginalis omnibus communis.*

51. *Temperance.*

52. *Iustice.*

53. *Chastitie.* Amb. Hex. l. 5. c. 21.

Et certe apes semina non coeundo concipiunt. Item, *Omnipotens creator apibus prolem sine concubitu dedit.*

Illum adeo placuisse apibus mirabere morem, Quod non concubitu indulgent, &c. They ingender not as other liuing creatures: onely they suffer their Drones *v.* among them for a season; by whose Masculine virtue they strangely conceiue and breed for the preseruation of their sweet kinde. Which strange kinde of breeding the Philosopher saith to be apparent vnto sense and reason. *Cum in genere piscium talis quædam sit generatio nonnullorum, ut sine coitu generent; hoc idem in apibus etiam evenire videtur, quoad sensus ratioq, apparens admoneat.*

54. Cleanlinesse.

For cleanlinesse and neatnesse, they may be a Mirror to the finest Dames. *Mundissimum omnium hoc animal est.* For neither will they suffer any flutterie within, if they may goe abroad, *Amoliuntur omnia è medio, nullaq inter opera spurcitiæ jacent*; neither can they endure any vnsauorinesse without nigh vnto them. *Odere fœdos odores: Nulla harum assidet in loco inquinato, aut eo qui malè oleat.* And for their persons (which are louely browne) though they be not long about it, yet are they curious in trimming and smoothing them from top to toe, like vnto sober Matrones, which loue as well to goe neat as plaine: pied and garish colours belong to the Waspe, which is good for nothing but to spend and waste.

55. The age of Bees.

Aneht the age of Bees there are diuers opinions: some thinke that they may liue foure or fiue yeares, yea some sixe or seuen: *Neq, enim plus septima ducitur æstas.*

Aristotle speaketh of a longer time. *Vita apum anni sex, nonnulla etiam 7. possunt complere: quod si examen 9. aut decē annos duraverit, prosperè actū esse existimatur.* Which opinions are grounded vpon this, that they see a stall sometimes continue so long, before the Bees die altogether. But this continuance is onely by succession: and so might they liue in *secula*, if the rottennesse of their combes, the hardnesse of their Honie, & the abundance of noisome stopping *v.* would suffer them to abide the Hiues. *Nam genus immortale manet.*

But

Margin notes:
August. de Trinit. l.3.
Idem de bono coniugali.
Georg.
V. s. 4. n. 3. &c.
Generat. an. l. 3.c.10.
Hist. an. l.9. cap. 40.
Nat. hist. li.11. c.10.
Hist. an. l.9.c.40
Var. l.3.c.15.
Georg. 4.
Hist. l.5.c.22.
V.c. 6.n. 20.
Georg. 4.

and of their Queene.

But the truth is, a Bee is but * a yeares Bird, with some aduantage.

* Which is a long life in comparison of the Silk-wormes, which liue but foure moneths; or of the Waspes, which liue but fiue: or of the Drones, which but six.

For the Bees of the former yeare, which vntill *Gemini* in the next yeare doe looke so yourhfully, that you cannot discerne them from their full growne Nymphes, which that spring they haue bred; doe from thenceforth change with manifest difference: for the young Bees continue great, full, smooth, browne, well-winged; the old waxe little, withered, rough, whitish, ragged-winged: and withall so feeble, that when they come loaded home, if any thing stand in their way, yea many times, though there be nothing, they fall downe, and being loaded cannot rise againe: and then either a little cold or wet in the day, or the nights dew killeth them: you may daily finde, specially in *Cancer* and *Leo*, some dead, some halfe-dead before the Hiues, and some aliue and lustie, which yet can neuer rise againe. Some of them will hold out so long, till their wings are more then halfe worne: but by *Libra* you shall scarce see one of them left.

The young Bees, as best able, beare the greatest burdens: for they not onely worke abroad, but also watch and ward at home both early and late: when need is, they hazzard their liues in defence of the rest, they beat away the Drones, and fight with other Bees and Waspes, and assault with their speeres whatsoeuer else offendeth them, they carrie their dead forth to be buried, and performe all other offices. But the labour of the old ones is onely in gathering, which they will neuer giue ouer, while their wings can beare them: and then when they cease to worke, they will cease also to eat: such enemies are they to idlenesse. And therefore generally they die in their delightfull labour, either in the field or comming home: *Atque animas sub fasce dedere.* Sometimes as well in Summer as Winter *v.* the Bees take pleasure to play abroad before the Hiue, specially those that are in good plight, flying in and out, and about, so thicke,

56.
The difference betweene the young Bees and old.

57.
The office of the young Bees.

58.
And of the old.

Virg.
V. *l.* 3. *n.* 59. &
62.

59.
Bees wont eftsoones to play.

Of the Nature and properties of Bees,

and so earnestly, as if they were swarming or fighting: when indeed it is onely to solace themselues: and this chiefly in warme weather, after they haue beene long kept in. *Exercitationem interdum solennem habent: spatiatáq̃, in aperto & in altum data, gyris volat, ueditis, tum domum redeunt.*

Nat. hist. l. 11. c. 20.

60. *They are soone killed with cold.*

The Bee is by nature very tender, soone chilled and killed with cold, which the Dorre, the Waspe, yea the Moth, the Gnat, and other little flies can endure, and most of all then, when by reason of long restraint, their bellies are ouer full. The first that faileth in them, when the cold beginneth to preuaile, is their wings: so that they cannot rise to their Hiues to helpe themselues by the heat of their fellowes. How to recouer them, yea when they are quite dead, See *Cap. 7. n. 63.*

61. *How to reuiue them.*

62. *The Bees excellencies.*

The Bee therefore excelling in many qualities, it is fitly said in the Prouerbe,

As ⎧ *Profitable* ⎫ as a Bee.
    ⎪ *Laborious* ⎪
    ⎪ *Loiall* ⎪
    ⎪ *Swift* ⎪
    ⎪ *Nimble* ⎪
    ⎨ *Quicke of sent* ⎬
    ⎪ *Bold* ⎪
    ⎪ *Cunning* ⎪
    ⎪ *Chaste* ⎪
    ⎪ *Neat* ⎪
    ⎪ *Browne* ⎪
    ⎩ *Chillie* ⎭

63. *Bees a chiefe exemplar of the diuine power and wisedome.*

Du Bartas. Fift day.

These wonderfull parts and properties of this little creature, what are they but so many euident proofes of the infinite power and wisedome of the Creator?

For, if old times admire Calicrates
For Iuorie Emmets; and Mermecides
For framing of a rigged ship so small,
That with hir wings a Bee can hide it all;
Admire we then th' All-Wise Omnipotence,
Which doth within so narrow space dispence

and of their Queene.

So stiffe a sting, so stout and valiant hart,
So loud a voyce, so prudent Wit and Art.
Their well rul'd State my soule so much admires,
That, durst I loose the raines of my desires,
I gladly could digresse from my designe,
To sing a while their sacred discipline.

Chap. II.
Of the Bee-Garden, and Seats for the Hiues.

Or your Bee-garden, first choose some plot nigh your home, that the Bees may be in sight and hearing; because of swarming, fighting, or other suddaine hap, wherein they may neede your present helpe. While the stalls are few, your Garden of Hearbs and Flowers will serue. *Hortis coronamentisq́ maximè aluearia & apes conueniunt, res præcipui quæstus compendijq́, cum sauit.* But when they are growne to a sufficient number, they require a square greene plot fitted for the purpose. *v.n. 8.*

2. See it bee safe, and surely fenced, not onely from all Cattell, (which if they breake in, may quickly spoile both the Bees and themselues) and specially from Swine (which by rubbing against the Hiues, and tearing the hackles in a wantonnesse, are most apt to ouerthrow the stalls;) but also from the violence of the winds: that when the Bees come laden and wearie home, they may settle quietly. *v.n. 5.*

The North fence of your Garden should bee close and high, that the cold wind of that coast, (which blowing against the Bees comming home wearie, would throw downe

1. Of fiue things requisite in a Bee-garden, the first is that it be nigh at hand.

Nat. hist. li. 21. c. 12.

2. That it be safely fenced from cattell and winds.

3. The North and East fences should be high.

and kill many) may bee altogether kept from them. And therefore, if it may be, set your Bees on the South side of your house.

The East-fence also would bee good and high to keepe from the Bees as well the sunne, as the winde. For the sunne rising doth oftimes till them forth, when the ayre is colder then they can endure; and the East-wind being cold & sharp, is very vnkinde for Bees, specially in the Spring.

But in no wise let the place be shadowed from the South-sunne: for that doth not onely dry the Hiues and relieue the Bees in the Winter and Spring, but also causeth them to swarme in Summer, if it be not extreme hot and drie *v*.

Nor yet from the Sunne-setting: because in calme and pleasant weather the Bees will be in the field after the Sunne is downe, euen as long as they can there see: and if when they returne, they finde it darke at home, many of them, their sight being but dim, *v*. fall short or wide: which flying and running to and fro till they be wearie, at length yeeld to the cold dew.

Otherwise let the fences be as good against the South and West-winds also, as may be: for although they be not so cold and bitter as the other; yet are they no lesse violent, and more frequent: so that they also doe much harme, specially in the Spring. And therefore if at that time of the yeare, in rough and boistrous winds, you finde that the Garden-fences doe not sufficiently guard and defend them; then is it good to set vp wixed or lined hurdles, or some other skreene betweene them and the weather. For though they can shift abroad in the strongest winds, as a ship that hath sea roome; yet are they easily ouerthrowne at the Hiue, as a shippe is soone wrecked at the Hauen.

A house or wall is fittest for the North fence: and a Quick-set-hedge for any of the other three: it may serue also for the first, specially if it be thicke.

3. That the place be sweet, not annoyed with any stinking sauour. I haue knowne a stall in the Spring, being sufficiently prouided of Honie, and hauing bred young, to forsake all, because of Poultry that roosted in a tree ouer them.

Odere

4.
The South and West fence must be also good, but not so high as to hide the Sunne from the Hiues.
V. *c*. 5. *n*. 19.

V. *c*. 1. *n*. 43.

5.
In rough winds the Bees need a skreene.

6.
3. *That it be sweet.*

and Seats for the Hiues.

Odore fœdos odores, procul, fugiunt: And yet the smell of vrine doth not offend them: nay, they will bee very busie where it is shed. It is thought they vse it for Physicke. *Remedium contra alui concitationem est vrina hominum vel boum.*

4. That it be neither verie cold in Winter, nor very hot in Summer. *Locus æstate non feruidus, hyeme tepidus, v:* A bare flower is naught in both seasons: because in Winter it is ouer cold, and by that meanes quickly chilleth the Bees that light vpon it; and in Summer it causeth them to lie forth through excessiue heat, *v.* A grassie ground therefore is best at all times: but let it be kept notte in Summer, and not wet in Winter: for long grasse and weeds about the Hiue, doe but harbour the Bees enemies, *v.* and hinder both their passage in and out, and their rising againe when they fall short: and water if it stand, as it will bee offensiue to your selfe, so is it dangerous to your Bees for chilling and drowning them. And as the parts about the hiues are to be kept notte & bare, so are other places also, where the swarmes doe vse to play and pitch, whether within or without the Garden, to bee freed likewise from long grasse and weedes, much more from Beanes, Pease, Hempe, and such high things: for the young weake Nymphs falling in those shadie places, except the weather be warme and drie, are in danger to be chilled before they can rise againe. For which cause the swarmes doe vsually refuse to stay and settle about such places: and then if windie or cloudie weather suffer them not to goe further, they must either goe home, or light vpon some other Hiues: where, without your present skill and diligence, they are like to be all lost.

5. That it be conueniently beset with trees and bushes fit to receiue the swarmes, as Plum-trees, Cherry-trees, Apple-trees, Filberds, Hazels, Thornes, &c. Which they will the more delight to light vpon, if, conuenient boughes hanging out alone from the bodies, the twigs below standing in their way be pruned, and the weeds and grasse vnderneath be cut away close to the ground. Although, if they be willing to stay, they will not refuse a dead hedge, a Lauender Border, or the like, or sometime the bare ground. For want of trees, some

Nat. hist. l. 11. c. 18.
Nat. hist. li. 21. c. 12.

7. Neither very cold in Winter, nor ouer hot in Summer.
Hist. l. 9. c. 40.
V. c. 7. in c. 3. n. 36.
V. c. 5. n. 19.

8. A grassie ground is best, but kept notte and drie.
V. c. 7. n. 43.

9. Beset with trees and bushes.

Of the Bee-Garden,

some haue stucke vp greene boughes, and the Bees haue lighted vpon them.

THe place being thus fitted, the seats are to be prouided; which, whether they be stooles or benches, must be set a little shelving, that the raine may neither runne into the hiue, nor stay at the doore.

To set many stals vpon a bench (as many vse to doe) is not good: for that in Summer it may cause the Bees to fight; as hauing easie accesse on foot to each other, and standing so neere, that they shall sometime mistake the next Hiue for their owne: and in Winter the bench will bee alwaies wet, which looseth the cloome, rotteth the bottome of the Hiue, and offendeth the Bees: and the Mouse at all times hath free passage from one to an other, without feare.

The single stooles therefore are best. And yet it is not amisse to set most of your swarmes vpon benches, aboue the old stalls: from whence remoue them to the stooles, when the stalls are taken: and then set vp the benches till an other yeare. Yet I preferre single stooles set two foot apart, though they bee laid flat on the ground: but it is better to reare them with foure legges, though little and short. If they be twelue or thirteene inches, three or foure inches may bee forced into the ground for their surer standing.

The best stooles are of wood: those of stone are too hot in hot weather, and (which is worse) too cold in cold.

For their size, they should not be aboue halfe an inch or an inch without the Hiue: saue onely before, where there needeth the space of three or foure inches, that the Bees may haue roome enough to light vpon: specially then, when the sight of a rainy cloud sendeth them thronging home. Which fore-part from one side to the other, is to be our shelving that it may the better auoid the raine. And therefore if the Hiue be fifteene inches ouer, the stoole should not be aboue sixteene or seuenteene inches one way, and nineteene or twentie at the most the other way.

These stooles would be set toward the South, or rather a point or two into the West: that the Hiue may somewhat

breake

10.
Two sorts of seats.

11.
The benches not so good as single stooles.

Vid. 7. n. 2.

12.
Swarmes may be set on benches.

13.
Wooden stooles better then they of stone.

14.
The size of stooles.

15.
Which way the stooles should be set.

and Seats for the Hiues.

breake the East-winde from the doore, *v.* and that the doore may be lightened by the Sunne-setting, when they returne late and loaded from field, *v.* and therefore it is to be wished that the Garden-fences did stand accordingly.

They should stand in straight rankes or rewes from East to West, fiue foot one from another (measuring from doore to doore) and from North to South, six foot one before another.

Likewise let them stand as farre from three of the fences, as they doe one from another. And so a plot of fiftie foot square, will receiue seuen rankes of nine stooles a peece, with the space of eight foot before them: which if it were bigger, were so much the better.

For want of roome or stooles, or wit, many doe set their stalls neerer together. But the greater distance is much better: not onely that you may haue roome enough to goe round about euery one, to see and amend what is amisse; but also that the Bees, when they come home in haste, specially when a swarme goeth backe againe, may be sure to flie into their owne Hiue. For if they stand neare together, at such time many will take the next Hiue for their owne, and then they fall together by the eares; *v.* and the Nymphs, when they go first abroad, wil by that occasion the sooner mistake: which if they doe, they dye.

The manner of placing the stooles in your Garden, with the distance of the rankes, I haue here expressed.

V. not. 3.

V. not. 4.

16. *How neere to each other.*

17. *How neere to the fences.*

V. c. 5. n. 79.

IV.

Of the Bee-Garden,

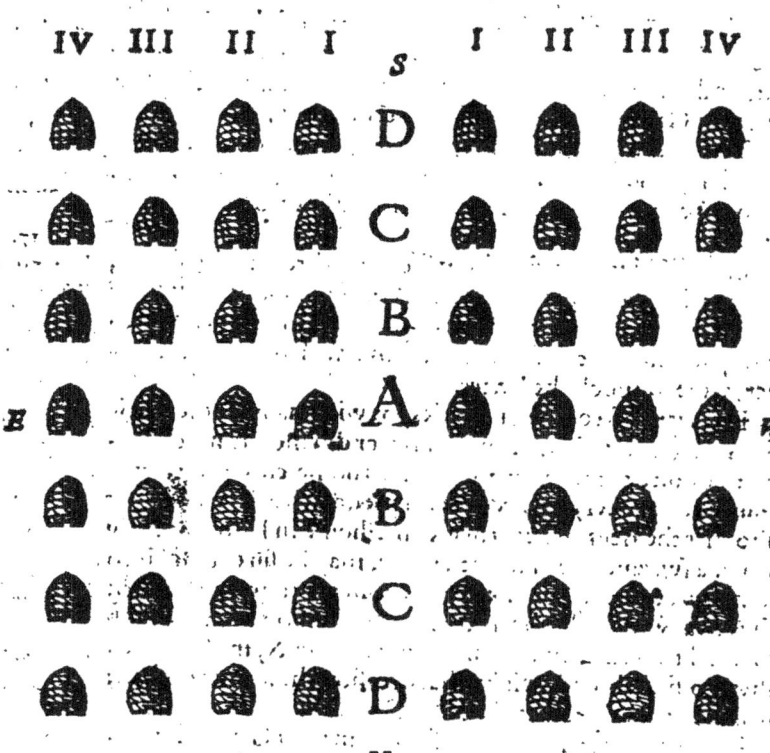

This Climactericall number of nine times seuen, is a competent or rather complete store for any one Garden, though large and alone: which being well ordered, will yeeld the Bee-master the better part of a liberall maintenance: if any be so happy to attaine vnto it. So that I see no euill at all in this Number: although the sixtie three yeare of mans age, being likewise called *Climactericall*, (because it ariseth of ✶✶✶ 6 septenaries, as so many Climacters or Ladder-rounds) be counted of some, and those no small fooles too, a parlous and ominous time: more dangerous for death, then all the

18.
Annus climactericus.

othe

other yeares of their life *. For which conceipt if you see no reason, thinke it is grounded vpon good obseruations: for this is certaine, that a ladder of nine rounds hath beene fatall vnto many.

* Ptolomæus obliquè eos notat, qui climactericos annos ficiunt ex numerorum sola obseruatione, ut enneadicos & hebdomaticos. Vnde multis molesta senilis superstitio super anno sexagesimo tertio, quoniam primi anguli tigrid-q; formidant: sed peccat in his vulgus errore veniali, qui Philosophi esse volunt, quia excusaueris. Pic. Miran. Lib. 6. c. 19.

19. *The Bees Register.*

V. c. 10. p. 1. x 3

Answerable vnto this climactericall squadron, it is meet you haue at hand a *Register*, containing the seuerall ages and yearely increases of all your stalls. Whereby you may be directed euery yeare, which are to be taken and which to bee kept for store: o: which is the chiefe point of a thriuing Beemaster. This Register may bee a *Synopsis* or Table drawne vpon a sheet, or halfe-sheet of Paper, diuided into sixtie three squares, or as many as be needfull for the stalls in your Garden: hauing first the foure Coasts; E. S. W. and N. noted in the out-sides: secondly, the middle row of squares from S to N. distinguished by Letters, the first square being marked aboue with D, the second with C, and the third with B, which are Southerne: The fourth (being the chiefe and middle-most, vnto which all the squares in the Table haue reference) with A, the fift with B, the sixth with C, the seuenth with D, which last three are Northerne: and thirdly, the first rew of squares next the Letters on both the E and W side, noted in the top or South part with one I, the second on both sides with I I, the third with I I I, and the fourth with I V.

The Table thus drawne, when you haue set a swarme vpon any stoole in the garden, marke in what letters ranke it is, what number from the Letter, and whether Eastward or Westward: and in the square answering thereto begin his Register, setting downe first the two last figures of the yeare of the Lord, then for a prime swarme, a double circle, for a castling halfe a double circle, then the day of the moneth in which he was swarmed, writing M for May, I for Iune, I for Iuly. The next line begin with the next yeare: if he did swarme,

Of the Bee-Garden.

swarme, set down a crossed circle, and the day of the moneth: if he swarmed againe, set downe in the same line a halfe circle, with a downe-right stroke, and the day of the moneth: if he did not swarme, but were full to the doore, set downe a circle with a full point in it : if he did also lye out, set downe a circle with a blotted circle in it : if hee did neither lie out nor were full, set downe a void circle.

⊚ ☾ ⊕ ⊣ ⊙ ● ○

And then doe likewise all the yeares that this stall endureth. When the Table waxeth full, after the vindemie make a new: taking out of the old the Register of those that liue. By this meanes you may certainly know the age, and yearely increases of any stall in your Garden : and so guesse whether he be fitter to kill or to keepe. *v. c. 10. p. 1. n. 3.*

20. The stooles height

Also the stooles should not stand aboue two foot from ground, because of the wind : nor vnder one foot for the dampnesse of the ground in winter, which would make the Hiues moist and mustie ; and for the heat of the ground in Summer, which in hot and dry weather would make the Bees lye out, and so hinder both their worke and swarming. *v.*

v. c. 5. n. 19.

The best heighth is betweene eighteene and twentie inches. Yet if you haue many, it is conuenient that the more North-ward rankes should stand higher, and the more South-ward lower, descending by degrees from two foot to one : as if there be two rowes of stooles, let the first stand two foot from ground, the next eighteene inches, & the benches or swarme-stooles one foot or lesse. *v.* If there be three rankes beside the benches, let the second be twentie inches, and the third six-teene, &c.

v. n. 13.

This vnequall heighth of rankes may as conueniently be effected, though the stooles be all equall, by the vnequall le-uelling of the ground : which in a great Bee-fold is best.

21. How to be footed.

The stone-stooles must be footed as they may : the fashion of each place where they are vsed will direct you. But the plankes or wooddon stooles are either to haue foure feet made of the heart of Oake, or of some other lasting Wood, or

Of the Hiues, and the Dressing of them. C. 3.

to be fastned to the seat with two woodden pins: which seat let be made of sound timber fiue or six inches ouer, and of that length, that it may be set betweene sixteene and eighteene inches in the ground.

Chap. III.
Of the Hiues, and the Dressing of them.

IN some countries they vse strawn Hiues bound with briar: in some wicker Hiues made of Priuet, Withy, or Hazel, dawbed vsually with Cow-cloome tempered with grauelly dust, or sand, or ashes.

1. Two sorts of Hiues.

The strawne Hiues when they are olde and loded, do vsually sinke on the one side, (specially if they take wet) and so break the combes and let out the hony: for which cause, first see that they be hard wrought, and then spleet them strong with a Cop, v. fitted to the top of the Hiue.

2. Strawne Hiues with their inconueniencies and remedies. V.2.11.

The Wicker Hiues will still be at fault, and lie open, (if they be not often repaired) vnto Waspes, Robbers, & Mise. Any of these, if shee finde but a little chap, will dig her way in: and the Mouse (vnlesse the twigs be close wrought) though shee finde none.

3. Wicker-Hiues with their inconueniencies and remedies.

Both these Hiues, if they be not well couered, are subiect to wet: which maketh them musty, and, if it be much, rotteth the combes, and destroyeth the Bees. But the heat in Summer, the cold in Winter, and the raine at all times doth soonest pierce the Wicker Hiues: for which cause it is good to double-dawbe them.

4. Strawne Hiues best.

All things considered, the strawne Hiues are best, specially for small swarmes. The

5.
The fashion of Hiues.

The Bees do best defend themselues from cold, when they hang round together in manner of a Sphære or Globe (which the Philosophers account the most perfect figure): and therefore the neerer the Hiue commeth to the fashion thereof, the warmer and safer be the Bees. But of necessitie the bottome must be broad, for the vpright and sure standing of the Hiue, and for the better taking out of the combs: and the top must rise some two or three inches higher then the iust forme of a Globe, to stay the hackle, and to shunne the raine: which yet, where the Hiues are couered with panns, is not necessary. Otherwise let your Hiues vary no more from this round figure, then needs must: as where it is within from the top to the skirts seuenteene inches, in the middle or widest place through the center fifteene inches, and at the skirts thirteene, after this forme.

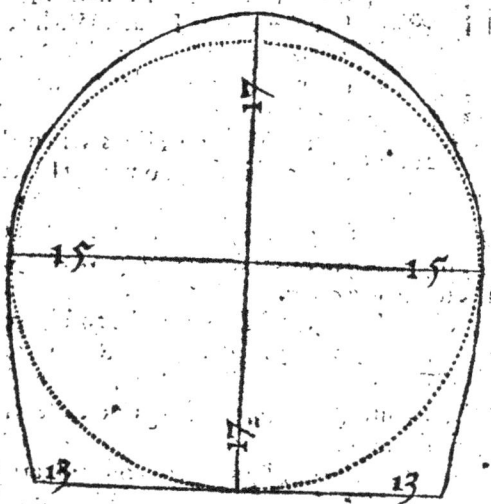

This forme with his dimensions wil conteine three pecks: and the abating of one inch in each dimension, abateth a gallon in the content.

The best that I haue seene are wrought by *Thomas May* of *Sunning*, about one mile from *Redding*.

and the Dressing of them. C. 3.

Hiues are to be made of any size betweene a bushell and halfe a bushell : that any swarme, of what quantity or time soeuer, may be fitly hiued. *v* : Lesse then halfe a bushell will not containe a competent stall ; and more then a bushell is found too bigge for any company to continue, and thriue together.

The midling size of three pecks, or within a pottle, vnder or ouer, as fitly conteining the naturall quantity of a good stall, is most profitable.

Haue alwaies Hiues enough of all sorts (but most of the midling size) in store, lest they be to seeke when you should vse them.

The best time for making them, whether they be Strawne or Wicker, is in the three still moneths of Winter, *Sagittar. Capr.* and *Aquar. v*: for then the * straw, briers, and twigs are best in season : and then is it best to prouide them, because then they are best cheape.

* *The best straw is most yellow without blacke spots, which is strong and tough.*

6. *The size of Hiues*
Vs. 5. B. 43.

7. *When Hiues are to be made and prouided.*
V. n. 54.

YOur Hiue being ready is thus to be dressed : First, take away all those staring strawes, twigs, and other offensiue jagges that are fast in the Hiue, making the in-side as smooth as may be : for these obstacles being many, if they cause not the Bees to forsake the Hiue, yet will they much trouble and hinder them : you may heare them (specially in the night) scraping and gnawing three or foure daies after they be hiued, yea sometime a weeke together, as though there were mise in the Hiue : and in strawne Hiues a long time after.

If you need but few Hiues you may prune them cleane with your knife : if you must vse many, then, hauing wet the skirts with a cloth, singe or sweale the in-side : but first and last rub it well with a Rubber, which is a peece of rough grind-stone or sand-stone, as great as your hand can hold.

2. The Hiue being pruned, put Spleetes in it, a three or foure, as the largenesse of the Hiue shall require : the vpper ends whereof set together at the top of the Hiue, and the nether ends fasten below in equall distance, about a handfull

8. *How Hiues are to be dressed before they receiue the swarmes.*

9. *The pruning of Hiues.*

10. *The spraying or splining of them.*

F aboue

above the skirt. In a wicker Hiue let the vpper ends rest against the middle of the staffe, & the nether ends against the parts of it betweene the Wickers; and in a strawne Hiue, set the vpper ends together in a Cop, and the nether ends against the briars or threads, between the third & fourth roule.

11.
The making of the Cop, and of the Spleets.

The Coppe is a round peece of wood an inch or two thicke, whose lower *superficies* is flat, with a hole in the middle halfe an inch deepe, for the spleets to rest in; and the vpper is conuex, turned or hewed fit to the concauitie of the top of the Hiue.

And for the Spleets, take a streight hazel or willow-sticke, quarter it if it be bigge enough, else slit it: then shaue and smooth the clefts, and hauing brought them to a conuenient [b] strength & length, cut the lower ends forked, to stay against the Hiues sides, and the vpper ends somwhat picked, and of that bignesse that they may fitly ioyne in the Cop or middle of the staffe, with their backs leaning [c] hard and fast one against another.

[a] If the Hiue conteine aboue three peckes, it may well receiue foure Spleets: otherwise three will suffice.

[b] Stiffe enough to keepe vp the Strawne Hiues from sinking, specially when they are turned, v. c. 5. n. 22. & 23.

[c] If you put foure Spleets in a Hiue, then cut their backes, where they must leane one against another, to square angles, such as be foure in a circle: if but three, cut them to obtuse angles, such as are three in a circle: (you may readily try them, before you put them in, by Moulds made iust to those formes) and so will they stand close and firme together. The first two of three, and the first three of foure are loose: it is the last that makes all fast.

And this is a handsome, easie, and sure way of spleeting: it is also good for drawing the Combes without breaking, and for keeping the Hiue from sinking and from tearing at the top. Besides which there are diuers sorts of spleeting, needlesse to be rehearsed: for euery Countrey hath his fashion.

12.
The seasoning of them.

3 Lastly, in swarming time season the Hiues that you meane to vse, rubbing them with sweet herbes such as the Bees loue, as Tyme, Sauourie, Marioram, Baulme, Fenell, Hysop, Mallowes, Beane-tops, &c. And when the swarme is

and the Dressing of them.

is setled, take the Hiue that you thinke fit for it in bignesse, *v.* and with a branch of Hazell, Oake, Willow, or any of the foresaid herbs, but chiefly with a sprig of that tree whereon the swarme lighted, wipe the Hiue cleane; and then dipping it into Meth, or faire water mixed with a little hony, or with milke and salt, or, for a need, with salt onely, besprinkle the same.

But if the Hiue haue beene vsed before, after you haue pared away the wax as cleane as may be; if you thinke the former dressing will not make it sweet enough; then let a hogge eat two or three handfuls of mault, or pease, or other corne in the Hiue: meane while doe you so turne the Hiue, that the fome or froth, which the hogge maketh in eating, may goe all about the Hiue. And then wipe the Hiue light-lie with a linnen cloth, and so will the Bees like this Hiue better than a new. But besprinkle it also, when you doe vse it, as is shewed before. And so serue a new Hiue when the Bees are so froward, that they will not otherwise abide.

And thus are the Hiues to be prepared and Dressed, before they receiue the Bees. Now will I shew you how they are afterward to be fitted and furnished.

1. First, let them be alwaies well couered, that they may be safe in Summer from heat, lest the wax melting, the Combes fall downe; *v.* in Winter from cold, lest it kill the Bees; *v.* and at all times from raine, lest it corrupt first the Hiue, afterward the Combes, and at last the Bees also. *v.*

In some places (where the stalls are not many) they vse earthen couers: but these doe not defend the lower part, and in Summer are too hot.

The best couer for Hiues is a thicke Hackle. *Aluearia stramento operiri vtilissimum.* Which is thus to be made, Take foure or fiue handfulls of * Wheat or Rie leased out of the sheafe: which being bound vp seuerally, beat out the corne; and then casting away their bands, draw out the eares of each handfull longer on the one side than on the other: and putting the long sides together (so to make the Head in forme of a Pyramis or Suger-loafe, for shooting the raine)

F 2   binde

C. 3.

V. c. 5. n. 43.

13.
The seasoning of an old Hiue.

14.
How Hiues are to be ordered when the Bees are in them.

15.
The Hiues alwaies well hackled.
V. c. 7. n. 53.
V. c. 7. n. 54.
V. c. 7. n. 58.
Nat. hist. li. 21. c: 14.

16.
How to make a hackle.

* In want of such straw, Wood-benet, or Sedge, or Rushes may serue.

17. *The Cap of two sorts.*

18. *The wreathed Cap.*

binde them all in one vnder the eares, as hard as you can.

The Head is to be couered or bound fast with a Cap: of which there be two good fashions, the one wreathed, the other platted.

The wreathed Cap is thus made; hauing bound the bundles all fast together with a thong, cord, or other strong string, leafe out of the sheafe almost a handfull of the strongest straw, and lay it in soake about a quarter of an houre. Being thus prepared, take out of that wet bundle a litche of 40. or 50. reedes or strawes; and laying halfe of them one way, and halfe the other, that the band may be of equall bignesse, take them vp together; and then mingling one end of the litche with the middle reeds of the Head, and twisting them fast together in your hand, let the band harle or double in the very top of the Head: and so begin to binde the Head round, working downeward, and still twisting the band as you goe. When that litche is well-nigh wrought vp, take out of the wet bundle so many more reedes prepared as before: and when you haue mingled one end thereof with the end of the first litche, holding them in your hand twist them fast together: and so continue your worke, alwaies binding as hard as you can, & bearing vp euery roule close to his fellow. When you are come down to the string, loose it, and binde the last or lowest roule in the place therof, making fast the end, by forcing it vp betweene the Head and the Cap with a forked sticke and a mallet.

19. *The platted Cap.*

The platted Cap is wrought contrary to the wreathed: for whereas that is begun in the crown, & wrought downward toward the right hand, and is made fast in the necke; this is begun at the necke, and wrought vpward toward the left hand, and is made fast in the crowne, after this manner.

First take a litch of strong reedes, and hauing wetted and wound it a little, put it about the necke of the hackle, and knitting the ends in a half knot, girt the hackle hard with it: (your assistant holding one end, while you pull the other) then to make this collar fast, wrap each end about it, forcing them betweene the collar and the head with the forke and mallet: Otherwise you may make a strong collar of a small

With.

and the Dressing of them.

With. The collar thus fitted to the necke, set the hackle betweene your legs, as you sit or stand, with the knot outward: and then, to begin, take vp a litche of the eares (about the bignesse of the top of your finger) next vnto the fore-said left end of the collar, and laying this end betweene it and the head, turne the top of the end downeward, and so leaue it: then take the next litch, and laying the first betweene it and the head, turne the first downeward, and so leaue it: then likewise take a third litche, and laying the second betweene it and the head, turne the second downeward, and so leaue it: likewise the fourth, and so forth, working thus round, till you come to the crowne, and platting still the litches hard, and close to the head. But when you come to the other end of the Collar, take that in for a litche. If the litches be too short for the worke, plucke them vp higher about the necke as you goe. When you haue wrought vp to the Crowne, knitting the foure last or top-litches in a true-loues-knot, make all fast.

The hackle thus made of foure or fiue handfulls will conteine in compasse about the necke, close vnder the Cap, betweene sixteene and twenty inches: sixteene will serue for the smaller Hiues, and twenty for the greatest, although they be fiue foot about. *20. The bignesse of the hackle.*

For the length of the hackles, each one is to be fitted to his Hiue, so that the skirts thereof may reach to the stoole, or within halfe an inch of it round about; saue onely before, where it must be pared somewhat shorter, that the Bees passage be not hindered. *21. The length of it.*

And then with a small pliant Garth or Belt of Bethwyn, Bramble, Brier, or the like, gird the hackle close to the Hiue*, lest the wind disorder it. If there be any crooke or bout in the Belt, set that before, that the hackle, bearing in that place farther out, may shoot the water from the doore: otherwise, for that purpose, set the Belt somewhat higher before, then behinde. *22. The belt or garth.*

*In the Winter, place the Belt below the middle or biggest part of the Hiue, to keepe it warme in extremity of cold. In Summer aboue, that the nether part of the hackle hanging out from the Hiue, the Hiue may be the cooler: and then because the Belt will be apt to rise, it would be held

23.
The hackle now and then to be taken off.

24.
The Hiues alwaies close cloomed.

Nat. hist. li. 11. cap. 14.

25.
Then seldome to be moued.
V. n. 4. 49. 53. 67. &c. 8. & 2.

26.
How a Hiue lifted vp is to be set downe againe.

27.
The Hiue-doore.

28.
The Gate or Summer-doore.

Of the Hiues,

borne to the place with two forked stickes, the fork resting vpon the Bels, and the other end vnder the Cap.

The Hackle thus fitted and placed, is now and then to be remoued, not onely to meet with Mise, Moths, Spiders, Ere-wigs, &c. which harbour vnder it, and to see what breaches the Mouse and Tit-mouse haue made; but also to ayre the moist Hiue: and this in a warme and windy day after much wet.

Next keepe the Hiues alwaies close for defence of the Bees against their enemies. The best cloome for that purpose is made of Neats dung: *circumlini alueos fimo bubulo vtilissimum*: but to harden it, temper it with Lime or Ashes, with sand or grauell, which are also good against the gnawing of Mise. With this cloome close vp the skirts & brackes of your Hiues: that there be no way into them, but onely by the doores.

And being thus safely shut, moue them not without vrgent occasion, *v.* for often lifting vp the Hiue, and leauing in the open aire doth discourage the stall.

But whensoeuer you are occasioned so to doe, (the Bees being stirring) lest any be crushed betweene the skirts and the stoole in setting it downe againe, reele vp one side with a little tile-shard: which, when the Bees are quiet, take away, and set the Hiue close cloomed againe.

The Bees entrance, as anon in this Chapter is shewed, must be sometime larger, sometime lesse, sometime nothing at all. And therefore euery Bee-Hiue must haue his Gate or Summer-doore, a Winter-doore or wicker, a Barre or shutting of the wicker &c.

The Gate or Summer-doore must be made of that size, that the Bees in Summer, when their number is greatest, may haue rome enough, with free egresse and regresse, not letting one another. The space of foure square inches is sufficient for any stall.

This Summer-doore is made thus: First cut away the lowest roule the space of fiue inches: and, with the Briar or Threed which bound that part, make fast both ends. Then fill vp againe the two extreme halfe-inches of the space, with two Doore-posts. The

and the Dressing of them.

The Doore-posts are two spleets halfe an inch broad, and fiue or six inches long, whereof the lowest inch is twice so thicke as the other, with a shouldering on the in-side. These Posts forced vp through the middle of the roules in their place, to the shouldering, as they serue to size out the Summer-doore to his due space of foure square inches; so are they fit to receiue the Winter-doore, when it shall be ioyned vnto them.

If the Hiue be with the least, you may set vp the Posts without cutting the roule.

In a Wicker-hiue the Summer-doore is made more easily.

Sometime, namely when a Hiue is reared, moueable posts are requisite: which may serue also at other times. A moueable Post is an inch-square peece of wood, with a shouldering aboue to rest against the Hiue: and an other in the inside of the doore to fit the wicket: the forme is this.

Of the doore-posts, and the vse of them.

29

30.
The Winter-doore, or Wicket.

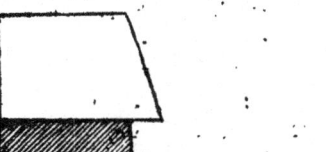 

The Winter-doore or Wicket is made of a peece of wood, an inch and a quarter thicke, almost an inch high, and fiue inches long. At each end whereof cut away halfe an inch all saue before, where that halfe inch in length must be leaft a quarter thicke, with his full heighth to fit the doore-posts: then in the middle of the neather side, cut, through the thicknesse, a hollownesse or passage, almost halfe an inch high, and three inches long: and then there will remaine at each end of the hollownesse halfe an inch vncut, besides the two extreme halfe inches leaft a quarter thicke, and fitted to the Posts.

The fashion of which wicket you may see in this figure.

The

31. The vse of it

The vse of the Winter-doore is to straighten the passage when there needeth not so much roome, that the Bees may the better keepe out the Robbers, that the Cold may haue the lesse force, and that the Mice may not enter, which in winter are wont to make much spoile. *v.c.7.n.3.*

32. The Barre.

V.c.7.n.6.

The Barre or shutting is to be made foure square of some heauy matter, as namely of Lead (that neither the rough wind nor craftie Titmouse *v.* may remoue it) in *length, depth, and thicknesse fitting to the wicket: with some little hollownesse next the stoole, that may let in the aire, and not let out the Bees.

** The length may be three inches and an halfe, the thicknesse three quarters, the depth halfe an inch: and the length of the hollownesse two inches and an halfe, the depth halfe a quarter of an inch.

For want of Lead or other mettall, you may with a hammer and grind-stone fit a Tile-shard: but let that be somewhat broad, that it may lie the faster on the stoole.

33. The vse of it.

† With this Barre you may shut or halfe shut the Wicket, as you shall see cause; to defend the Bees in the more dangerous times from Frost, Snow, Titmise, and Robbers.

For small stalls, the Gate, Wicket, and Barre, may be all of a lesse size.

34. The Settle.

It is also conuenient for each hiue to haue his Settle before him: which may be a planke of the bredth of the stoole, and of that length that it may stand leaning from the ground to the fore-part of the stoole: that thereon the Bees may settle when they come wearie or thronging home, and so ascend to the doore; and that there they may sunne and refresh themselues being chilly and wearie. Otherwise you may make a narrow planke or boord to serue, fitting the length of it to the bredth of the stooles, and then the one edge leaning to the fore-part of the stoole, let the other bee

borne

and the Dressing of them.

borne vp with two forked stakes set fast in the ground, or by some other props.

BEe-hiues being thus fitted with all necessaries, are afterward at diuers times of the yeare to be diuersly ordered. The *Melissæan* yeare is most fitly measured by the Astronomicall monthes (which begin with the Sunnes entrance into the seuerall signes of the Zodiack, and are therefore called by their names) because as the Sunne, entring into the twelue signes, and so beginning these twelue moneths, doth notoriously alter his course, making the daies longer or shorter, the aire warmer or colder, and the earth more fruitfull or barren, making also both the *Æquinoctia* and *Solstitia*, in which the foure quarters of the yeare, Spring, Summer, Autumne and Winter take their beginnings; so the most notable alterations about Bees, in things either to be obserued in them, or to be done for them, doe likewise fall out in the beginnings of these moneths.

But the foure Quarters the Bees begin one moneth sooner then the Astronomers. For their Spring or first quarter beginneth with *Pisces*, when the Sunne beginneth by his quickning heat to reuiue the flowers, which all the dead of Winter lay buried in the ground; and the Bees hauing tasted thereof beginne to breed, *v.* and to increase their companies for the fruits of ensuing Summer, which from the former Summer hitherto haue daily decreased: the other Spring-moneths are *Aries* and *Taurus*, *v. n. 63. &c.*

Their Summer likewise containeth *Gemini*, *Cancer*, and *Leo*, most rich and plentifull in flowers and dewes, *v:* wherewith the multiplied Bees doe now store their Cells against the penurie of Winter. *v. n. 37.*

Their Autumne or Haruest, hath *Virgo*, *Libra*, and *Scorpio*: in which the Bee-masters *v:* and the Master-Bees *v:* doe reape the ripe fruits of many Bees labours. *v: n. 44.*

And their Winter consisteth of the three *still* moneths: *v.* in which the Bees liue altogether vpon their Summer-store, and get nothing. *v. n. 58.*

Heere note, that although Winter and Summer doe properly

35. *How to order the Bee-hiues throughout the yeare.*

36. *The moneths and quarters of the Melissæan yeare.*

V. c. 4. n. 12.

V. c. 6. n. 38. &c.

V. c. 10. p. 1. n. 20.
V. c. 7. n. 25. &
28.
V. n. 59.

Psal. 74. 17.
Prou. 20. 4.
Za. 14. 8.

perly betoken two of the 4. quarters of the yeare; yet * sometime they be taken, according to the common account, for two halfe parts or moities thereof: the one containing the warmer season, as from the end of *Aries* to the end of *Libra*, the other the colder, as from the end of *Libra* to the end of *Aries*.

* Namely, when they are mentioned together in a kind of opposition: as c. 3. n. 7. where you reade, neither very cold in Winter, nor very hot in Summer. *Locus æstate non feruidus, hyeme tepidus, &c.* Which two opposite parts the Poet doth fitly distinguish and describe by the two times of foddering and of pasturing Sheepe and Goats.

Georg. lib. 3.

———— *Victumq; feres & virgea lætus*
Pabula, nec tota claudes familia Bruma :
At verò Zephyris quum laeta vocantibus Æstas,
In saltus utrumq; gregem & Pascua mittes.

Metam. lib. 6.

But they are more certainly notified by the comming of the Fieldefare, and of the Swallow: the one bringing cold Winter, the other warme Summer with her. Hir Sister *Philomela*, that shrowdes hir selfe in the woods, is wont a little to preuent hir, obseruing more the time of the yeare, then the disposition of the aire: For she is heard commonly the last weeke in *Aries*, though it bee then cold and winterly weather: whereas *Progne* stayeth after that vntill she finde it warme abroad. If some foolish one or other chance to start out of hir Dormitorie sooner, the Prouerbe then is verified, One Swallow makes not a Summer.

37.
SVMMER.

V. n. 28.

The Spring hauing replenished the Hiues with plentie of Bees, the Summer is readie with his plentie of Honie to entertaine them. During which season the Hiues must haue their largest entrance. *v :* lest the thronged multitudes be pestered for want of aire, or doe let one an other as they goe and come earnest in their worke, or bee stayed in swarming when they should passe at pleasure. Neither can the opennesse of the Hiues be hurtfull vnto them, seeing now there is no feare of enemies.

38.
In **GEMINI**
set the doores
wide open.
V. n. 28.

At *Gemini* therefore set the doores *v :* wide open, without Barre or Wicket: and so let them stand all this quarter.

39.
CANCER.

40.
To make the Bees
swarme.

Gemini being past, if the weather be vsually coole, when there commeth a calme warme day, take off the hackles from those Hiues that are likely to swarme. But if the weather be extreme hot and dry, then is it good to keepe on the hackles to coole the Hiues, &c. *v. c. 5. n. 21.*

At mid-*Cancer* double the stalls that lie out. *v. c. 5. n. 22. 23.*

When

and the Dreſſing of them.

When you would haue no more ſwarmes, as namely after the firſt blowing of Blackberries, v: which is commonly within a ſeuen night after Midſummer: ſet vp thoſe Hiues that are full with three Tile-ſhards, or other things of like thickneſſe, and cloome vp the ſpace betweene the hiue and the ſtoole: If yet they chance to ſwarme, as ſoone as they are hiued, put them backe to the ſtocke, v. c. 5. n. 11.

Alſo reare the ſwarmes that being vnder-hiued doe lie forth, with bolſters of that thickneſſe that may but let in the Bees.

In *Leo*, or preſently after the laſt ſwarme, kill the Drones, of thoſe ſtalls you meane to take, with a Drone-pot cloomed to the doore. V. c. 4. n. 35.

And if you ſee any other ſo peſtered with multitudes, that they are loath to meddle with them; you ſhall doe well to helpe them ſome warme afternoone, and then will they take the worke out of your hand, and ſpend the leſſe time about it.

To the plentifull Summer ſucceedeth waſtfull Autumne. At *Virgo* therefore, or a little before, (which is the moſt dangerous time for Bees, becauſe of Waſpes that then, if not ſooner, learne the way into the Hiues, but chiefely of robbing Bees, which then begin to ſpoile) v. To the Gates of the weaker ſtalls, (whether they be ſmall ſwarmes, or ſtocks that haue caſt twice and late) ſet vp the Winter-doores, and faſten them with good cloome, v: and ſee that the Hiues bee cloſe in all places. (Thoſe that haue lien forth or otherwiſe be verie full, you may let alone and not ſtraighten their entrance till the weather bee colder, for ſuch are ſafe enough.) But firſt view your ſwarmes whether they fit their Hiues: thoſe that haue not now wrought downe within a handfull of the ſtoole, if you meane to keepe them (to the end they may lye warme the Winter following, and be ready at the doores to keepe out robbers) cut off ſo much of the skirts as will ſerue the turne (the bigger the Hiue is, the more you may leſſen him) and ſo ſet him downe, cut a Summer-doore v: in the skirt, and put to the Winter-doore. Without ſuch help the cold will kill many, and weaken all, whereby they become

---

41. To keepe them from ſwarming. V. c. 5. n. 11.

42. LEO

43. How and when to kill the Drones.

44. HARVEST

45. VIRGO.

46. To keepe the weaker hiues from robbing. V. s. 7. n. 28.

47. Set vp the Winter-doores. V. n. 24.

V. n. 28.

Of the Hiues,

Hist. l 9. c. 40.
48.
And keepe them shut til they offer to go abroad.

become vnlustie in all their doings: as the Philosopher well noted, *Si alueus justo amplior sit, desidiosiores redduntur.*

Moreouer, because the Waspes and robbing Bees will bee stealing betimes, before the true Bees be stirring; it is good in the euening, when the Bees are all in, to barre vp the Wickets of those that are weake, that a Bee cannot passe: and not to open the same the next day till the weather be warme, and the Bees offer to come abroad, though it be not before nine, or ten, or eleuen a clock: and then you may either open it, or halfe-open it, according to the flight of your Bees, *v.*

V. n. 33.
49.
The reared stalls now to be set downe againe.
V. n. 41.
V. c. 1. n. 55.
V. c. 4. n. 25. &c.
V. n. 26.
50
In Virgo try whether the Bees will liue.

The stalls which you reared in the end of *Cancer* for feare of swarming or want of roome, *v:* (now that the death of the old Bees *v:* and of the Drones *v:* hath made roome) are to be set downe againe, *v:* lest their swarming be hindred the next yeare: vnlesse they be swarmes that haue wrought downe to the stoole.

Also in this moneth, about the middle, those Hiues which you deeme to be weake because the Bees are gone vp from the doore, knocke with your hand, one after an other: they that at the first or second stroke doe make a great noise both aboue and beneath, continuing the same for a space, haue store of Bees, and are therefore in lesse danger: but those that make a little short noise, though they be heauy and haue Honie enough (such as are commonly those of three yeare old, & vpward, that haue cast twice or oftner that yeare, and did not by *Virgo* beate away their Drones) yet haue they but few Bees, and are therefore ill able to resist the violent multitude of Robbers: which, when they perceiue their weaknesse, will neuer leaue them, as long as there is a drop of Honie in the Hiue.

V. c. 7. n. 43.

If you see them once fighting, *v.* either presently take them, or make their entrance so narrow, that but one Bee may passe at once: and before *Libra* bee sure to take them. For though they escape this robbing-time through your care and diligence; yet at the Spring they will surely yeeld, or die of themselues, or flie away. Note yet, that those stalls which are very full, will make but a little noise when you knocke them, (but different from the other, as being quicke, smart,

and

and the Dressing of them.

and all ouer the Hiue) vntill toward the end of this moneth, when they be gone vp from the doore, and their number is somewhat diminished.

In the end of this moneth is the time to kill and driue Bees, *v. c.* 10. *part.* 1. *n.* 2. & 13. Some Bees faile after *Virgo*: and therefore it is good to make triall of them in *Libra* also, by poysing and knocking the Hiues; for as they that then make * a little noise will die for lacke of company; so they that are light will die for lacke of meat. And alwaies haue an eye to those that the Robbers doe eagerly haunt: which is a signe that they perceiue in them some defect or other: and therefore will not be answered without their errand.

* A little short noise aboue in the Hiue, specially when in the end some few single Bees endeuour by their earnest and continued sound to seeme many, bewraieth their paucity and decaying.

Such as by these meanes you finde vnlikely to liue, take or driue: those that you suspect, and yet are willing to keep; marke them, feed them in due time, and proue them againe in *Pisces* and *Aries*.

At *Libra*, or before if you see cause, set vp the Winter-doores of the best, and then diligently in the euenings shut all those in with the Barre, that haue least watching at the doore. For in the cold mornings, while the true Bees keepe in, because it is not fit time for them to gather in; the theeues, both Waspes & Bees will be abroad, seeking where they may breake in and steale. But still let the weaker haue their Wickets halfe-shut.

This shutting & opening of the Wickets must be continued throughout *Scorpio* also; vnlesse abundance of cold raine do sooner chasten the Waspes. But for the poore stalls, it is best to keepe them halfe-shut all the day long, as in *Virgo* and *Libra*.

At *Scorpio* dresse your Hiues for Winter. First lift vp the stalls (except those that be full of Bees, which will not need your helpe) and sweepe the stooles cleane: then setting them downe againe warily, *v.* that you hurt no Bees, cloome them close, and mend all brackes and faults about them: and where the hackles be worne, set new in their steads, that may keepe

---

51. *Now take the Combes.*

52. **LIBRA.**

53. *Try them againe in Libra also.*

54. *Now set vp the wickets to the best, and keep the rest shut till the Bees offer to goe abroad.*

55. **SCORPIO**

56. *Continue the shutting and opening of the wickets this moneth also.*

57. *How to dresse the Hiues for winter. V. n. 26.*

the Hiues dry and warme. And now remember also to shut the wickets of them all.

58. WINTER.

59. SAGIT. CAPRIC. AQVAR. three still moneths.

After Autumne, the Sunne drawing neere the Winter Tropicke, with a short and low course aboue our *Horison*, there follow three *still* moneths, *Sagittarius*, *Capricornus*, and *Aquarius*: in which as the plants lie still in the earth waiting the Sunnes returne to reuiue them; so the Bees lie *still* in their Hiues, passing this fruitlesse time in sleepe and slumber. Yet so, that if there happen a milde and warme houre, they presently perceiuing it awake out of their swiuet, and hye them out of doores with all alacrity: that they may take the fresh aire, recreate themselues, drinke, exercise their wings, carry out their dead and other noysomenesse, and lighten their little bellies, which are oft times so stuffed, when the weather suffereth them not to goe abroad, that they can hold no more: so loth are they to defile their nests. And hauing thus refreshed themselues, at their returne, they take their repast, and then betake them againe to their rest. But many such daies, specially in time of scarcity, are dangerous, as causing them to spend much of their store, which in *still* frosts they would spare.

60. *How the Bees spend their time in them.*

61. *The first sharpe weather in Capr. shut the Bees in.* *V. c. 7. n. 6.*

The first foule and cold weather in *Capricorne* shut the Wickets close, to saue the Bees from the Tit-mouse, *v.* and from the cold, as well within the Hiue as without. For as the frost and snow and cold winds, yea and the ordinary disposition of the aire doth chill many of them, whom the flattering sun-shine enticeth abroad; so the great frosts, striking through the doore, doe freeze the nethermost in the Hiue to death: so that by little and little many stalls in some winters haue beene thereby wholly destroyed: the which, by keeping them warme, might haue beene preserued. But when you shut them in, be sure the Hiues be alwaies close and sure: for the Bees when they awake will striue by all meanes to come forth, though they neuer finde the way in againe. Yet when there happeneth any pleasant day (namely when the sunne shineth, the winde is still, or bloweth mildly out of the South or West, and the earth is without frost & snow) it is very behouefull to giue them leaue to play, *v.* and to refresh them-

62. *And in pleasant weather let them loose, if it may be, once a fortnight.* *V. n. 59. & c. 1. n. 59.*

and the Dressing of them.

themselues: once in a fortnight or three weekes is to be wished, specially after *Capricorne* is past: but if you or the weather shut them in much longer, they will be so faint and feeble through their long restraint, that without very pleasant weather at their comming abroad, a number of them will be chilled while they rest themselues but a little in the open aire. And therfore as often as, for this purpose, the doore is a little opened; alter it not, vntill the weather alter: and when *Aquarius* is halfe spent, if, for feare of a piercing night-frost, you barre them vp in the euening; let them goe againe in the morning, vnlesse either snow or boysterous windes forbid you. In winter prouide your Hiues. *v. n. 7.*

The still Moneths of Winter being past, the new yeere entreth with *Pisces*, the first moneth of the Spring: when the Plants begin to sprout, and the Bees to breed againe.

Now therefore, if not sooner, the weather being faire, halfe open the wickets of the better sort, and so let them stand day and night. For the night-cold, being now shorter and weaker, is not dangerous to such: and the day-cold doth them more good then hurt, causing them to lie still and spare their store, vntill it be fit time to goe abroad. But for the weaker swarmes (which are more subiect to cold, and robbing that now beginneth afresh, *v.*) shut them close in the euenings; and open them not in the mornings vntill it be warme: and then giue them but roome for a Bee or two to passe, specially those that stand most warme in the Sunne-shine, which maketh the robbers able to endure the siege, whom otherwise the aires chilnesse would quickly discourage.

And now (the Bees beginning to breed, *v.*) is the time to dresse and fill their Troughs, which all the winter lay neglected.

At this time, in a morning before the Bees come much abroad, lift vp your Hiues: and quickly sweeping the dead Bees and other noysomenesse away, and scraping cleane the stooles, set them downe againe, *v.* and cloome them close as before. For albeit the Bees in time would rid them cleane themselues, yet shall it be good for them to haue it done at once,

---

63.
The SPRING.
64.
PISCES.
65.
The first faire day in Pisces, set the Bees at libertie.

V. c. 7. n. 27.

66
Now dresse their Troughes.
V. c. 4. n. 12. & c. 6. n. 53.
67.
Clense the stools.
P. n. 26.

once, that they be neither hindered, nor annoyed therewith: and now and then the carrying out of a dead Bee at this time of the yeere doth cost a quicke Bee hir life: for being drawne with the weight of the corps to the cold ground; while she standeth panting a little, she is chilled, and so not able to rise any more.

This cleansing of the stooles, after a calme *Aquarius*, when the Bees haue beene much abroad, is not so necessarie, and specially for the better stalls.

<small>68.
And feede or driue light stalls.</small>

Those that by their lightnesse you perceiue to lacke honey, you may now saue by feeding, *v. c.* 8. *n.* 11. or driuing them into others that haue store. *v. c.* 10. *p.* 1. *n.* 15.

<small>69.
ARIES.
70.
The second chiefe robbing time.</small>

Aries is almost as dangerous a moneth, for robbing, as *Virgo*: and therefore you must haue a care in the euenings to shut the Wickets, & in the mornings not, before it be warm, to halfe-open them againe: and where the drie winds and hot sunne haue shrunke the cloome, be carefull to fill vp the chinkes againe.

The poore stalls this moneth would be halfe-shut all the day, as in *Virgo* and *Libra*.

<small>71.
In TAVRVS remoue the bars.</small>

At *Taurus*, and sooner, if sooner you see * cause, remouing the Barres from the better stalls, set the Wickets open: and for the weaker sort, let them all this moneth be shut in the euenings: and in the mornings, as soone as it is warme, be but halfe-opened.

* That is, when either they keepe watch at the dore in the euenings, or be so encreased that they cannot easily passe too and fro in their worke: for if the passage seeme too streight onely in their playing fit, *v. c.* 1. *p.* 59. that maketh no matter.

<small>72.
In GEMINI the Winter-doores.</small>

At *Gemini* take away the Wickets from the better, & the Barres from the weaker stalls: and when this moneth is halfe past, make them all alike: leauing the doores as they were in *Gemini* before. *v. n.* 38.

CHAP.

Chap. IIII.
Of the Breeding of Bees, and of the Drone.

HE Drone, which is a grosse Hiue-Bee without sting, hath beene alwaies reputed a greedy lozell: (and therefore hee that is quicke at meat and slow at worke is fitted with this title) for howsoeuer he braue it with his round veluet cap, his side gowne, his full paunch, and his lowd voice; yet is he but an idle companion, liuing by the sweat of others brows. For hee worketh not at all, either at home or abroad, and yet spendeth as much as two labourers: you shall neuer finde his maw without a good drop of the purest nectar. In the heat of the day he flieth abroad, alost, and about, and that with no small noise, as though he would doe some great act: but it is onely for his pleasure, and to get him a stomach, and then returnes he presently to his cheere. *Fuci eum exeunt, efferunt sese fusim in sublimi, gyroq; volitant: quod ubi satis iam fecerint, redeunt domum, & epulis perfruuntur.* But for all this there is such necessary vse of him, that he may not be spared, as without whom the Bee cannot bee.

The Drone no labourer.

Hist. an. li. 9. c. 40.

The generall opinion anent the Drone is, that he is made of a hony-Bee, that hath lost his sting: which is euen as likelie, as that a dwarfe hauing his guts pulled out, should become a gyant. Others seeing the fondnesse of this opinion, haue thought and taught that the Drone is a different *species*, and that as Bees breed Bees, so Drones breed Drones: which conceit (if the Author had obserued, that at the time of their breeding and many moneths before, there is not a Drone left aliue to breed them) hee would haue liked as well as the

Diuers opinions of the Drones originall.

H former.

Of the breeding of Bees,

former. These opinions then, being one as likely as another, let them goe together. The truth is, they are of the same *species* with the hony-Bee, but of a different *Sex*.

> 3.
> The Drone is the Male-Bee.
> *V. c. 1. n. 53.*
> *V. c. 6. n. 6. & 7*

For albeit he be not seene to ingender with the hony-bee, *v.* either abroad, as other *insecta* doe, or within the Hiue, (where yet you may by means behold what they do;) *v.* yet without doubt is he the Male-Bee, by whose naturall heat and masculine vertue the hony-Bee, which breedeth both hony-Bees and Drones, *v.* secretly conceiueth.

> *V. n. 18.*

> 4.
> Diuers reasons prouing the Drone to be the Male.
> The first reason is, that they are suffered in breeding time onely.
> *V. n. 18. & 19.*
> Nat. hist. li. 11. c. 11.
> *V. s. 5. n. 4.*

The reasons that moue me thus to thinke, are these. First, because although they be great wasters of the Bees store, yet vntill they begin to leaue breeding, and haue conceiued for the next yeere, (which some doe about *Leo*, most before *Virgo*) they suffer them: afterward they begin to beat them away. Which if some doe not, before *Scorpio* they die naturally: and from thenceforth all the Winter, vntill the Bees breed new againe, *v.* there is not a Drone to be had *In rerum natura*. When they are quite gone, then doe the Bees lay no more seeds that yeere, but onely hatch and breed vp those that are already in the celles.

> 5.
> The second reason is, that the Drones being taken away in breeding time, the Bees breed no more.

Secondly, as the rather and the more the Drones are, the more and greater are the swarmes; (*Certe quo major fuerit fucorum multitudo, eo major fiet examinum proventus;* *v.*) so where the Drones are few and late, there is small increase: and therefore if you kill the Drones of a Hiue before the Bees haue done swarming and breeding, (as some fondly haue done before Mid-sommer, to saue their hony from these lazie lurchers) neither will the swarmes come forth that were formerly bred, nor the stocke thenceforth breed any more.

> *V. c. 6. n. 18.*

After which time bringing in *Ambrosia*, *v.* as much as before, and hauing no young ones to spend part, they lay it vp carelessly in their cells, where it corrupteth and turneth to stinking stopping, *v.* which will cause them so much to mislike their Hiue, that the next *Virgo* they will easily yeeld to the Robbers, *v.* And if by your industry they be then preserued; in *Pisces*, when breeding time is, finding their wombes barren, and therefore loathing euen themselues and all, they yeeld their goods to them that will take it; and

> *V. c. 6. n. 19. & 20.*
> *V. c. 7. n. 25.*

after

after a while, when the strange Bees and they smell all alike, by conuersing together in the same Hiue, and sucking the same hony, away they goe with them to their Drones. But euery faire day they will returne to fetch that they least behinde them: you may see them flie so thicke to and fro that hiue, as if it were full of Bees: but when night is come, they are all gone.

Thirdly, because *omne simile generat sibi simile*, Euery liuing thing doth breed Male, or Female of his kinde, and experience doth teach vs that the Bees doe yeerely breed, as well Drones as honi-bees; *v.* seeing the honi-bees are females, it followeth necessarily that the Drones are the Males of the same kinde. And therefore in the learned Languages the Drone hath his * Masculine appellation, as the Honi-bee hir feminine.

* *Hic fucus, ὁ κηφήν: At bec apis, ἡ μέλισσα,* הדבורה, *cum* ה *feminina. Melissa the daughter of Melissus King of Crete, being one of Jupiters nurces, is said to haue beene by him transformed into the Honi-Bee: which retaineth still her gender, sex, and name. Didymus ait duas Melissi fuisse filias, Amaltheam & Melissam, quæ Iouem puerum captiuo lacte & melle nutrierunt.* Lact.lib.1.instit.c.22. *Nec saue rustico dignum est sciscitari, fueritne mulier pulcherrima specie Melissa, quam Iupiter in Apem conuertit.* Columella.lib.10.c.2.

Fourthly, we see the like in the likest *insecta*, the Waspe and the Dorre: for the manifesting wherof I wil briefly shew you the breeding of them both.

The Waspes neast is begun by one great Waspe, which you may therefore call the Mother-waspe: the which in *Cancer* (or in hot and dry springs somewhat rather) within some hole, vsually made in the ground by a Moale, Mouse, or other meanes, worketh a Comb of the vtter drix of pales, or other timber, in forme of a round tent hanging by the top to the ouer-part of the hole. This combe containeth about six Cells, of the bignesse and fashion of the Bees cells, wherin she breedeth so many young ones: which, when they are fledge, doe breed as well as their dam: and so enlarge the combe to some eight inches ouer. Then, making more roome beneath by moining and carrying out the earth, they hang an other combe vnder the first, by little pinns, and so an other, and

---

6. *The third reason is, that they are bred by the Bees.*
V. * *in annot. & n 12, &c.*

Deborah.

7. *The fourth reason is, that the waspes and dorres haue drones, which are their males*

8. *The breeding of waspes by drones.*

and an other, increasing still in the same place till Summer be done. For they goe not forth in swarmes as Bees doe. *Missio, ut apum, nulla vel crabronum vel vesparum fieri solet: sed qui subinde oriantur novelli ibidem manent, & alveum, terrâ egestâ, faciunt ampliorem.* When their breeding draweth toward an end, namely in *Virgo* and after, (besides the small or ordinary Waspes, which lie in all the vpper combes) in the last or lowest combe, made for the nonce with larger cells fit for larger bodies, they breed also two other sorts, Drones or Male-waspes (which are somewhat bigger and longer then the small Waspes, and without stings as the Drone-bees) and Mother-Waspes, which are like the small ones in all respects, saue that they are twice so bigge. These when they are fledge hauing conceiued, as the Bees, by the Drones; in *Libra*, and sometime sooner, doe flie abroad (as their Drones also doe) gathering for themselues, and searching and prying into euery corner as they goe, for their Winter-lodging: and after a while, when the aire waxeth cold, leauing both Drones and small Waspes to the mercy of Winter (which with his first cold-wet wether chilleth and killeth them as they flie abroad) doe forthwith betake themselues to some warme place, as the thatch of an house, a mortice in a post, an auger-hole, or the like; but specially into hollow trees, (which is the cause, why in grounds adioyning to Woods their neasts will be most rife) where they abide till the next spring without any meat, as it were in a dead sleepe: out of the which neuertheless a little warmth of the fire, or of your hand will awake them at any time. At the blowing of Palme, if the wether be warme, they flie abroad for food: and in *Cancer* or *Gemini*, as I haue said, they begin to nestle and breed. He that killeth one of them, killeth a whole neast of Waspes.

Hist.l. 9. c. 42.

* When the old Mother-Waspe hath done Breeding, and hir wings are so worne, that she is not able to helpe her selfe, the little ones keepe her so long as they liue together. Before the young Mother-Waspes are bred, you may easily finde her among the little ones: but when they are fledge, you cannot know her from one of them, but by hir ragged wings.

And

And that the Drone-waspes are the males, some were of opinion in the daies of *Aristotle*: for thus he writeth; *Si vespam ex pedibus ceperis bombilarег, fœceris, advolant quæ aculeo carent: quod non faciunt quæ aculeata sunt. Itaq; argumento quidam hoc utuntur quod altera mares sunt, alteræ fœminæ*: which argument seemeth not vnprobable, seeing the Fowlers counterfeiting the call of the Hen-Quailes catch onely the Cocks.

Hist. li. 9. c. 41.

The Dorre likewise beginneth hir neast single, being more like the Bee then the Waspe is, in that she maketh Honie, and more vnlike in the fashion of hir Combs: for she hath onely a few round cels of the bignesse of grapes, lying flat on the ground one vpon another without any order, else which are made after this manner. First either vpon the ground in the grasse, or in some shallow hole within the ground, shee prepareth a little stuffe which is soft like Wax, but browne and more brittle, of the bignesse of hir head; and therein she layeth about six or seuen seedes together, compassing them round with the same stuffe: which increaseth by little and little as the seedes doe: and when they begin to liue, it groweth into so many seuerall Cells, as there are grubs, each one hauing one to himselfe. When they be come to their bignesse, the Cells, which before were browne and brittle, doe now wax white and tough, that you can scarce teare them. And when the Dorres are ripe, they gnaw their way out at the top. Vpon these they make more in like manner, and the void open Cells they fill with Honie, wherewith they feed both themselues and their young, when the weather suffereth them not to flie abroad. All this neast is couered with a little Mosse like a Birds-neast. Vntill *Lammas* they breed females onely as the Waspes doe: and then last of all, for propagation of their kind, they breed their Drones, being likewise, as the Drones of Bees and Waspes, without stings. And those, to put the matter out of doubt, within a moneth after when they are ripe, doe openly engender with their females; as the chasers doe, but their hiues they chuse in the neast, and are carried away by them. After which time the females breed no more till the next Summer, though

9.
The breeding of Dorres by drones.

Of the breeding of Bees,

though you may see them gathering, and flying about somewhat longer then the Waspes. In *Sagittarius* they betake themselues to their Winter-rest, where they lie single as the Mother-Waspe in a sleepe or swouet. But the Drone-dorres, as the Drone-waspes, are destroyed by the weather: not one afterward to be seene till next *Leo*, when the females breed new againe. But one thing in the Dorres and Waspes is more strange, then in the Bees. For whereas the Bees assoone as they haue bred their first brood of females, doe presently breed Drones, *v.* (both which, when they are ripe, multiply together) the young Dorres and Waspes in the beginning of Summer, doe not immediatly take the Drones (for then there are none) but receiue from their dams, togither with their nature and being, that Masculine seed, whereby when they are ripe they breed all the Summer following, vntill in the end they likewise conceiue by their late-bred Drones for the next yeare, both for themselues and the young that shall come of them.

V. n. 19.

10.
The fift reason is the apparent signes of their Sex.

By this time thou wilt say with me, that the Drone is the male-Bee: Whereof if some curious Chirurgion would make an Anotomie, he should easily discerne *Duos amplos & candidos testes,* two lawfull witnesses of his Masculine Sex.

11
Aristotles Objection answered.
Hist.l.5.c.21.
Generat.l.3.c.10.

This truth began to appeare many yeares agoe, euen in *Aristotles* time. *Aliqui* (saith he) *mares esse fucos, fœminas vero apes esse contendunt.* Which opinion he reciteth in another place. *Sunt qui fucos mares esse, apes fœminas arbitrentur.* Where though he doe not approue it; yet hath he no other reason against it but this, *Arma ad pugnam viresq, exercendas nullis fœminæ à natura tribuuntur.* Nature hath armed no female for fight and force against the male: but the Bees haue power and weapon to chastise the Drones *v.* and therefore the Drones cannot be their males.

V. n. 12.

The weaknesse of which reason I maruaile he did not see, seeing in all the kinde of *Hawkes* the female doth command the male, as being both stronger and better armed. Whereunto may bee added the example of the *Amazons* reigning in his time: who by force of armes subdued many Kingdomes of men, and held them in subiection: like vnto which,

and of the Drone.

which, it is maruaile but there were then some mankind Viragoes in *Greece*, as well as there be now in other Countries. Which thing, if nothing else, the experience of his Masters † Master might haue taught him.

* The first instance is beyond exception: neither doe I see how the other can be answered, valesse peraduenture it be replyed that such rule is against Nature.

† *Aristotle* his Master was *Plato*, whose Master was *Socrates*, whose Master was *Xantippe* that thundring showring Queene of Shrewes. *Xantippé Socratis Philosophi vxor morosa admodum fuisse fertur & iurgiosa: iracundiáq́, & molestiarum muliebrium per diem peráq́, noctem scatebat.* A. Gellius l. 1. c. 17. *Socrates, cum in eum Xantippe priùs conuitia & maledicta ingessisset, posteà vero & sordidis aquis perfudisset, Nonne* (inquit) *dicebam Xantippen tonantem quandoque pluituram?* Laertius lib: 2. in vita Socratis.

But you must vnderstand that the Philosopher speaketh thus, not *dogmaticè* but *disputatiuè*, onely by way of reasoning: for in the end of the same chapter he yeeldeth himselfe to haue no certaine knowledge thereof. *Non tamen satis adhuc explorata quæ eueniant habemus.*

To returne therefore to our purpose, the Hony-Bees hauing, as those other *insecta*, conceiued by the Drones; the best about *Pisces* when they first gather vpon flowers, others in *Aries*, and the weaker later, begin their breeding: which is continued all the Summer, euen to the end of *Virgo*. But the chiefe time is in *Aries*, *Taurus*, and *Gemini*: which monethes yeeld *Ambrosia* the *Schadons* food, in greatest plentie, varietie and vertue.

The Bees will be sure to serue themselues first, their first generation being alwaies females: which they breed after this manner.

Close vnder the Honie (which is at that time altogether in the vpper parts of the Combs) in the middle of the bottomes of the void Cels, as the Waspes doe on the one side, they lay their seedes, about the bignesse of those which the Butter-flie leaues vpon the Cabage-leaues: but of different colour, the Bees being white like Wasp-seedes, and the Butter-flies yellow. And so they descend by degrees toward the neather part of the Combes, filling one Cell after an other. Although when the chiefe breeding is past,
they

12. When the Bees begin to breed.

13. The chiefe time of breeding.

14. The first breed are females.

15. The manner of their breeding.

16.
The Bee-seed is first turned into a Worme.

they doe not precisely obserue this order, but lay vp their Honie promiscuously among the young Bees, where they finde the Cells void. The Bee-seed at the first sticketh vpon one end, vntill it be a liue Worme or Grub: as soone as it liueth it is loose, and lyeth in the bottome of the Cell round like a ring, one end touching the other, till so the bottome can no longer containe it: after that, it lieth along in the Cell till it be growen to the full bignesse of a Bee: and then doth the Worme die, and becommeth void of all motion and sense: and so is shut vp in the Cell, the Bees couering the top close with wax.

17.
The Worme being dead groweth to the shape of a Bee and then liueth againe.

The Grub being now dead, presently beginneth the alteration from a Worme to a Bee: which, is two-fold, in shape and in colour: the first alteration in shape, is the diuision in the middle; then the other diuision betweene the head and shoulders, whence it is called *insectum*: after that, the growth of the head, legges, wings, and other parts into their shape and fashion. The first that altereth in colour from white to browne is the vpper part, and of the vpper part the head, and of the head the eyes.

The vniforme shape and white colour of the Worme, being thus altered into the proportioned shape and brownish colour of a Bee, she beginneth to moue againe, and to liue hir second life: and then breaking the couer wherewith she was inclosed in the Cell, she commeth forth a flying Bird,

Hist.an.l.5.c.22

Fœtu posito incubant, exclusus inde vermiculus, dum paruus est, jacet in fauo obliquus: postea sua ipse facultate se erigit, cibumq, capit. Fœtus apum & fucorum candidus est: ex quo vermiculi fiunt, qui in apes fucosq, transeunt. And all this within the space of a moneth. Yea in swarming-time, when the Hiues haue more heat, partly from the aire, and partly from the multitude of Bees; when also the *Schadans* neuer want their fill of *Nectar, Ambrosie*, and faire water continually brought in fresh and fresh vnto them, I haue knowne this effected in three weekes: although *Plinie* speakes of more then twice so long a time. *Fœtus intra 45. diem peragitur.*

18.
The breeding of the Lady-Bees.

But the Lady-bees are bred in the seueral Palaces of the
Queene,

and of the Drone.

Queene, *v.* after a peculiar and more excellent manner. For the golden matter whereof they are made, is not turned into a Worme at all; but immediatly receiueth the shape of a Bee. *Primordium regum colore cernitur fulvo, corpulentia mellis crassioris, magnitudine ilico proximâ suæ futuræ soboli: nec primùm ex eo vermiculus gignitur, sed statim apis.* Item, *Higinius negat ex vermiculo, ut cæteras apes, fieri ducems; sed in circuitu favorum paulo majora, quam sint plebeij seminii, inveniri foramina repleta quasi sorde rubri coloris, ex qua proximus alatus rex figuratur.*

When the old Bees haue ended their first broods of females, then last of all after the same manner in wider Cells made for the nonce, *v.* they breed the Male-bees or Drones: as was long since obserued, *Sunt fuci sine aculeo velut imperfectæ apes, nouissiméq̀, à fessis & jam emeritis inchoata, serotinus fœtus.* And therefore some stalls doe not dronie before *Cancer*, not many before *Gemini*, nor any before *Taurus*: although you may see the* Nymphes of good stalls abroad in *Aries*, of others in *Taurus*, and of all in *Gemini*. By chance some few Cephens may be bred betime with the femals: but they, as comming out of season, are not suffered to liue.

Vir. c. 6. v. 11. & 12.

Hist. l. 5. c. 22.

Colum. l. 9 c. 11

19. *When the Drones are bred.*

Vir. c. 6. v. 10.

Nat. hist. li. 11. c. 11.

20. *When they come abroad.*

* The young Bees are called Schadons: *Schadones sobolem dico.* Hist. l. 5. c. 22. The brood of females, when they haue the shape of Bees, are called Nymphs, and the young Drones Cephens: *Cætera turba, cum formam capere capit, Nymphæ vocantur, ut fuci Cephenes.* Pl. li. 11. c. 11.

These Cephens or Drones, when they are fledge, doe not onely serue for generation; (as hath beene shewed) but also doe helpe the females much, by reason of their great heat, in hatching their broods. *In fœtu adjuvant apes, multùm ad calorem conferente turba.* And for these causes they are alwaies in breeding-time mingled with them throughout the Hiue. Although afterward (when they haue beene much beaten, and can goe no where single, but one or other will be on their jackes) they gather all together in a cluster, for their safetie in one side of the Hiue: so that it is true at some time which the Philosopher spake indefinitely, *Tenent alvei locum penitiorem.* And yet their hanging together will not serue

21. *Two vses of the Drones.*

Nat. hist. li. 11. c. 11.

22. *Where they lye.*

Hist. l. 9. c. 40.

serue their turne: for the Bees, when they are difpofed, will quickly make them part, and depart. When there is no vfe of them, there will be no roome for them.

23.
The male-Bees are ſubiect to the females.
Nat. hiſt. li. 11. cap. 11.

For the Drones are but vaſſals to the Honie-bees: which as they doe excell them in vertue and goodneſſe, ſo doe they alſo in power and authoritie, ruling and ouer-ruling them at their pleaſures. *Sunt quaſi ſeruitia verarum apum: quamobrem imperant ijs.* For albeit generally among all creatures the males, as more worthy, doe maſter the females; yet in theſe, the females haue the preeminence: and, by the Grammarians leaue, the Feminine gender is more worthy then the Maſculine, *Hæc apes* then *hic fucus*, *hæc Nympha* then *hic Cephen*. But let no nimble tongued Sophiſters gather a falſe concluſion from theſe true premiſſes, that they, by the example of theſe, may arrogat to themſelues the like ſuperioritie: for *Ex particulare non eſt ſyllogizare*, and he that made theſe to command their males, commanded them to be commanded. But if they would ſo faine haue it ſo, let them firſt imitate their ſingular virtues, their continuall induſtry in gathering, their diligent watchfulneſſe in keeping, their temperance, chaſtitie, cleanlineſſe, and diſcreet œconomie, &c. And then, if they meete with ſuch dull Lubbers as theſe Drones are; they may with leſſe blame borrow a point of the Law, and enioy their longing. Yet when they haue it, let them vſe poore Skimmington as gently as they may; eſpecially in publike, to hide his ſhame.

And this they may note by the way, that albeit the females in this kinde haue the Soueraigntie, yet haue the males the lowder voice: as it is in other liuing things, Doues, Owſils, Thruſhes, &c. the males being knowne by their ſounding and ſhrill notes from the ſilent females. Yea the wiues themſelues will not ſuffer that Hen to liue, which preſumeth to crow as the Cock doth: nature teaching, that ſilence and ſoft noiſe becommeth that Sex.

24.
When the Bees leaue breeding, and beat away their Drones.

The Bees breeding or laying of ſeeds beginneth to ceaſe, in ſome by *Leo*, in ſome not before *Virgo*. After which time theſe * *Amazonian* Dames, hauing conceiued for the next yeare, begin to wax wearie of their mates, and to like their roome

and of the Drone.

roome better then their company. At first not quite forgetting their old familiaritie, they gently giue them Tom Drums entertainment: they that will not take that for a warning, but presume to force in againe among them, are more shrewdly handled. You may sometime see a handfull or two before a Hiue, which they had killed within: but the greatest part flyeth away, and dieth abroad.

* Amazones bellicosæ erant Scythiæ mulieres, quæ cum viris exulantes in Cappadociæ ora juxta amnem Thermodonta consederunt: ubi, viris plerisq; per insidias accolarum trucidatis, reliquos qui domi remanserant, ut ipsæ solæ rerum potirentur, interficiunt: & armis sumptis etiam cum contemptu hostium se strenue tuentur, & imperium longe lateq; in Europam & Asiæ partem tandem proferunt, Ne vero genus periret, finitimis tanquam maritis utuntur: quos officio functos abigunt: Atq; quos pariunt virgines fovent, & armis exercent; masculos vero duræ enecant: vnde eas Æorpata i. Viricidas appellant Scythæ, ut tradit Herodot. l. 4. Prima harum regina Marthesia vel Marpesia dicebatur: quæ plures quidem peperit filias, Antiopen, Orithyam, Menalippen, & Hypoliten: è quibus duæ majores natu matri successerunt, cæteræ imperium non sunt adeptæ. Amazonum itaq; regnum apum rempublicam aptissime refert: Marpesia apum reginam quæ plures solet producere fœtus: Antiope & Orithya primores filias, quæ primum & secundum examen educunt, iisque moderantur: Menalippe & Hypolite eas principes quæ aut nequaquam aut nequicquam dominantur. Nam post secundum examen aut in alveis morantes morte mulctantur, v. aut egressæ fere fame pereunt, v. c. 8. n. 4. Vtriusq; etiam populi mores non minùs conveniunt: nam & apes fœminæ sunt bellicosæ, quæ non modo Europam & quandam Asiæ partem, ut illæ; sed universa orbis terrarum imperia possident: quæ sui sexus prolem summa itidem cura enutrientes, mares omnes tam viros quam filios cædere solent: ut & ipsæ vere Æorpata dici possint.

25. The Bees compared to the Amazons.

V. c. 1. n. 7.

But because in the same Hiue they doe not leaue breeding all at once; therefore neither doe they kill their Drones all at once: but at the first taking away onely the superfluous, they suffer as many as they need, to remaine longer: some sometime a whole moneth after.

26. They rid not their Drones all at once.

The forward stockes, that haue cast their last swarme in *Gemini* or soone after, begin at *Leo*: yea of those in the beginning of *Gemini* some somewhat sooner, the backward, that cast not their last swarme much before *Leo*, may stay till the end of the same moneth: but vsually about *Virgo*, or a weeke after, they make a cleane riddance of them.

27. When forward stalls begin.

28. When the backward.

Those

Of the Breeding of Bees,

29. *When full stockes that haue not swarmed.*

Those stockes that being full haue not swarmed at all, because they are rich and feare no want, vse to suffer them so long and sometime longer, euen to the end of this moneth.

30. *When those that are ouer swarmed.*

Those that haue ouer-swarmed themselues, finding their pouertie and weaknesse, wax desperate and carelesse of their estate: and therefore sometime keepe their Drones till toward the end of *Virgo*, sometime kill them not at all: but let them alone, vntill they die by nature: which is not long after. For few of them can liue till *Libra*, and the youngest not to the end of that moneth. *v.* Take heed to such stalls, for they are likely to die.

V. n. 4.

31. *Sometime the Bees cast out euen the white Cephens.*

Some are so prouident, that, to preuent this trouble and saue their Honie, they draw the poore Cephens out of their Cells before they be ripe, or come to their second life. Such you may safely trust.

32. *Timely ridding of Drones a good signe.*

Those that soonest rid their Drones, are likely to be forwardest the next yeare.

33. *Sometime they rid their Drones in the Spring.*

Sometime the Drones are beaten away in the Spring. For when forward stalls (which in their heat are bold to fly abroad when others dare not wagge) haue lost many of their Nymphes in a tempestuous and stormie Spring; they will therefore destroy their Drones also. But hauing formerly conceiued by them, they then begin the world anew, as after an other Winter: and first breeding Nymphs, in the end they breed Cephens againe. Which if they can compasse before swarming time be past, they will swarme that yeare: otherwise they will be fat and full, and excellent good either to keepe or kill.

34. *And afterward breed new again.*

35 *Sometime it is good to helpe the Bees in this work.*

Because the stockes that haue cast often, doe beare with their Drones so long, although there be twise so many as bee needfull for the Bees that are least; therefore (to saue the Honie which those Wolmores would deuoure) it is not amisse to preuent the Bees, and presently after the last swarme to diminish their number, with a Drone-pot cloomed to the doore: specially of them you meane to take, or see much opprest with superfluous multitude, *v. c. 3. n. 4.*

CHAP.

Chap. V.

Of the Swarming of Bees, and the Hiuing of them.

THE stocks hauing bred and filled their Hiues doe send forth swarmes. A swarme doth consist of all such parts as the stocke doth: namely of a Queene-bee, Honie-bees as well old as young, and Drone-bees.

  If any man desire to see the Queene, he hath now opportunitie, when she goeth forth with hir swarme : *v.* and dead ones hee may finde many before the stooles, when the stocks haue cast their last swarmes, *v.* and also when many meet in one swarme, *v. c. 1. n. 7.* But then, being dead and shrunke together by the force of the poison, they lose much of their stature and comlinesse.

  Men thinke that the swarme consisteth onely of young Bees, and that the old Bees onely tarrie behinde: but indeed (though it may seeme strange) the swarme is no younger, then the stocke: for there are in both of both sorts. The young Bees remaine in the stock with the old for their defence, and for the greatest labours ; *v.* and the old ones goe with the young in the swarme for their aid and guidance in their worke.

  The Drones they take with them for propagation of their kinde. *v.* And therefore those swarmes that haue many Drones will surely prosper: and if they be rathe will swarme againe, vnlesse they bee ouer-hiued : whereas those that haue few or none, will increase little or nothing all the Summer after.

  A warme, calme, and showring spring causeth many and rathe

1.
The parts of a swarme.

2.
When you may see the Queene-Ry.
V. n. 34.
V. n. 35.

3.
The swarme no younger then the stocke.

V. c. 1. n. 57.

V. c. 4. n. 3.
4.
Many Drones in a swarme a good signe.

5.
A kinde Spring for swarmes.

Of the Swarming of Bees,

V. c. 7. n. 60.
Hist. l. 4. c. 22.

rathe swarmes, though sudden stormes doe hinder them. *vt Augent mella siccitates, sobolem imbres.*

*Dry weather makes plenty of hony, and † moist of swarms.

V. c. 4. n. 13.
V. c. 6. n. 38. 39.
&c.

But note that the chiefe time for breeding swarmes is the Spring, *v.* and for honie-gathering the Summer: *v.* so that when a dry Summer followeth a moist Spring, the Bee-folds are rich. If the Summer be also moist, the increase of Bees will be greater: but, because of the scarcity of hony, this increase will prooue a decrease: the more swarmes you haue at the end of this Summer, the fewer stalls shall you haue at the beginning of the next. For, except some faire rathe swarmes, and some good stockes, which cast betimes or not at all, they die all for hunger; when they haue spent their owne pittance, and spoiled their fellowes. How to preuent this pouerty, see *note* 11. & * in 20. and to preuent the losse & spoile that would come thereof, take the light stocks, together with the small and late swarmes, *v.* feed the midling sort, *v.* and be sure they be not ouer-hiued. *v. n. 45.*

V. v: 10. p. 1. &
iij. & iiij. in n. 3.
V. c. 8. n. 5.

* The reason is, that in hot and drie weather the hony dewes are raised, and the aduentitious moisture is drained from the flowers, the pure naturall iuice onely being lest in them: of both which they gather all the day long without interruption.

† The reason is, that the weather keeping them in, they can doe nothing but breed and hatch their schadons: and when they goe abroad, they bring in grosse Bee-meat, *Ambrosia* and water, wherewith to feed them; but can finde nothing fit to lay vp in store. So that moist weather giues them two causes of swarming, plenty of Bees, and penury of hony: the one makes them able, the other willing: and then neither winde, nor cloud, nor raine can stay them. Whereas in times of plenty it is otherwise. *v. n. 20.*

6.
Swarming weather.

V. n. 20.

Likewise, in warme and calme weather the swarmes delight to arise, but specially in a heat-gleame, after that a showre or gloomie cloud hath sent them home together: in extreme hot and dry weather not so: *v.* in so much that stalls being full and ready to swarme with the first, are sometime so kept backe with cold dry windes in *Gemini*, and with extreme heat and drought in *Cancer*, that they haue not swarmed at all that yeere.

7.
The swarming houres.

The swarmes vse to come forth betweene the houres of
nine

nine and three, and sometime an houre sooner or later: but chiefly betweene eleuen and one. They choose rather the fore-noone, if the weather please them: otherwise they will stay for a faire houre in the after-noone. This time of the day therefore, in the swarming moneths, your Bees must continually be attended.

The swarming moneths are two, *Gemini* and *Cancer*: one moneth before the longest day, and an other after.

The two swarming moneths.

In some very backward yeres, such as was 1621. & 1622. there haue bin swarmes a weeke in *Leo*, which did well, (the Bramble, that was wont to be a fortnight or three weekes rather, *v.* not blowing before that time:) Likewise in warme Countries in a kinde Spring, some haue come somewhat before *Gemini*, but this also is rare.

V. c. 6. n. 39.

Those that come before the Solstice, in the ascending of the Sunne, are rathe swarmes. Those that come after, in his descending, are late swarmes. But there are few that come in the first fortnight, and they very good: few also in the last fortnight, namely after S. *Peters*-tide, and they all as bad: vnlesse the backwardnesse of the yeere, when it happeneth, doe mend them.

9. *Rathe swarmes.*
10. *Late swarmes.*

Note heere that in the Heath-countrie, swarmes are vsually lateward, namely in the latter part of *Cancer* and the forepart of *Leo*: which some yeeres proue better then the rathe.

Those that swarme before the blowing of knap-weed, come in very good time: before the blowing of blackberies, *v.* they may liue and doe well: but blackbery-swarmes, specially castlings, are seldome to be kept, as being more likely to die then to liue: and if they liue, they seldome swarme the next yeere. And moreouer they weaken the stocks from whence they came, which otherwise the next yeere would swarme betime: and then one such swarme is worth three of those lateward ones. Wherefore put such backe againe into the stocke: which you may easily doe, so soone as they are hiued, by knocking them downe vpon a table close to the doore: their fellowes that are behinde will soone be in with them. And if they rise againe, serue them so till they cease. But if you spie them rising before the Queene be come forth, shut them in a while, and that will stay them.

V. c. 6. n. 39.
11. *Blacke-berieswarmes are seldome to be kept.*

A

12.
A prime swarme and an after-swarme.

13.
A stall may cast foure times.

14.
Diuers causes of breaking the prime swarme.

15.
One prime-swarme worth two after-swarmes.

v. n. 67. & 68.
16.
The vulgar Bees appoint the rising of the fore-swarmes, & that vpon 4. grounds.

V. s. 1. n. 6. & 7.

17.
Fiue signes of the first swarming.
V. s. 4. n. 10.

A good stocke doth naturally and vsually cast twise; a prime swarme, and an after-swarme: specially if the prime swarme be so rathe, that the castling may come before the bramble-buds be open: yea and rathe prime swarmes not o-uer-hiued, in a plentifull yeere may swarme once or twice: although some full stalls doe not cast once, some but once, and some hauing many princes (specially when the prime-swarm is broken) doe cast three or foure times. For sometime it happeneth that, in the swarming, a blacke cloud rising stay-eth part of them that are alreadie come forth, and lie about the hiues-doore: sometime when they are all vp, either fearing a cloud, or disliking the lighting-place, or being troubled in the hiuing, part doth returne.

One prime-swarme is worth two or three after-swarmes, except it be broken: and then if the residue come forth in one entire swarme, that after-swarme may bee the better of the twaine: but if it be diuided into two or three, then will they all be but indifferent: such, except they be timely, or vni-ted, v. can hardly liue till the next Summer.

The choice of the time when the first colonies, or prime-swarmes shall go forth, the rulers referre vnto the commons: who by reason of their continuall trauell and businesse both without and within, doe best know when all things are rea-die and fit for them: First within they will be sure that they haue a Prince ready to goe with them: for without a Gouer-nour they will not be, v. Then that their Hiue be full, so that it may be diuided at the least into two or three sufficient companies: one to remaine with *Murpesia* the old Queene, an other to go forth with *Antiope* the Prince, and a third hap-lie, which, together with the vnripe brood in the celles, may make an other swarme to serue *Orithya*. Without like-wise they will see, first that the flowers be in state presentlie to furnish them with store of wax and hony: then that the weather do please them, as being warme and calme, & moist: vnlesse, being continually vnseasonable, they haue no choice. *v. t. in n. 5.*

When the Hiues begin to be full, they will dronie, or yeeld forth sledge-drones: v. which is a signe that the first
brood

and the Hiuing of them.

brood of nymphes haue beene a good while flying abroad, and are now able to endure both weather and labour.

Other signes of the Hiues fulnesse and readinesse to swarm are at the Hiue-doore, First, the Bees houering in cold euenings and mornings. Secondly, the moistnesse or sweating vpon the stoole. Thirdly, their hasty running vp & downe. Fourthly, their first lying forth in foggy and sultrie mornings & euenings, & going in again when the aire is cleere.

When they will swarme, sometime they first gather together without at the doore, not onely vpon the Hiue, but vpon the stoole also: where when you see them begin to hang one vpon another in swarming time, and not before, and to grow into a Cluster that couereth the stoole in any place; (specially if there be Drones among them) then be sure they will presently rise, if the weather hold. The first that come forth wil increse that Cluster to some fourth part of the swarme: and then begin they to flie away, first out of the Hiue, and after from the Cluster. But commonly some few of them doe first flie forth and play to & fro the Hiue-doore, so to till out more company vnto them : and when by this meanes they haue gotten out so many, that you may see them begin to dance *v* aboue the Hiue ; then doe they hastilie issue forth and swarme.

But heere you must note, that as to fill the Doore, or to lie forth a little now and then in foggie or sultrie mornings and euenings, (which is because then they are most offended by heat within, and can best indure the aire abroad) and otherwise to go in againe, is a signe that the Hiue is full, and therefore ready to swarme; so to lie forth continually (as in extreme hot and dry summers they vse to doe) vnder the stock or behinde the hiue, &c. (specially after *Cancer* is come in) is a signe and cause of not swarming. For the Bees, knowing by nature that the greatest companies doe prosper best, vntill they finde themselues so pestred with heat and throng of multitudes, that the Hiue can scarce hold any more, will haue no minde to swarme : and when they haue once taken to lie forth, the hiue will alwaies seem empty, as though they wanted company.

One cause of their lying forth, is stormie and windie weather

K

18. The signes of present swarming.

V. s. 34.

19. To lie forth continually is a signe they will not swarme.

20. The causes of their lying forth.

Of the Swarming of Bees,

ther, not suffering them to swarme when they are ready: for when their number is growne so great through their continuall breeding, that the Hiue cannot hold them, seeing they may not swarme, they must needs, for want of aire & roome within, lie without: which when they haue once caught, they will hardlie leaue: and the longer they lie out, the lother they are to swarme.

An other cause of their lying forth, is continuall hot and drie weather, specially after the Solstice: which causing plentie of hony both in plants and dewes, their mindes are so set vpon that their chiefe delight;

Virg. (*Tantus amor florum, & generandi gloria mellis*) that they haue no leisure to swarme: although they might most safelie come abroad in such weather, which would not suffer the weakest Nymph to fall.

And when by continuance of such honie-weather they are once sufficientlie prouided, they will then be loth to leaue the sweet fruits of their labours, and to change their full store-houses for that which makes giddie House-wiues. But if they haue once begun a combe without where they lie, the matter is out of doubt. Whereas contrarily in wet and scanty Summers, no weather will stay them from swarming as soone as they are readie: although by that meanes (vnlesse they be rathe, or the weather sodainelie mend) most as well of the stockes as swarmes are like to die for hunger: *v.* and therefore, as neere as you can, so * order the matter, that your swarmes may come betime. For rathe swarmes and their stocks, that haue the summer before the, proue alwaies good.

V. n. 5.
* By hauing faire and fat young stockes, in a good standing, not ouer-hiued, and well kept.

But for those stockes, which not swarming in *Gemini* happen afterward to lie forth, this may be a remedy.

¶ 1.
The remedy and meanes to make them swarme.

First keep the Hiue as coole as may be, by watering and shadowing both it, and the place where it standeth: and then enlarging the doore to giue them aire (alwaies prouided that there be no backe-doore in the shadie parts of the Hiue) moue the cluster gentlie with your Brush, and driue them in.

2

If yet they lie forth and swarme not; (though they haue had fit weather two or three daies) then the next calme and warme day, betweene 11. and 1. of the clocke, or within an houre sooner or later, (when the Sunne shineth, and you see

no

and the Hiuing of them.

no clouds comming to hide it) put in the better part, at the least, of them that lie out, with your Brush; and the rest gentlie sweep away from the stoole, not suffering any to cluster againe. These rising in the calme heat of the Sunne, and flying about before the Hiue, will make such a noyse, as if they were swarming: which their fellowes hearing, will happlie come forth vnto them, and so begin to swarme.

If this doe not serue, but that returning to the Hiue they lie forth againe; then reare the Hiue high enough to let them in, and cloome vp the skirts all but the doore.

But if notwithstanding all this they doe not swarme; then assure your selfe that either they haue no Prince bred to goe forth with them, or else they are fat and full of honie, which they are resolued not to leaue.

And then if it be before Mid-*Cancer*, & the hony-weather hold; your best way is to double the stall, by turning the skirt of the Hiue vpward, and setting a leere prepared Hiue fast vpon it: into which they will ascend, and worke and breed there as well as in the old. *v.* In the end of *Virgo* driue them all into the new Hiue, (which then, if the weather haue held good, will be full of wax and hony) and take the olde for your labour. But if Mid-*Cancer* and the hony-dewes be past, (because they want time and meanes to store the void Hiue) let them stand: such a stall will be verie good to be taken; or, being young, to be kept. *v.* But first replenish some ouer-swarmer with his excesse or lying out (specially if you meane to take him) thus.

When all hope of their swarming is past, in some euening (while it is yet light) holding a Hiue vnder those that lie out, cut them off from the stoole with a * tight thread: and carrying them to an ouer-swarmer that you would mend, knock them downe on a Table close before his Hiue: into which, because they come without a Prince, they are quietly admitted, and quickly vnited vnder one common Commander.

The manner of doubling a stall is this: Hauing first measured the Hiue about in the largest place, prouide a leere spleeted Hiue of the same size and compasse: make ready also two square stickes 13. or 14. inches long; and an inch thicke at one end, and halfe an inch at the other: these two sticks

---

C. 5.

3

22.
What is to be done to these that by no meanes will swarme.

V. n. 24.

V. c. 10. p. 1. m. 3.

23.
How to replenish an ouer-swarmer.

* Held straight betweene two hands.

24.
How to double a stall.

sticks lay parallel ouer the hiue fiue or six inches apart, and each of them a like distance from the middle of the Hiue, with both the thicke ends one way to size out the doore for this doubled stall: and so tie them with needle and thread to the skirts fast in their places. These stickes doe also serue to keepe the Hiue from slipping, and to saue the Bees, that otherwise might be prest to death betweene the two skirts. Then in a faire night, so soon as it is dark, reare the full Hiue with three bolsters, two on the West side, and one on the East, some foure or fiue inches high, (or with a double rest) to let the Bees in: and couer both it and the stoole with a large Mantle. Then make a Brake behinde the stoole of foure stakes, 2. two foot, and 2. foure foot long, pitched fast in distance equall, and fit to conteine the full Hiue: which you may be sure of by fitting it to the leere Hiue, being of the same compasse. One of the short stakes set close to the middle of the backe of the stoole, the other Northward opposite to it: one of the long ones on the West part, and the other on the East. Then right in the middle, betweene the stakes, digge a hole in the ground halfe a foot deepe; and of such compasse, that being halfe filled with a wisp of straw, it may fitly receiue the top of the Hiue, and so the Hiue may stand vpright and fast in the Brake. Then pare away the inner edges of the tops of the short stakes, that the Hiue in the setting downe may not stay against them: and taking vp the West-stake, sticke it by you.

The Brake.

These things thus prepared, your selfe standing on the West side of the Brake, and your assistant on the same side of the stoole at your right hand, (both in your complete harnesse) *v*. let the assistant take hold of the Hiue, &, yeelding the top toward his breast, reare the fur-side of the skirt from the East-bolster. When you see it fitting, embracing the hiue as neere the skirt as you may, lift it vp sheere from the other two bolsters, and set it downe warily in the middle of the Brake, with the top in the hole as vpright as you can, and the doore to the backer part of the stoole, that it may stand South-ward as it did before. And presently let your assistant, being readie, place the leere prepared hiue ouen vpon it, with the thick ends of the stickes South-ward: and doe you

V.c.1.n.40.

and the Hiuing of them.

you put the long stake into his place againe. Then cloome the Hiues together with rolles, flatted, that none of the cloome fall in among the Bees, leauing open the space betweene the sticks ends for the new doore of this double hiue. Lastly put on the hackle, and gird both it and the long stakes to the leere-hiue, about the middle with a Belt, and about the top with a With. And so let them stand till after the end of the *Dog-daies*, when Bees are taken. *v*. But in no case let the doing hereof be deferred beyond the time prescribed, *v*: lest you haue little or nothing for your labour. *V. s. 10. p. 1. n. 1.*
V. n. 22.

25. *How to driue all the Bees into the new hiue, and so to take the old.*

At the Vindemie, in a faire calme morning before any Bees be abroad, shut vp close all the stalls in your Garden: and those that stand next couer with sheetes and blankets, lest some of the younger sort mistake, and tarrie at their doores till they be chilled. And when the Sunne is an houre high, and the aire waxeth warme, hauing first parted the new Combs and the old with a long knife, take off the vpper hiue or *Receiuer*, & set him vpon the stoole in the old place: B. *v* 1 be sure, &c. *as it followeth, v. 10. p. 1. n. 15.* If you see the *Receiuer* be very fat, or feare the Queene be hurt, or not in the *Receiuer*, your best and safest way is to take them both: for if they be ouer-fat or want a Ruler, vndoubtedly they will not prosper.

26. *The signes of after-swarmes.*

The signes of after-swarmes are more certaine. For whereas the rising of the prime swarme is appointed by the vulgar, whose chiefe rule is the fulnesse of the Hiue; the Hiue being now well emptied, for other swarmes there needeth some other direction, which the Rulers themselues doe giue by their voices: without which that stocke will swarme no more that yeare. And yet the choice of the houre, yea and of the day among foure or fiue is permitted vnto them, as best knowing the disposition of the weather.

27. *The rising of the after-swarmes is appointed by the Rulers.*

28. *The Bees Musick*

When the prime swarme is gone (if the stocke shall cast any more) the eighth or ninth euening after, sometime the tenth or eleuenth, the next Prince, when she perceiueth a competent number to be fledge and readie, beginneth to tune in hir treble voice a mournefull and begging note, as if she did pray hir Queene-mother to let them goe. Vnto which voice if the Queene vouchsafe to reply, tuning hir

K 3   Base

Base to the young Princes *Treble*, (as commonly she doth, though sometime scarcely intreated in a day or two) then doth she consent. And therefore, vnlesse foule weather stay them till it bee too late, *v:* you may assuredly looke for a swarme. Which seldome ariseth the next day, although the weather be verie pleasant; or the next day, vnlesse the weather bee verie pleasant: but after the third nights warning, they will accept indifferent weather, such as the prime-swarmes will not come abroad in. And as the Queenes voice is a grant, so hir silence is a flat deniall: the Prouerbe heere hath no place, *Qui tacet consentire videtur* : For without this Concent there is no Consent.

v. n. 36.

29. The Princes part.

This song being contained within the compasse of an *Eight* from *C-sol-fa-vt* to *C-sol-fa*, the Prince composeth hir part within the foure vpper Cliefes *G, A, B* and *C* vsually in triple moode, beginning with an odde *Minim* in *G-sol-re-vt*, and tuning the rest of hir notes, whereof the first is a *Semibriefe*, in *A-la-mi-re*. Sometime she taketh a higher key, sounding the odde *Minim* in *A-la-mi-re*, and the rest in *B-fa-b-mi*. Sometime, specially toward their comming forth, she riseth yet higher to *C-sol-fa*, holding the time of three or foure *Semibriefes*, more or lesse. Now and then shee beginneth in duple time some two or three *Semibriefes*, but alwaies endeth with *Minims* of the triple Moode.

30. The Queenes part.

The Queenes part, contained within the foure lower Cliefes, consisteth of *Minims* altogether in triple moode; commonly in *Fa-fa-vt*, sometime in *C-sol-fa-vt*, sometime in the other two *Cliefes* betweene them: continuing hir tune the time of nine or ten *Semibriefes* more or lesse.

31. The other Ladies parts.

Sometime a third Princesse imitating the Queenes voice in time, though differing haply in tune, ioyneth with them, the more, with their full noise, to incite the swarme to goe, that hir turne may come the sooner. And sometime a fourth also interposeth hir *Minims* to fill vp the Quire. But none dare counterfeit the voice of the chiefe Prince; for that were treason to hir person (and yet sometime one of them, in hope to part the swarme, will steale out with hir:) which, if the swarme be not parted, or being parted be put together, costeth her hir life *v:* as well as the liues of some of hir followers.

V. c. 1. n. 7.

lowers. Notwithstanding each of these, when hir elder sister is gone, and hir turne next, changeth hir note, begging in *Orithya*-tune leaue to be gone too: which as sometime the Queene granteth vnasked, beginning first hir selfe; so sometime by hir silence she denieth, though mournfully intreated: and then the swarme tarieth, and the poore Ladie must die.

With these various and harmonious notes, answering one an other, and some pawses betweene, they goe solemnly round about the Hiue, so to giue warning vnto all the company. This they continue daily vntill their swarming: but you may heare them best euenings and mornings. Which Musicke as it cannot but please and delight them that listen to it; so must it be most sweet and pleasant to the young Prince hir selfe, vnto whom therby is proclaimed a Warrant, not onely of hir life, but of a Kingdome also: both which otherwise she were sure to lose.

In this *Melissomelos*, or Bees Madrigall, Musicians may see the grounds of their Art: first their *Moodes*, sometime the triple or *imperfect* of the more, sometime the *duple* or *imperfect* of the lesse: then the tunes of the six notes, *vt, re, mi, fa, sol, la*; whereof the Queene soundeth the first foure, and the Prince the other two, together with the doubling of *fa-sol* in two higher Cliefes, to make vp the full *Eight*: and lastly the six Concords, an *imperfect Third*, a *perfect Third*, a *Diatessaron*, a *Diapente*, a *Sixt*, and a *Diapason*. And if any man dislike the harshnesse of the *Seconds* and *Seuenths*, which now and then hit among them; he sheweth himselfe no experienced Artist, which knoweth not that as well in *Musick* as *Oeconomick*, there must sometime be Discords: yea and that in either they haue their laudable vse, as seruing to make sweet Concords the sweeter. So that if *Musicke* were lost, it might be found with the * *Muses* Birds.

The seuerall parts of whose Song comprizing these mentioned notes, with pauses interposed (as I haue at seuerall times by a Winde-instrument, whose notes can neither rise nor fall, attentiuely obserued) I thought good heere to prick downe, that you may see in them all these particulars of their Naturall Art. Onely I cannot altogether warrant the Conclusion: because in that confused noise, which the buzzing Bees in the busie time of their departing doe make, my dull hearing could not perfectly apprehend it: so that I was faine to make vp that, as I could. But I am sure, if I misse, I

In the Bees song are the grounds of Musicke.

* Var. l. 3. c. 15.
V. Præfat.

MEANE

AS of all states the Monarchie is best, So of all Monarchies that Fe-mi-nine, Of
They work in common for the common weale: Their labour's restlesse to maintaine their state: Their

famous Amazons excels the rest, That on this earthie Sphære haue euer bin, Whose lit-tle heams in
Hexa- gonia no Be-za- leell, for curious Art may passe, or imitate, One Sou'raign and but

weaker sex (so great in field) No powrers of the mightiest Males can make to yeeld: They liuing aye,
one commands this people loyall, the great Marpese with plenty blest of issue roy- all: An- ti- o- pe,

most sober and most chast, Their paine-got goods in pleasure scorne to wast.
and Ori- thyia faire, Wish o- ther Princes his In- fantaes are.

When so increased is this prudent Nation,
That their owne limits cannot them suffice;
To seeke new Cities, for new habitation,
They send abroad their num'rous Colonies:
    Antiope the prime Prince gone,
        Orithya soone
Of hir Queene-mother, making mone,
    Begs the like boone:
That with hir traine hir fortune she may seeke:
And this she sings in measures mournfull sweete.

TENOR.

AS of all states the Monarchie is best, So of all Monarchies that Fe- mi- nine, Of
They worke in common for the common weale, Their labour's reftlesse to maintaine their state: Their

famous Amazons excels the reft, That on this earthlie Sphære haue euer bin, VVhofe lit- tle hearts in
Hexx. gonia no Beza- leell, for curious Art may paffe, or imitate. One Sou'raign and bu

vveaker fex (fo great in field) No powers of the mightieft Mates can make to yeeld: They liuing aye,
one commands this people loyall, the great Marpefe with plenty bleft of Iffue roy- all: An- ti- o- pe,

moft fober and moft chaft, Their paine-got goods in pleasure fcorne to waft.
and Ori- thyia falyre, VVith or ther Princes hir In- fantaes are.

To whofe graue accents if hir Princely Grace
Vouchfafe with Trine Afpect reply to make,
To fweeteft Treble tuning fweeter Bafe:
Hir mournefull fuit a ioyfull end doth take:
  And then, when fit time they efpy,
    Some thoufands ftrong
  This Armie royall gallantly.
    Doth march along.
Harke, harke, me thinkes I heare in Notes of choice,
This faireft Ladies fweeteft mournfull voice.

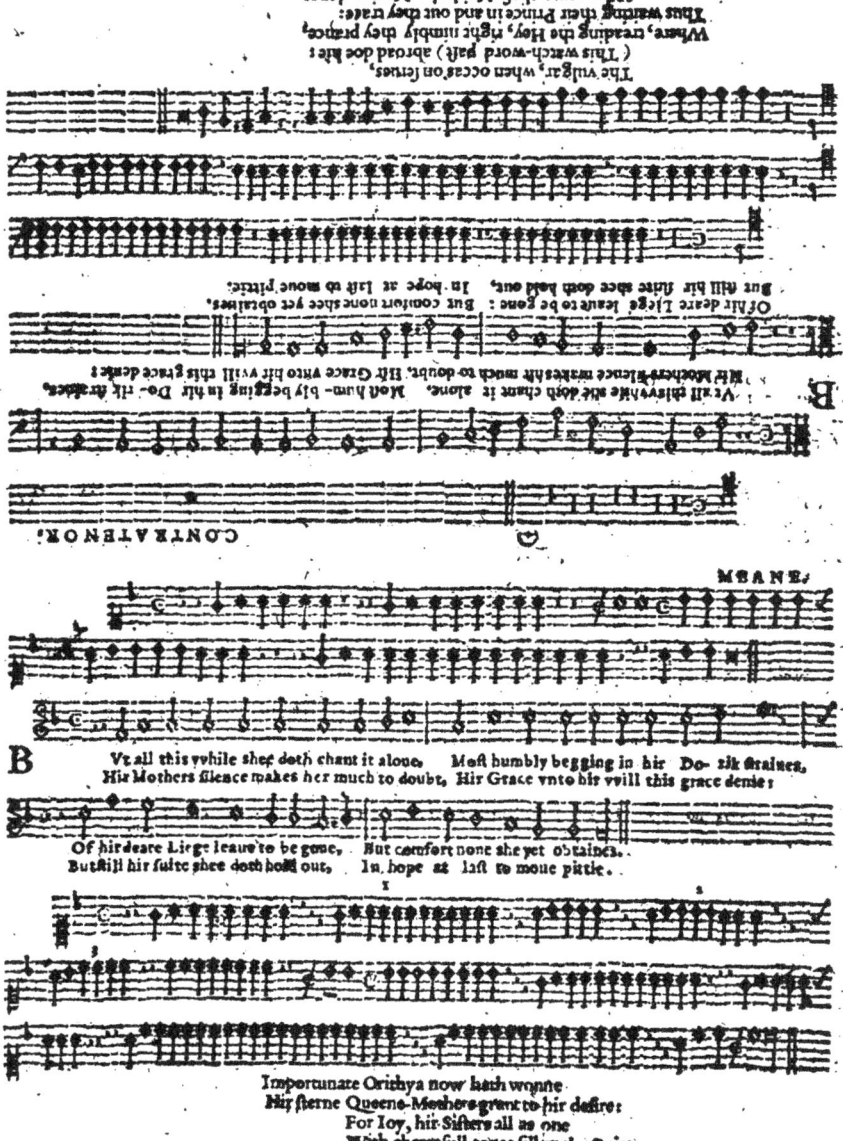

Vt all this while shee doth chant it alone.   Most humbly begging in hir Do- rik Straines,
Hir Mothers silence makes her much to doubt, Hir Grace vnto hir vvill this grace denies
Of hir deare Liege leaue to be gone,   But comfort none she yet obtaines.
But still hir suite shee doth hold out,   In hope at last to moue pittie.

Importunate Orithya now hath wonne
Hir sterne Queene-Mothers grant to hir desire:
For Ioy, hir Sisters all as one
With cheerefull tones fill vp the Quire.
These Ladies Musicall Consort assures
The Prince his much-desired Sou'raignitie:

The

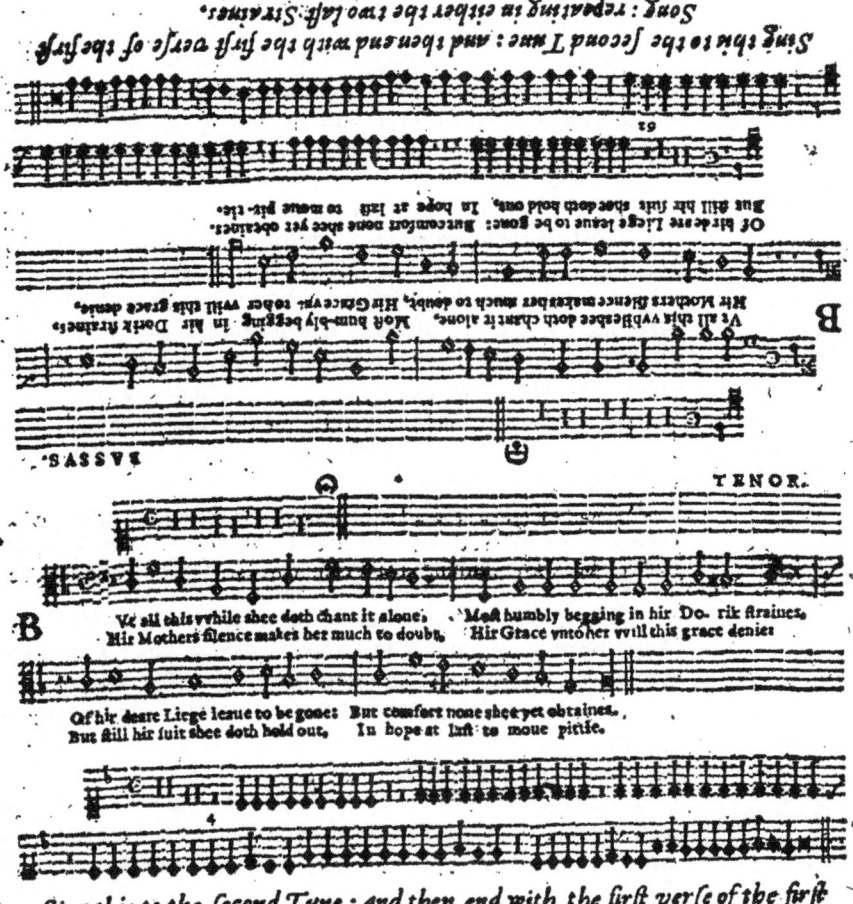

*Sing this to the second Tune: and then end with the first verse of the first
Song: repeating in either the two last Straines.*

The vulgar, when occasion serues,
(This watch-word past) abroad doe hie,
Where treading the Hey, right nimbly they prance,
Thus waiting their Prince in and out they trace:
Who come, these Maids the Morice dance,
Along vnto their resting-place.

Of the Swarming of Bees.

33.
Before swarming the voices come downe to the stoole.

In the morning before the swarme come abroad, these Ladies come downe neerer the stoole: and there they hold on their melodie somewhat longer, singing sometime aboue twentie notes together, and with shorter pauses.

34.
The manner of their swarming.

At the very swarming time they descend to the stoole: where answering one another in more earnest manner, with thicker & shriller notes, the mainie begins to march along; thronging one another for haste, and buzzing with their wings in great iolitie.

As soone as these gallant Nymphs are aloft, they doe most nimbly bestirre themselues, sporting and playing in and out as if they were dancing the Hey; in this manner waiting for the comming of their Prince. Now when some two third parts or three fourth parts of the swarme is passed, the Musicke ceaseth, and * then commeth forth this stately Dame *Orithya*: who walking a turne or two before the doore (of purpose, you would thinke, to be seene) she takes hir leaue, leauing but a small traine to follow her, which high them after as fast as they can.

* Sometime when ill weather hath kept in the swarme ouer long, shee will come forth before them, as it were checking their slacknesse and timiditie: but then returning in, she commeth forth afterward in hir due place.

This decent order the great Lords of the earth seeme to haue learned of this little Ladie: who in their Country-progresses, goings to Parliament, and other solemne processions, doe send the greatest and fairest part of their retinew before them, hauing behinde but a small troope of necessarie attendants, to guard their persons.

35.
The prime swarme being broken, the next may call and swarme within the eighth day.

If the prime swarme be broken, the second will both call, and swarme the sooner; it may be the next day: and by that occasion haply a third also may arise, yea and sometime a fourth.

But all within a fortnight after the prime swarme.

36.
All the swarmes of one hiue come within a fortnight.

Except in some extraordinarie plentifull yeares both for Breed and Honie. Such as was 1626. wherein not onely many swarmes did swarme as old stockes; but also old stockes hauing beene swarmed twice, about six weekes after began to swarme a third, as in an other yeare: and so had, in effect, two Summers in one.

After

After the second swarme, I haue heard a young Ladie-bee call: but the Queene, not willing to part with any more of hir companie, did not answer: and the next day she with seuen more were brought forth dead, &c.

Sometime though the Queene giue consent to a third or fourth, the Bees seeing the stock little enough to liue, shew themselues loth to goe: and then also there is no way with her, but one.

When the swarme is vp, and busie in their dance, it is a common vse, for want of other Musicke, to play them a fit of mirth with a Pan, Kettle, Bason, Candlesticke, or other like Instrument, so to stay them, forsooth, from flying away. Indeed where other Bee-folds are not farre off, this vse hath a good vse: for thereby the place and time of their rising is publikely notified, and so a iust and open claime laid vnto the Swarme, that otherwise some false neighbour might chalenge for his: which vndoubtedly was the originall cause of this custome. But the pretended reason is to me a meere fancie: although I know it to bee as ancient as common. For Claudian long agoe could say,

    ———— *Cybeleia quassans*
Hyblæus procul arua sedet reuocare fugaces
Tinnitu conatur apes.————

And before him *Virgil*,

Hinc vbi iam emissum caueis ad sidera cœli
Nare per æstatem liquidum suspexeris agmen, &c.
Tinnitúsque cie, & matris quate cymbala circum:
Ipsæ consident medicatis sedibus, ipsæ
Intima more suo sese in cunabula condent.

And before him old *Aristotle*,

Gaudere etiam plausu, & sonitu apes videntur. Quapropter tinnitu æris aut Psithiis conuocari eas in alueum aiunt.

If you see them begin to flie aloft (which is a token they would be gone) cast dust among them to make them come downe. If they will not be stayed, but, hasting on still, goe beyond your bounds; the ancient Law of Christendome permitteth

V. c. 1. n. 7.

37.
What vse there is of tinging the swarme.
V. n. 34.

Dee consolatu Honorij.

Georg. 4.

38.
What to doe if the swarme be way-ward.

Of the Swarming of Bees,

permitteth you to pursue them whithersoeuer, for the recouerie of your owne.

Fugientes persequi possumus in ——— alienum vel inuito Domino aut volente. Lege Thesaurus § ad exhibendum. Quia id cuique acquisitum ei conseruari debet. Lege Patre. § de ijs qui sunt. Secus si apes feras nuper in alieno pradio captarem. § Apium, in fine de rerum divisione.

But sometime they flye so fast and so farre before they pitch, that though you follow them neuer so fast, you must be content to leaue them, happily to the happy finder. For when you haue lost the sight and hearing of them, you haue lost al right and propertie in them.

Examen quod ex alveo tuo evolaverit, eousq; intelligitur esse tuum, donec in conspectu tuo est, nec difficilis persecutio ejus est: alioquin occupantis est. Iustinian. l. 2. institutionum juris. tit. de rerum divisione.

39. Some swarmes prouide them houses aforehand.

Sometime they will be prouided of a house before they swarme, which some Harbingers haue found and viewed, and dressed against their comming: as either a hollow tree, or a void Hiue: and then will they away presently, and by no meanes settle till they come thither. Vnto which place they will flie, not, as at other times, vncertainly this way and that way; but as directly as they can guesse.

40. And then they fly away directly to the place.

A poore Woman hauing taken a poore swarme to keepe for halfe, by New-yeares-tide lost hir owne part and hir Partners: and being carelesse of the Hiue when the Bees were dead, she let it stand abroad till she had forgotten it: The next Summer comming into hir Garden, she found some Bees passing to and fro hir Hiue, which were then busie in cleansing and dressing it: shee wisely fearing that the Bees came to carrie away the Wax that was leaft, bade hir Daughter take the Hiue and carrie it in. The Wench following hir play did happily forget hir mothers command: and by that meanes the Hiue stood still, till the vnexpected swarme came, that afterward stored hir garden. It is not amisse therefore to follow the counsell of *Columella*: *Oportet autem vacua domicilia collocata in apiarijs habere. Nam sunt nonnulla examina qua cum processerint, statim sedem sibi querant in proximo, (Seu potius prius quasitam, lustratam, & paratam adeant. v. n. 39.) eandemq; occupent quam vacuam repererint.*

41. *Vacua alvearia stent semper parata in Apiario.*

When

and the Hiuing of them.

WHen your swarme hath made choice of a lighting place, you shall quickly see it knit together in forme (if nothing let) of a *Cone, Pine-aple, or cluster of grapes. As soone as it is setled, or at least as soone after as may be, hiue them. For the longer they hang, the lother they are to be put from the place, the more time they lose from their worke, and the more in danger are they to be gone, either home againe, or quite away. For when they are once setled, they presently send forth spies, to search out an abiding place: who if they returne with good newes before swarming-time be past that day, they rise presently, and are gone: otherwise they will stay till swarming-time the next day. But whensoeuer the spies haue sped, they returne with all speed, and no sooner doe they touch the Cone or Cluster, but they begin to shake their wings like as the Bees doe that are chilled: which the next perceiuing doe the like: and so doth this soft shiuering passe as a watch-word from one to another, vntill it come to the inmost Bees: whereby is caused a great hollownesse in the Cone. When you see them doe thus, then may you bid them farewell: for presently they begin to vnknit, and to be gone. And then though you Hiue them neuer so well, they will not abide.

When you see your swarme, first choose out a fit hiue, neither too big nor too little, but proportionable to the quantitie and time of the swarme: so that the Bees may fill it that yeere, or at the least within a handfull, which they may make vp the next yeere in good time.

A swarme before *Mid-gemini*, put into a Hiue that conteineth twice so much as the *swarme is: a swarm at *Cancer*, into a Hiue that conteineth so much, and halfe so much: and for a swarme at *Mid-cancer*, a Hiue, that will hold it or little more, may suffice. The rest betweene these let be fitted in like proportion vnto these.

For example, a swarme of three gawns, or a †good Primeswarme before *Mid-Gemini*, will aske a Hiue of three pecks: such a one at *Cancer*, a Hiue of fiue gawnes. Likewise a double-prime swarme comming betime, is fitted with a bushell-Hiue: and all pecke-swarmes, and other single swarmes

42.
The Hiuing of Bees.

43.
When they are to be hiued.

*A Cone is a round *Pyramis*. *Figura rotunda ex lato in acutū desinens*: and therefore is a Pine-aple, of his figure, called *Conus*.

44.
The token of their flying away after they be setled.

45.
How to fit the Hiues to the swarmes.

Of the Swarming of Bees,

swarmes after *Mid-Canicer*, with the least, or halfe-bushell hiue. *v.* But little and late swarmes are rather to be vnited. *v.*

* The aire being sultry-hot, causeth the swarme to hang hollow, and so to seeme greater than he is.

† The goodnesse or greatnesse of a swarme you may most certainelie know, by the weight: it being a good one that weigheth fiue pound, a reasonable good one that weigheth foure, and a very good one that weigheth six. Heereby also it will not be difficult, which seemeth impossible, to know what number of Bees is in a swarme; if you know first that 4480. is a pound, because 280. weigheth one ounce, as 35. one dragme. So that two good swarmes vnited weighing 10. or 12. pound, doe conteine betweene 40. and 50. M. the number of a Campo-Royall: which company cannot wel be larger vnder one Leader, in the largest Hiue. *v. c.* 3. *n.* 6. Of such a number did *Alexanders* victorious Army consist. For *Diod. Sic. l.* 17. reckoneth vp some 48. M. with those 3500. left behinde with *Antipater*. And *Iustin. l.* 9. not mentioning this company; numbreth 36500. which number is also great enough for a very faire swarm; as conteining the quantity of two reasonable swarmes vnited: there being also few single swarms so good, as to amount to 30000.

The weight of any swarme is to be knowne when the Bees are newly hiued, and the number in any weight when they are newly taken.

If this iust proportion be not precisely kept, the Bees may doe well enough in a middle-sized hiue: for being vnder-hiued, they will cast somewhat the sooner, though peraduenture the lesse swarme; and being but a little ouer-hiued, though they spend some time in supplying the former yeeres defects, they may yet swarme in good time, and the fairer swarme. And indeed all swarmes, whether bigger or lesse, by decreasing or increasing, doe naturally draw towards this quantity.

But if the disproportion be much, it must be amended; whether you spy your error the same day, or afterward.

If the same day, your remedy is to knocke out the Bees vpon the mantle betweene two single Keffs, and to set a fitter Hiue ouer them: but this is not to be done before the swarming-houres be past, lest some of the Bees take a misse, and goe home againe. Otherwise you may set the Hiue in a Brake, *v.* with his bottome vpward, and the fitter Hiue vpon.

If afterward you see by the Bees lying out, that they are

vnder-

and the Hiuing of them.

vnder-hiued, your remedy is to reare the Hiue with a skirt, or Bolsters, as much as will let them in. If at *Virgo* you see, by their not filling the Hiue, that they are ouer-hiued; your remedie is then to cut off the skirt vnto the combes, or neere to them.

But generally it is safer and more for your profit, to vnder-hiue a swarme, then to ouer-hiue him.

Your Hiue being fitted and dressed, *v.* you must haue also in a readinesse a Mantle, a Rest, and a Brush.

The Mantle may be a sheet, or halfe-sheet, or other linnen cloth, an ell square at the least.

A Rest is either single or double. The single Rest is a *Prisme* or three square *Columne*, eighteene inches long, and three inches deepe, hauing the vpper edge full of nicks for the space of six inches at each end, and the middle space, of six inches, smooth. It will be safer for the Bees, and lighter for cariage, if the length of tenne inches in the middle of the bottome be cut away one inch high, abating the new edges; and the foure inches at each end be hollowed in the middle of the bottome from end to end, at the same height of one inch: and so this will be the forme of the side,

And this of the end. It is most fitlie made of a quarter of a young tree.

Vpon sheluing or hanging ground, one single Rest may serue: but if the ground be somewhat leuell, it is better to vse two: because the Hiue-skirt is set downe vpon them with lesse danger to the Bees, then vpon the ground or other flat thing. And these two Rests are to be placed with the vpper edges about nine inches apart: so that the Hiue standing vpon them, may hang out ouer them some two or three inches.

46.
Better to vnderhiue a stall then to ouer-hiue him.
V. c. 3. n. 8.
47.
Three things requisite to hiuing.
48.
The Mantle.
49.
The single Rest.

Of the Swarming of Bees,

C. 5.

V. n. 45. 56. 69.
V. n. 57.

50
The double Reſt.

In ſome caſes two ſingle Reſts are moſt conuenient, *v.* but in moſt the double: *v.* which is alſo lighter for carriage, and more ready for vſe.

The double Reſt conſiſteth of two parts or ſides, an inch thicke, of the ſame length and depth with the ſingle Reſt, hauing ſuch vpper edges ſo nickt at both ends, and the lower edges ſmooth, with ten inches of the middle cut away halfe an inch high, and then made ſharpe againe: which two ſides are to be faſtned one to another, at the iuſt diſtance of nine inches from edge to edge, with two Rounds or Braces tennanted into them three or foure inches from the ends. Theſe ſides are fitly made of inch-board, or of a cleaft Lug of Withie or other wood.

51.
The Bruſh.

The Bruſh is a handfull of Roſemary, Hyſſop, Fennell, or other herbes; of Hazell, Withie, Plum-tree, or other boughs; or rather of boughes with hearbs, bound taper-wiſe together.

52.
What the Hiuer muſt doe.
V. c. 1. n. 27.

V. c. 1. n. 40.

All things neceſſary thus prepared, let the Hiuer, which muſt weare no offenſiue apparell, *v.* firſt drinke of the beſt beere, and wet his hands and face therewith: and then let him goe about his buſineſſe ſoberly and gently, taking good heed where hee ſets his foot, and how hee handleth them: for if he tread vpon a Bee, or by any other meanes cruſh one of them; they preſently finding it, by the ranke ſmell of the poyſonous humor, will be ſo angry, that he ſhall haue worke enough to defend himſelfe, vnleſſe hee haue on his complete harneſſe: *v.* and being thus diſquieted they wil be the worſe to hiue. Moreouer, the troubling of them doth oft times make them riſe and goe home againe: ſometime it breaketh the ſwarme, cauſing part to returne, whereby the reſt are diſcouraged, being leaſt vnſufficient: yea ſomtime it diſperſeth and ſpoyleth the whole ſwarme: it may be alſo the death of the Queene: and then they will not continue to the next Summer, howſoeuer prouided. And experience hath taught me, that few ſwarmes much troubled in the hiuing do proſper. And therefore in any caſe Hiue them as quietly, and with as little buſineſſe as you may.

53.
The manner of Hiuing.

The manner of hiuing is ſo manifold, by reaſon of the many

and the Hiuing of them.

many & different circumstances of the lighting or pitching places, that it can hardly be taught by precepts; but is rather to be learned by vse and experience, guided with reason and discretion. Neuerthelesse for the helpe of nouices, I will set downe some speciall directions, which he that marketh, may readily hiue a swarme in most lighting places: and a little practise will fit him for any.

First therefore note that a swarme is to be hiued by 1. shaking, or 2. cutting the bough whereon it hangeth; or by 3. wiping the Bees down, or 4. driuing them vp into the Hiue.

If your swarme light vpon a bough, first spread the Mantle vnder it, and lay the Rest or Rests in the middle thereof, with the ends toward two corners of the Mantle.

Then if the swarme be so high, that you or some assistant may conueniently put the Hiue vnder it; hauing first remoued the twigs round about, that stand in your way, shake the Bees into the Hiue: and when you haue set the Hiue right vpon the Rests, take vp the two corners of the Mantle at the ends of the Rests, and pinne them together vpon the top of the Hiue, to stay the Bees running out sodainely: and then returning to the bough, shake it againe, and turne it aside out of his place, or couer it with your body, or with some cloth: and then presently loose the corners of the Mantle, and spread them againe. When they begin to cease running into the Hiue, if you see them lie thicke vpon the Mantle, shake them to the Hiue-skirts: and the rest, as well vpon the Hiue as the Mantle, driue in gently with your Brush. So shall you easily and quietly Hiue them. Otherwise hauing first taken away the twigs that may let you, cut off the bough or boughes (for sometime they wil hang vpon many): and if you doubt that some of them may fall in the cutting, let another second you with the ready Hiue, holding it directly vnder them. The bough being cut, lay the *Cone* betweene two single Rests, and set the Hiue ouer them. Or else put the *Cone* first in the Hiue, and then set the Hiue downe vpon the Rests.

But if they hang so neere the ground, that you cannot conueniently put the Hiue vnder them; then placing the Mantle

54.
Foure meanes of Hiuing a Swarme.

55.
How to Hiue a Swarme that lighteth vpon a bough.

56.
Either high.

57.
Or low.

Mantle and Rests right vnder, shake them downe: and setting the Hiue ouer them vpon the Rests, take vp the two corners of the Mantle, and doe as before.

And in case some of the swarme be first fallen to the ground, whence they make no haste to rise againe; then, placing a double Rest without a Mantle as well as you may, not killing any Bees, either shake the rest downe to them, and so set the Hiue ouer them all, or else set the Hiue ouer that part, and the rest, hauing cut the bough, lay beside the Hiue, and moue them with your Brush.

58. How if it light vpon a high tree.
If they pitch vpon a high tree, it is not best to shake them into the Hiue, but rather with a sharpe knife cut the bough if you can conueniently: and either put it into the Hiue, and couer it with a Mantle, or bring it downe gentlie in your hand. But if you want a ladder or other meanes to bring it downe, then let it downe by a cord tied to some crooke of the bough.

59. How if vpon the body of a tree.
If they pitch vpon the body of a tree, or vpon some great arme; then set one side of the Hiue right ouer the Bees, and with the Brush driue them vp by mouing still the lower and wayward part. But if you haue no meanes to fasten the Hiue by tying it aboue, or propping it beneath with prongs or the like, or if they be vnwilling thus to take the Hiue; then parting them from the tree with a tight *v.* thred, wipe them downe into the hiue, and set them vpon the Mantle & Rest vnder the tree. If they be so high that you must clime for them, then couer them presently with a Mantle, and so carry them downe. But looke that many will rise againe: which let alone vntill they be knit, and then sweepe them likewise into another leere Hiue, and put them to their fellowes. If yet some of them will vp againe, you must not cease to trouble them, by wiping them off gently with your Brush, by laying on Mug-wort, Margerom, Wormewood,

White Nettle.
* Archangell, or other Weeds, or Hearbs, or by couering the place with a cloth: and after a while they will all to their fellowes in the Hiue.

V. n. 23.

But if they be so neere the ground, that you cannot conueniently put the Hiue vnder them; then with a tight thred
sweep

and the Hiuing of them.

sweep them downe vpon the ground, hauing first layed the Rest either with or without the Mantle, and set the Hiue ouer them.

And if they be of that distance from the ground, that you may set a stoole close vnder them; then make fast one side of the Mantle vnto the tree close vnder the Bees, and the rest of the Mantle lay vpon the stoole with the Rest: then hauing sodainly swept downe the Bees vpon the Mantle, set the hiue ouer them: and presently loosing that side of the Mantle from the tree, lay it ouer the Bees close to the Hiue.

60. How if it light vpon the top of any thing.

If they light on the top of a stub, pollard, dead hedge, or the like, set one side of the Hiue ouer them, propping the other side with a prong or two, and driue them vp as before.

61. How if it light in the middle of a dead hedge.

If they light in the middle or bottome of a dead hedge, your best way is softly to vnworke the hedge till you come to them: otherwise you must violently knocke the hedge on the other side, so forcing the Bees into the Hiue: and then setting them downe, trouble the place as before. But then be sure to be troubled your selfe: for it is hard so to get them from such a hold.

62. How if it light on some hollow side of a stub, or tree.

If they light on some hollow side of a stub or tree, which they will be loth to leaue; beware in any case you wet them not: for that doth not onely drowne many, but also maketh the rest more eagerly keepe the place: because some through the wet cannot flie away, and their fellowes finding them there will still resort vnto them. But when you haue moued them by other meanes as much as you may, put some morter or cloome into the hollow place, mouing it forward by little and little, so that you burie none of the Bees, vntill you haue spread it ouer the place: and then will they forsake that, and take some other part of the tree or stub, where you may more easily hiue them.

63. How if it flie into a hollow tree.

When they flie into a hollow tree, so that by none of the foresaid meanes you can hiue them, then must you remoue them by some offensiue smoake, and make them chuse a new lighting place: which is thus to be done. If the Bees lye aboue the hole where they went in (as they will doe if they may) then boare a hole aboue them: if beneath, beneath them:

them: but bee sure that the vpper hole bee wide enough: rather then faile make two or three with a two-inch auger, or, with a hatchet, one as great. Then fire a peece of Match, or for want of Match, take a little Hay, or other thing that will smoake moderately, and not flame; and put it into the tree beneath them: and you shall see them fly forth aboue for life, and presently pitch in some place where you may hiue them. But this is to be done the same or the next day at the farthest: for afterward they will abide the smother, and rather lose their liues then leaue their goods.

64.
How if it light vpon another hiue.

If a swarme by reason of the coldnesse of the aire, and roughnesse of the wind being not able to get away, do offer to light vpon any other Hiue; quickly couer the Hiue close with a Mantle, lest the Bees entring be pittifully murdered.

65.
The swarme is alwaies to bee kept together, lest the Bees kill one another.

But in all manner hiuings this one rule is generall. The swarme must bee continually kept together: for if at that time part remaine from the company but the space of halfe an houre or lesse; afterward when they finde them, and would returne vnto them, they are vsed as Strangers and Robbers: as fast as they come they are beaten and killed. And those that escaping thence goe backe to their old home, finde no better entertainment: and those few that escape thence, desperatly runne into any other Hiues, and so leape out of the Frying-pan into the fire. And therefore when the swarme is hiued, if you see part begin to gather together by themselues; remoue them as speedily as you can, that they may goe to their fellowes in time.

66.
The swarme to be set neere the lighting-place.

And alwaies if you may chuse, set the swarme in the morning Sunne, and as neere the lighting-place as may be: which if some inconuenience will not suffer you to doe, yet set it within the length of a Pearch, or at the least within sight and hearing: and then (lest those which are least at the lighting place, by losing their company a while, lose their liues also) first trouble them by the meanes mentioned *n.* 59. and then cause some of the hiued part to arise by shaking them off the bough, and by wiping them downe that are on the out-side of the Hiue. Which, when they are vp, will make such a noise, that their fellowes may easily finde them. And

if

if any yet hankering behinde chance to be set vpon when they come to the Hiue; be sprinkle the Mantle, the Hiue, and the Bees with a little strong drinke, and you shall part the fray.

And if any man maruaile why they of the same swarme should so soone be strange one to an other, seeing that Bees of one Hiue being pent a whole day in an other, are yet welcome to their fellowes at the last; I can giue no other reason but this, that they knowing a swarme may part, and so each part become a seuerall company, they deeme these to be such by their long absence. And if you aske why they should finde so hard entertainment in their old home from whence they came, it is because they went away with a Leader of their owne, and so became a seuerall company. And therefore if she bide away, as many as come backe, (vnlesse they come presently) are vsed as strangers: but if part haue brought hir home againe, the rest doe safely returne afterward, either that euening, or the next morrow.

If the swarme part, as sometime it will, and settle in diuers places so neere that they may see each other; let the greatest part alone, specially if it bee best to hiue, and trouble the other in the setling with shaking, gentle rubbing with weeds, and spitting and blowing in the place, that they may goe to their fellowes. If they bee setled and hang vpon a bough, cut the bough and bring them to them. If they bee setled in some other place, then put them in a hiue without Spleets: and if they be within a pearch of the other part, moue them both, one towards an other by little and little till they be close together. After they haue stood so about halfe an houre, lift vp the spleeted hiue from his Mantle and Rest, and shake the Bees out of the vnspleeted hiue vpon the same: you may first knocke the hiue downe, and then presently clap it twice or thrice betweene your hands. This done, sprinkle both parts with good drinke, and then without any stay set the spleeted hiue ouer them, and they will straight way vp into it. But lay the vnspleeted hiue along hard by, not where it stood, but on the other side: and those that remaine in it will follow their fellowes. But if the parts

67. What to doe if a swarme part.

be

be farther a-part then a Pearch; then put them together the same night, as if they were two swarmes. *v. n.* 69.

In like manner, when you haue little swarmes vnder the quantitie of a Pecke, specially after *Cancer* is well entred; put two or three of * them together, whether they rise in the same day, or in diuers.

* After this time, the chiefe breeding being past, the swarmes desire most to vnite themselues, that thereby they may make their company sufficient: which by breeding they haue not time to doe.

68. *Vniting of swarmes is profitable.*

For being thus vnited they will labour cheerefully, gather store of wealth, and stoutly defend themselues against all enemies: whereas if they were kept asunder, they would surely perish the next robbing-time, or winter; or liuing would doe you little good. And therefore if two swarmes rising at the same time do weld and knit together; (as lightly they will doe, if they be within hearing one of an other) neuer trouble your selfe to part them, nor be sorrie for the chance. For those two being all one, are better then three such that are alone. Indeed sometime it falleth out, that they fall out, and fight at the first: but that is because they are yet diuers companies vnder diuers Commanders. For so soone as the inferior being taken away, there remaineth one supreme Monarch ouer all; the strife presently ceaseth, and they are thence-forth linked in perpetuall peace and vnitie together. Wherefore they are little acquainted with the nature of these politike creatures, that fetch their similitudes from them, to crosse that Rich, Mightie, Renowmed, thrice happy VNION, vnder one Prudent, Potent, Peacefull, thrice Noble Soueraigne.

69. *The manner of vniting.*

The way to vnite two swarmes is this. In the euening some two or three houres after Sunne-set, or when it waxeth darke, hauing spread a Mantle on the ground, neere vnto the stoole, where this vnited swarme shall stand, and set a paire of Rests in the middle of it; knock downe the *Remouer* vpon the Rests, and then lifting vp the Hiue a little, and clapping it betweene your hands to get out the Bees that sticke in it, lay it downe on his side warily by the Bees, and set the

Receiuer

Receiuer vpon the Refts ouer them: and they will begin presently to afcend. If thofe that remaine doe not runne out to their company, of their owne accord; clap the place where they be gathered, and force them out: and lay downe the hiue againe fo, that the small remnant may follow their fellowes: if you fpy any cluftering by themfelues, or ftragling from the Refts, guide them thither. And when they are all in, either that night, or betimes in the morning, cloome the Hiue vnto his ftoole.

Otherwife about ten a clocke, or as foone as it is darke, fet the *Remouer* in a Brake *v:* with his bottome vpward, and the *Receiuer* vpon him, binding them about the skirts with a long Towell or two Napkins fowed or pinned together, and fo let them ftand till the morning: and then fet the *Receiuer* vpon his ftoole. After this manner I vnited two fwarmes without the death of any one Bee, fauing onely her that muft not be faued.

If yet there be not Bees enough in the Hiue, you may in like manner put another fwarme to them.

In the vniting of fwarmes, two fpeciall inconueniences are to be auoided. The one that being vnited, they exceed not the naturall quantitie of a fwarme: *v.* for if they doe, though they agree and gather, and grow fat, yea and caft the next yeare a faire fwarme; yet will they neuer come to their firft quantitie againe, nor fcarfe fwarme any more in that vaft roome. The other that they fight not, and deftroy one an other. Vnto which two inconueniences the fwarmes that vnite themfelues, if they be not aided, are obnoxious. To preuent the fruitleffe concourfe of more then need is, which is the firft inconuenience, when you fee a fufficient faire fwarme abroad, haue an eye vnto the reft of your ftockes: if you efpie an other about to rife, ftay him by prefent fhutting the doore with a Napkin, Apron, or other fuch cloth, vntill the firft fwarme be fetled: if then one rifing draw neere vnto him (as lightly he will doe if he can finde him) couer him quickly with a Mantle till that be fetled: if being now hiued, an other preffe into him; then before many be entred, (that you may be fure not to haue the Queene) carrie

70. Another wey. V. n. 34.

71. Two fpeciall inconueniences to be auoided in this worke.

72. 1. Superfluous multitude.

V. c. 3. n. 6.

73. 2. Ciuill warre.

74. To preuent the firft.

carrie away the Hiue with the swarme about two pearches off: and set a leere prepared Hiue in his place for that other swarme.

If none of these things bee done, but that swarmes doe runne together in greater quantitie than a good Hiue can conteine; then reare the Hiue with bolsters high enough to let them all in: which, when they haue once swarmed, the * next Vindemie take away thus.

* If you doe it in Winter, see the Bees be not chilled.

In a faire afternoone, about foure a clocke, picke away all the cloome betweene the hiue and the stoole: and in the morning, at the breake of the day, lay the Hiue along with the edges of the Combes vp and downe, vpon a Mantle spread on the ground: and there pare off the Combes ends euen with the skirts, and so set him againe on the Stoole vpon moueable v: Doore-posts, and a thin bolster behinde: and presently clome vp the Hiue as close as may be.

Concerning the other inconuenience, know this; that though two strange swarmes, with their seuerall Queenes, doe neuer meet in one Hiue without discontent; (which they expresse by running to and fro without, and making a tumultuous noise within: from which they sometime fall to fighting and killing) yet commonly this strife is soone at an end. For the first Queene hauing gotten the right of the whole Roome by the possession of the Capitol or Superior part, where she sitteth safe with hir Guard about her; the Inferior by a common consent, is straight-way dispatched: and so they become all fellowes and friends vnder one Soueraigne. And therefore when swarmes are vnited by you, be sure that the Bees in the *Receiuer* be not throwne downe among the other, lest the Superior Queene come downe with them, and so you make more strife than needs.

But the danger is when two Princes with their equall Colonies happen to be equally aduanced in the Hiue: and therefore neither yeeldeth to other, but fight it out on both sides with equall hope of victorie. When this chanceth, which is very seldome, the Controuersie is doubtfull; and the conflict like to be perillous, or rather pernicious, if it be not

not preuented. In this case you haue no other way, but the next morning, if still they fight, to cast them all out of the Hiue: and so will they either knit apart, or returne to their old stockes; from whence another time they may swarme more luckily. The six and twentieth of Iune, 1621. I had two faire swarmes vp at once, which going together ouerfilled a good Hiue: where neither of them yeelding their Queene to the other, the fight continued full two daies and two nights, euen from Thursday noone till Saturday in the afternoone: wherein such hauock was made, that the better part of these braue Souldiers (a mournfull spectacle) lay some dead, some halfe-dead sprawling on the ground. At the last it was my hap to spie one of these Queenes at the Hiue skirts in a Cluster: which taking vp, now, quoth I to one that stood by me, heere is shee for whose sake all this slaughter was made: about an houre after my sonne found the other dead on the ground. When they had thus mercilessly murdered both the Queenes, and the better part of the swarmes; they that escaped rose all out of the Hiue, and went into another swarme which stood behinde them: of which, because they brought no Ruler with them, they were quietly receiued.

77. A storie of a deadly feud.

Sometime a swarme being abroad, yea knit in the *Cone*, will not abide, but returne home againe: the cause whereof is windie, wet, or cloudie weather, the not finding of a fit lighting-place, trouble in hiuing, the hot standing of the Hiue without defence, and the missing of their Prince. And this specially in a plentifull season, they being then as readie to returne vpon little or no occasion, as loth to come abroad; euen in the safest weather. *V. n.* 20. I obserued once, that the Prince being scarce ready, fell downe from the stoole vnable to recouer hir wings: whereupon the swarme returned. She being put into the Hiue, the next day the swarme rose againe and setled, but the Prince hapned to fall beside the *Cone*. The swarme being knit, missing her, began to vnknit, and be gone: which I perceiuing presently hiued them: but they being still discontented, ranne vp and downe the Hiue, with a murmuring noise both without and within. Anone

78. The causes of a swarmes going home againe.

I had

I had espied about a handfull of Bees hanging vpon a Nettle on the ground: among which was the Prince. When I had cut off the Nettle, and set it by the Rest vnder the Hiues-kirt; presently the knot vnknitting, I saw the lost Prince with hir long traine stately walking into the Hiue. As soone as shee was entred, these Male-contents began to stand still and buzze, ioyfully shaking their wings, as they wont to doe when they are pleased; and so quietly kept the Hiue. To see the suddaine alteration among them presently vpon hir approach, and how they could haue notice of it all at once, as well they without, as those within, would euen make a man to wonder; but that indeed all they doe is nothing else but wonders.

79. How to stay them.

Swarmes that goe home, doe sometimes stay long before they rise againe: and when they rise (specially if they were hiued) they are likely to fly away: although I haue knowne a swarme to rise foure times in three daies, and at the last to be quietly hiued. If thereforeyou perceiue the swarme returning before many be entred the old stocke, shut the doore fast: if that will not serue the turne, carrie the old stocke away stoole and all, and set the swarme presently vpon a stoole in his place.

80. How to keepe them from other Hiues. V.c.2.n.17.

And if any of them be going into other Hiues, (as sometimes, where the Hiues stand neere together or are many, some of them, specially the young Nymphs that haue not beene abroad before, will doe; v.) couer them with Mantles: for as many as enter will die, or scape narrowly.

81. Set not a swarme neere an others hiuing-place.

If a swarme light neere the place where another was hiued a day or two before; be sure to set it as farre as conueniently you may, from the place where the former lighted and stood: the space of a Pearch or somewhat lesse may suffice: otherwise many of the first swarme resorting thither, will to the new swarme, and so be killed.

82. What to do when the swarme is new hiued.

When your Bees are hiued, those that hang on the outside, driue in gently with your Brush, and lay the corners of the Mantle that are farthest from the Rest, ouer the Hiue, with boughes also to shadow it, if the weather be hot. But if you finde them vnwilling to goe in (as in extreme hot weather

weather they will be, though they like the Hiue well enough) then striue not with them; but laying the corners of the Mantle ouer the Hiue, as before, with boughes to shade it, there suffer them till the heat be abated, and then driue them in: and if you thinke they cannot otherwise well endure that heat, couer the Hiue againe with Mantle and Boughs. And so let it stand till it wax darke, and all the Bees be come home.

Then knitting the foure corners of the Mantle together, at the top of the Hiue, and binding the Mantle about close to the middle of the hiue with a small line, carrie the swarme to his place. And after a while, taking away the Mantle, set it vpon his seat with the doore toward the South, or rather South-west: *v*. and then leauing onely a breathing place, for feare of stifling them, cloome it vp close, & put on a hackle *v*. and so let it stand till it be faire and warme the next day. For if the Hiue be left open; in the morning betimes they will resort to their former standing and there abide, sometime flying about, sometime setling on the ground: where if the cold or wet take them many dye. When you see the weather fit them, then hanging the Mantle, or other white cloth vpon the Hiue, let them go. But they will the sooner leaue the haunt of their hiuing-place, & fal to their work; if you shew them their new standing by knocking them out together vpon the stoole, when the weather is warme.

All swarmes, if the morrow be faire, will desire to be abroad betimes: and knowing their want, will bestirre themselues more lustily in their labour than other Bees. But if the foule weather keepe them in the first day, then are they much discouraged: so that the next day being indifferent, when other Bees worke hard, they will scarce looke out of the doore, not daring to commit their leere and thinne bodies to the could aire. And if they be quite kept in the second day also; then will they not wagge (though they dye for it) vntill the weather be very pleasant. They may liue fiue or six daies in the Hiue without Honie: but afterward they begin to string downe, hanging one at anothers heeles. *Pedibus connexa ad limina pendent.* Which is a certaine signe of

83.
How to remoue it in the euening.

84.
How to set it on his seat.
V. c. 3. n. 15.

V c. 3. n. 15. & 20. &c.

85.
How to vse it in the morning.

86.
Foule weather the first day doth much discourage a swarm.

87.
Foule weather continuing doth make it droupe and die.

88.
A swarme may liue six daies without Honie.
Virg.

89.
How to preuent the drouping and death of a swarme.

of death, if they be not presently relieued.

To preuent this euill, If the swarme light in your Garden within a Pearch of the Seat that is appointed for him, set it there at the first: and so will they lose no time in hankering about the hiuing-place. And if it light farther off, (whether in your garden or other place where they may stand safe, specially the weather being vnkinde or vnconstant) leaue them there till it mend. *v:* for those that are not remoued, but keepe still their first standing, becauſe they are not to seeke of their way home, they feare the foule weather as little as the best. And therefore need not to be shut in in the morning, as those that are remoued: or to haue any white ouer them for their direction.

V. c. 9. n. 2.

90.
How to cure a drouping swarm.

The meanes to recouer such a drouping swarme is this. The first Sunne-shinie day turne vp the Hiue to the Sunne, that his heat may reuiue them: and besprinkling the sides of the Hiue, the Spleets, and the Bees also a little with Mede or Honie-water; hold them so in the heat of the Sunne till you see many of them fly abroad. Then set downe the Hiue gently vpon his Seat againe, and couer it not til it be through warme, and the Bees play cheerefully, as at other Hiues.

Chap. VI.
Of the Bees Worke.

1.
Bees most industrious creatures.

Nto the industrious nature of Bees nothing is more odious than sloth and idlenesse: while there is matter to worke vpon (vnlesse they be let by vnkinde weather) their worke neuer ceaseth: yea the old Bees, which haue spent their daies in continuall labour, will not at the last allow themselues any immunitie or rest in their Hiues, as a recompence for

for their paines past, but continue still their trauaile vnto death: *v.* In the three still moneths indeed, *Sagittarius, Capricornus,* and *Aquarius,* because then there is nothing to gather, they worke not: (yet when a faire day or houre commeth, as wearie of rest, they will abroad, imploying themselues in diuers necessarie offices: *v.*) but so long as any good flowers grow, euen from *Pisces* or a little before, vnto *Sagittarius* and, some yeares, somewhat after, (which is full nine moneths) they lose no time, (*Nullus, dum per cœlum licuit, perit dies.*) but follow their businesse tooth and naile. Which incessant labour while the time permitteth, with the three singular effects thereof, the (1) working of Wax, the (2) making of Honie, and the (3) feeding of their young: *v.* the Poet in few words hath elegantly expressed all together.

Quod superest, ubi pulsam hyemem sol aureus egit
Sub terras, cœlumq; æstiua luce reclusit;
Illæ continuò saltus siluasq; peragrant,
Purpureosq; metunt, flores & flumina libant
Summa leues. Hinc nescio qua dulcedine lætæ
(3.) *Progeniem nidosq; fouent: hinc arte recentes*
Excudunt (1.) *ceras: &* (2.) *mella tenacia fingunt.*

V. c. 1. n. 58.
2.
In three monthes they cannot worke.
V. c. 3. n. 60. 61.
3.
All the yeares after they lose no time.
Nat. hist. li. 11. cap. 6.
4.
Three fruits of Bees labour.
V. n. 53.
Virg.

THeir first worke is the ground of the other two, the Artificiall Cells seruing both for Coffers to lay their sweet treasure in, and for neasts and nurseries to breed their young in. The matter thereof they gather from flowers with their Fangs: which, being kept soft with the heat of their little bodies, of the Aire, and of their Hiues, is wrought into Combs. This worke is so nimbly and closely done, that it can hardly be perceiued: insomuch that *Aristotle* plainely confesseth, *Nec vero quemadmodum operantur visum adhuc est.* But *Plinie,* willing to goe a little beyond him, telleth vs a tale of a Lanthorne-hiue made at *Rome,* through which, forsooth, their doings in the Hiue were discried: and in another place of another like deuice, *Multi aluearia speculari lapide fecère, ut operantes intus spectarent.* But vnlesse the Bees also were transparent as well as the Hiue, this cannot be: seeing they doe alwaies frequently compasse the Combs round

5.
The first, and ground of all, is Wax.

6.
How Wax is gathered and wrought.

Hist. l. 9. c. 40.

Nat. hist. li. 11. c. 16.

Nat. hist. li. 21. c. 14.

round about. A more likely way than that, were to haue a moueable peece in one side of the Hiue: which when you haue taken away, you may see the Drones and the Hony-Bees walking together to and fro, and with their doubled heat hatching their young: but their worke can you not see; though you remoue and part the Bees till the bare Combes appeare. But if your curiositie would so faine behold the manner of their curious and artificiall building, the onely way is this. In *Gemini* set vp a last yeeres midling swarme two or three handfulls aboue the stoole: and then when most of the Bees are abroad (but most fitly in the forenoone when they are most quiet) you may behinde the stoole behold them working on the edges of their combes: and hauing blowne their liquid and soft wax out of their mouthes (as the Waspes doe their drossie stuffe, which you may see them gather from pales with their fangs and so carry it away) to fasten and fashion it with their fangs and forefeet.

7. How you may see the working of the combes.

How much wax they bring at once, doth appeare by the new swarmes: whose first weekes worke is spent chiefly in building combes: wherein they are so earnest, that it falleth out with them as it is in the Prouerbe, *The more haste the worse speed.* For many of their burdens doe fall from them before they can fasten them to the Combes. You may then see great store of them vpon the stoole by the skirts of the hiue, like vnto the white scales, which fall from young birds feathers. And therfore some haue imagined, that they also are scales which the young Bees doe likewise shed from their wings. But put you some of those parcells together with warme fingers,& you will quickly be resolued of that doubt.

8. How much wax they bring at once.

The Bees combes are placed otherwise than the Waspes: for the Waspes hang theirs one vnder another, and the Bees theirs one beside another; beginning them in the top of the hiue, at that distace that a Bee may reach frō one to another.

9. The admirable Architecture of their combes and cells.

Their cells or little holes are made six square, according to the number of their feet: and of that length and widenesse, that each of them may easily containe a Bee. Which are so artificiallie wrought and ioyned together, that *S. Ambrose* in the consideration thereof saith, *Quæ castra quadrata tantum possunt*

Hexamer.l.5. c.21.

Of the Bees Worke.

possunt habere artis & gratiæ, quantum habent crates favorum, in quibus minuta ac rotunda cellula connexione sui invicem sufficiuntur? Quis enim architectus eas docuit hexagonia illa cellarum indiscreta laterum æqualitate componere, ac tenues inter domorum septa ceras suspendere, stipare mella, intexta floribus horrea nectare quodam distendere?

But heerein their Art is yet more exquisite, that whereas there are two courses of cells in the two sides of euery comb; the cel-bottoms in these two sides are neuer opposite one to an other: but each hexagonial bottom of one side answereth to three third parts of the hexagonial bases of three cotiguous cells on the other side, meeting all in one angle right in the centre of the opposite bottome: as in this forme: which is so artificiall, as well for strength as beauty; that no schadon, though the thin bottome of his cell should faile, can breake through into a cell of the other side. Hee that sees this, sees he not a wonder?

Besides these ordinary combes, there is commonly one Drone-combe in a hiue, wherin the Cephens are bred, made for the nonce with wider cells. *Sunt loculi ipsi fucorum ampliores, & finguntur seorsim quoq; per se favi fucorum.* Although in some hiues part of the Drone-combes be made out with Nymph-cells. The Drone-combe being no thicker than others, and yet the Drones longer than the small Bees; they increase the length of his cells by couering them, not with a flat couer, as they doe the rest, but with a deepe hollow one like an old wiues thrumbd cap: which afterward, when the Drones are bred, they take away. And when those cells are void of Cephens, they fill them as they doe the other with hony: yea and after swarming-time, if they want vpper cells for their hony, they will not tarry till their Cephens come forth themselues, but liking better their roome than their company, they draw them out of their seminaries before they be ripe. *v.c.4.n.31.*

10. *The Drone combe.* Hu.l.9.c.40.

But the Queenes cells are built single, euery one by himselfe: and that in diuers places of the Hiue, some aboue, and some beneath: that, as other princes, she may for her delight remoue at hir pleasure. But, for the most part, in the out-sides

11. *The Queenes cells are built single in diuers places.*

of the combes: for although it be fit for Princes to be neere their chiefe Cities; yet doe they not loue to be pestered in the midst of them. In fashion they are round: which is the most perfect figure, as the six square is most fit for comely ioyning many such buildings together. They are also larger than the rest: to shew that subiects houses should not match their Soueraignes in greatnesse. In these Palaces do they breed their young Princes. *v.* *Pliny* speaketh thus of them. *Regibus imperatoribus extruunt amplas, magnificas, separatas, tubercula eminentes.* The common people, finding them alwaies in those stalls that die, take them for certaine signes of death, and call them pipes, or taps: and therefore when they see them in a stal that they take, they say, This was taken in good time, for it is piped: and therefore would haue stood no longer. But seeing none are without, no not the yongest swarms, ordinary reason might teach them to forgoe that fond conceipt.

The Combes haue successiuely sundry colours: white, yellow, browne, blacke. Their first colour white, by the end of Summer is turned to a light yellow. Those that are taken and tried this first yeere, are called Virgin-wax, but the whiter the purer: and the rest are ordinarie. The second Summer this light yellow is changed to a sad. The third this sad yellow into a browne: which afterward, as they wax old and corrupt, altereth againe into a blackish and durtie colour: but these being tried will returne to yellow.

The time when Bees gather wax, is onely betweene *Taurus* and *Virgo*: (vnlesse *Aries* be milde and warme:) for then they may begin in that month.

BVt Hony they gather all the yeere: saue onely in those 3. still moneths, when the weather keepeth in both Bees and flowers. *v.* And it is of two sorts: the one pure and liquid, which is called *Nectar*, the other grosse and solid, which we may by like reason tearme * *Ambrosia*. For both serue for the food of these diuine creatures.

* Yea rather, this is the true *Nectar* & *Ambrosia* wherewith *Iupiter* was first nourished in the Ile of Crete, *v. c. 4. n. 6.* while the *Curetes* hid him fro *Saturn*: Which gaue occasion to the Poets of this fiction, that the Bees were his nurses.

C. 6.

12.
In fashion round.

P. c. 4. n. 18.
Nat. hist. li. 11. c. 11.
13.
The common errour anent these celles.

14.
The combes doe often change their hue.

Virgin wax and ordinary.

15.
Wax is gathered onely in foure months.

16.
Hony the second fruit is gathered in 9. moneths.
V. c. 3. n. 59.
17.
Two sorts of Hony.

Of the Bees Worke.

nifes. Dißas call veram παιδός ſole autem. Virg. Geor. 4. And afterward, when they would make him immortal, because of the long-preſeruing vertue that hony hath, (v. c. 10. par. 3. n. 1.) they fained it to be his immortall food. Iupiter Ambroſia ſatur eſt & nectare vivit. Mart. l. 2 1. Ep. 58.

The groſſe hony is gathered by their fangs: from whence it is conueied by the fore-legs to the thighes of the hin-legs. (*Quaſi flores comportant prioribus pedibus fœminia onerant propter id natura ſcabra, pedes priores roſtro: totaq́; onuſta remeant ſarcina paudata.*) and that ſo nimbly, that vnleſſe you haue a quicke eie, you can ſcarce perceiue it.

    18. *How Ambroſia or groſſe hony is gathered. Nat. hiſt. li. IX. c. 18.*

This worke may beſt be ſeene in the ſpring, when they gather vpon the blackthorne: for then by reaſon of the cold they are not ſo quicke.

When they haue brought theſe burdens home; they vnload them into the dry cells for the young to feed on, which are not yet able to flie abroad. And in the beginning and ending of the yeere, looke what they ſaue when the weather is faire, they lay vp for themſelues againſt a rainy day. Which, while it is good, they will feed on, to ſaue their *Nectar* as much as may bee. But this kinde of hony is like vnto freſh fiſh: it muſt not long be kept. For if being laid vp in the cells, by reaſon of plenty that comes in freſh and freſh, it lye vnſpent; after a while it corrupteth, and of ſweet becommeth the ſowreſt and the moſt vnſauory of all things both to taſte and ſmell: which then they commonly call Stopping or Coome. Where there is any ſtore of this ſtuffe, it doth ſo offend the Bees, that oft times it maketh them to forſake all. Moſt of them will that yeere goe forth in ſwarmes: and thoſe few that are leaſt will neuer proſper.

    19. *Ambroſia, is the Schadons food, as water their drinke.*

    20. *Being kept it is ſoone corrupted.*

    21. *And then becommeth moſt vnſauory ſtopping.*

    22. *Much ſtopping maketh the Bees forſake their hiues.*

Anent this leg-ſtuffe or groſſe hony there is a generall error. For, without all ſcruple or doubt, men doe count it and call it wax: (as did ſome alſo in time of old, whoſe opinion *Ariſtotle* doth thus deliuer: *Ceram apes perreptando flores capiunt priorum acumine pedum: mox priores in medios abſtergunt, & medios in blaſa poſteriorum.*) But againſt (as I ſhall ſhew you) both ſenſe and reaſon.

    23. *This Ambroſia is commonly taken for wax. Hiſt. l. 9. 40.*

If you put it to your tongue, it hath the taſte of hony: which wax hath not. If you feele it betweene your warme fingers,

    24. *Which error is diſproued by ſenſe.*

O 2

V. n. 14.

fingers, it muttereth apart: where wax sticketh fast together. If you put it to the fire, it melteth not, as wax doth. And whereas wax is all of one colour, *i.* white at the first, *v.* euen as those little fallings of the new swarmes; (which is wax indeed) this leg-honie is of diuers colours, white, blacke, yellow, greene, red, tawny, orenge, murry, and of sundry midling colours. Therefore sense doth say it is no wax.

25.
And reason.

The reasons are two. The first is, because when they gather abundance of this stuffe, they haue neuer the more wax. The other because when they make most wax, they gather none of this.

For proofe of the first, All the Bees betweene *Virgo* and *Taurus* doe gather abundance of it: and yet are not their combes in this time any whit enlarged. Also one of those old stalls that are full of combes, doth carry more of this matter all the summer long than many swarmes: and yet haue they no more wax at the end of the yeere than at the beginning.

For proofe of the other, The new swarmes within one weeke, if the weather serue them, will haue halfe filled their hiues with combes: and yet in all this space shall you scarce see one carry any of this. If you would know the reason why the stocks gather so much, and the new swarmes so little; it is because the stocks haue *schadons* which they feed with it, and the new swarmes haue none. And if any foolish Bee doe carry in *Ambrosia*, it is put in a dry cell where it turneth to Stopping, *v.* as I haue seene within a fortnight after the hiuing.

V. n. 21.

26
And by authoritie.
Nat. hist. l. 11.
c. 7.

And this, though now it seeme new, yet was it knowne many ages agoe. *Plinie* writeth of it thus: *Præter hæc (s. præter ceram & nectar) convehitur erithace, quam aliqui sandaracham, alij cerinthum vocant. Hic erit apum dum operantur cibus: qui sæpe invenitur in favorum inanitatibus sepositus; & ipse amari saporis.* Speaking in the last words of that which is corrupted *v.* And before him *Aristotle* himselfe thus: *Mel apibus tum æstate tum hyeme cibo est: sed recondunt alterum quoq; cibarij genus, cui duricies cera proxima, quod sandaracham nonnulli appellant.*

V. n. 21.
Hist. L. 9. c. 40.

The

Of the Bees Worke.

The *Nectar* or liquid hony the Bees gather with their tongues, whence they let it downe into their bottles, which are within them like vnto bladders: each of them will hold a drop at once. You may see their little bellies strut withall. Men thinke, because they see nothing on their legs, that they come in leere: when they are better and more heauily laden than the other. These bottles, as soone as they come home, they empty into their combes. *Mel ore euomunt in cellas.* This *Nectar*, being cleere as Crystall at the first and liquid as water, when it is two or three yeeres old, becommeth white and hard. *Concrescit autem mel concoctum jam tempore: initio enim, ut aqua, dilutum est, & primis diebus sine crassitudine cernitur.* While it continueth liquid, and will runne of it selfe, it is called liue-hony: when it is turned white and hard (euen like vnto sugar) it is called corn-hony, or stone-hony.

And the liue-hony is of two sorts: that which is gathered by a swarme, cleere and crystalline at the first, *v.* layd vp in virgin-wax, *v.* and taken the same yeere, is the right virgin-honie: the other, which is yellow and thicker, gathered by an old stall, and therefore kept in corrupter cells with drosse and courser hony, is called ordinary.

The first shoot whereof (specially in a plentifull yeere of *Nectar*-dewes) running sheere of it selfe, is a kinde of virgin-hony, *v.* and little inferiour to the right.

Nectar, whether it be ordinary or virgin-hony, is either finer or courser, according as the soile is where it is gathered: *v.* For the best countries, which yeeld the best wheat and the best wooll, yeeld also the best hony. And therefore the wood-lands of Hampshire haue better honie than the heath, and the champion or field country, better than the wood-lands. The reason is, because where the flowers are most fragrant and vertuous, as well of the fields as gardens, in the purest and sweetest aire; there the honi-dewes, which are extracted from them, are most fine and pure, *v.n.40.*

When the cells are full, they close them vp with little filmes of wax, which they will not breake vntill winter and hunger driue them to it. And thus doe they all the summer,

27.
How the pure Nectar is gathered.

Hist. an.li.5.c.22.
Hist. an.l.5.c.22.
28.
Two sorts of Nectar.
Liue-hony and stone-hony.
29.
Liue-hony of two sorts.
Virgin-hony.
V.c.10.p.2.n.15.
V.n.14.
30.
The finest ordinary is a kinde of Virgin-hony.
V.c.10.p.2.n.6.
31.
All hony, courser or finer, according to the soile.
V.c.10.p.2.n.12.

32.
The full cells they close with wax.

descending

descending lower and lower from one cell to another, vntill *Virgo*: after which time they lay vp no more in store. For honie then waxeth scarce abroad: and thenceforth they can gather no more wax to shut it in. As for that which they purchase by fight and forraging, it doth them little good. For the most part of it they presentlie spend: and if they saue any, they halfe fill a few cels with it: which being vncouered, either themselues or some other theeues quicklie deuoure: according to the Prouerbe, *Euill gotten goods are soone spent*.

> 33.
> *Nectar & Ambrosia made of many simples, whereof each mayneth yeeldeth varietie.*

This *Nectar* and *Ambrosia*, together with those sweet and holesome vessells that doe containe them, are gathered from infinite varietie of herbs, flowers, and trees, which God in his prouident bounty hath ordained to succeed one another. So that from *Pisces* to *Sagitt*, there neuer want some plants or other, containing these sweets: which the Bees featly draw from them, without any hurt to the fruits: *Fructibus nullis nocetur*.

> Nax. hift. lib.
> 11.c.8.

> 34.
> *Dandelion continueth longest.*

The Dent-delion, or after the French pronunciation Dandelion, may well be called *apiastrum* or *melissophyllon*. For the Bees gather vpon it almost all the yeare. The Dazy and Yelowcrea are next for continuance, but nothing so much regarded.

> 35.
> *What Pisces yeeldeth.*

The Winter Giliflowre and the Hazell are the first. For they spring in *Pisces*, and sometime before. After them the Dazy and the hearb Bearesfoot, the Violet, &c.

> 36.
> *What Aries.*

In *Aries* besides those before named, the Box, the Withy-palme, both greene yeelding *Nectar*, & yelow yeelding *Ambrosia*, Daffadill, Lide-lilie, blackthorne, &c.

> 37.
> *Taurus.*

In *Taurus* Slow-tree, Plum-tree, Goosebery not blowne, and blowne, Chery, Peare, Cockbell, which is a Woodflowre. About the middle of this month the chiefest plants begin to flourish in great abundance: as Apple, Crab, Barbery, Beech, Crowpickes, Charlocke, Rosemary, &c. But specially the plentifull Vetch and Maple. They gather on the flowre of the Maple a whole month together, and somewhat on the flowre of the Vetch when his time is, *v.* but the greatest store of hony is drawne out of the black Spot of the

> F.m. 59.

little

Of the Bees Worke.   C.6

have picked leafe of the Vetch, which groweth on each side
the two or three vpper-most ioynts. These they ply continually. I neuer saw Vetches, how farre soeuer from Hiues,
that for three moneths together (if the weather serued) were
not full of Bees.

In *Gemini*, the first moneth of fruitfull Summer, besides   38.
those prime Plants, Vetch and Maple, (which now are in   *Gemini.*
their prime) and the rest forenamed; Beanes also, which
with their flowers haue also blacke spotted leaues like Vetches, on which sometime they gather, Arch-angell, Barberie,
Fumitorie, Ribwort a kinde of Plantanie, Holme or Hollie,
Hawthorne, Elder, red Honie-suckle, Red-weede, white
Honie-suckle, which they like much better than the red, &c.

In *Cancer*, with the fore-named, the blossome of the   39.
Vetch, as well as the Leafe, Benet, Malowes, the soueraigne   *Cancer.*
Tyme, which yeeldeth onely Nectar: and therefore he was
deceiued that said *Crania Thymo plena*. Tyme, for the time it
lasteth, yeeldeth most and best Honie: and therefore in old   Plinius. hist. l.
time was accounted choise, (*Thymus aptissimum ad mulsificandum.*   11. c.21.
Pastus gratissimus apibus Thymum est.   Hist. l. 9. c. 40.
                                                                    Vir. Georg. 4.
Dum Thymo pascentur apes, dum rore cicadæ.)

Hymettus in Greece, and Hybla in Sicily were so famous
for Bees and Honie, because there grew such store of Tyme:
Propter hoc Sicilium vel Siculum mel amarum, quod ibi Thymum be-   Var. l. 3. c. 16.
nignum & frequens est. The Knap-weed flourisheth about the
middle of this moneth, and the Blackberie about a weeke
after: Both which (as sweet and plentifull) the Bees much
haunt.

But the greatest plentie of the purest Nectar commeth   40.
from aboue: which Almightie God doth miraculously de-   Of Honie-dewes.
still out of the Aire, (*aerei mellis cælestia dona*) and hath or-   Virg. Georg.
dained the Oake, among all the trees of the Wood, to receiue and keepe the same vpon his smooth and solide leaues,
(*Et quercus sudabunt roscida mella*) vntill either the Bees   Virg. Pollio.
tongue, or the heat of the Sunne haue drawne it away. When   41.
there is a Honie-dew, you may perceiue by the Bees: for, as if   *The Bees worke*
they smelled it, or by the sweetnesse of the Aire, they present- *most earnestly*
ly issue out of their Hiues, in great haste following one an-   *in a Honie-dew.*
                                                          other :   V. c. l. n. 44.

Of the Bees Worke.

other: and refusing their old haunts, search and seeke after the *Oake*: which for that time shall haue more of their custome, than all the Plants of the Earth. Sometime the Maple and Hazell, take part with the *Oake*: but little and seldome. While the Honie-dew lasteth, they are exceeding earnest, plying their businesse like men in Haruest: you may see them so thicke at the Hiue-doore passing to and fro, that oftentimes they throw downe one another for haste.

<small>42.
What the Honie-dew is.
Nat.hist.l.11.
c.12.</small>

What this *Mel Roscidum* should be, *Plinie* seemeth much to doubt where he saith, *Sive illud sit cœli sudor, sive quædam syderum saliva, sive purgantis se aeris succus*. But, if coniectures might be admitted, I would rather iudge it to be the verie quintessence of all the sweetnesse of the earth (which at that time is most plentifull) drawne vp, as other dewes, in vapors into the third Region of the Aire, by the exceeding and continuall heat of the Sunne; and there concrete and condensated by the nightly cold into this most sweet and Soueraigne *Nectar*: and then doth it descend vnto the earth in a dew or small drizling raine: that he might well say, *Constat materiam, ex qua mel gignitur, rori esse congenerem*. Which opinion is the more probable for these reasons. First because that when the yeare is backward in his fruits, the Honie-dewes are also backward: comming onely at such time as the flowers haue the most solid and best iuyce. Before, when the iuyce is weake and waterish, and afterward, when it is dryed and wasted, they are not. *v*: Secondly, because that in more hot & Southernly climats, where the fruits are more forward, the Hony-dewes also are more timely: as in *Italy* before *Gemini*. *Non omnino*, saith *Plinie*, *prius vergiliarum exortu*: *v*. whereas with vs they fall not vsually before *Cancer*. And thirdly, because the Countries that haue store of the best and sweetest flowers, haue euer the best Honie. *v. n.* 29.

<small>Galen. de aliment.li. 3.</small>

<small>*V.* * *in* 43.</small>

<small>Nat.hist.lib.11
c.12.
V.c.10.q.1.n.20</small>

<small>43.
When the Honie-dewes are most frequent.</small>

The hotter and drier the Summer is, the greater and more frequent are the Honie-dewes: cold and wet weather is vnkinde for them: much raine at any time, as comming from a higher Region, washeth away that which is alreadie eleuated: (so that there can be no more vntill an other fit of hot

and

Of the Bees Worke.

and dry weather) and in the end it dissolueth them quite.

The time in which these Honie-dewes fall, is vsually betweene the first and last daies of this moneth: although the continuance of hot and dry weather may cause them come somewhat rather, or last somewhat longer, euen vntill mid, *Leo* or * after. They may happen at any time of the day: but for the most part in the morning before it be light: *Sub lucanis temporibus. Itaq́, tum prima aurora folia arborum melle roscida inueniuntur.* And then shall you haue the Bees vp in a morning as soone as they can see, making such a shrill noise where they goe, that, as merrie Gossips when they meet, a man may heare them farther than see them.

* In the yeare 1613. almost two moneths after the vsuall time, namely in the later part of *Virgo*, there fell diuers Honie-dewes: which came to passe by reason that continuall wet kept them backe in their due time, and *Virgo* followed exceeding hot, fit weather for them. But because the state of the flowers was then weake, the state of those Honie-dewes also was so weake, that the Bees were little the better for them. The stalls, that were taken, proued light: and most of the swarmes and stocks, that were kept for store, died for want before the end of Winter. Except onely in the Heath Countries, where the Heath-flower being then in his prime, those late Honie-dewes made fat stalls.

In *Leo* Vetches, Malowes, Tyme, Knap-weede, Blackeberie, white Honie-suckle, Redweed, Thistle, Melone, &c.

Now also doe they gather on the Lauender, if their hastie Dames doe not gather it from them before it be readie.

In *Virgo* Knap-weed, Black-berie, Redweed, Dandelion, Malowes, Borage, &c. and the ample Heath, which yeeldeth Honie like vnto their Wooll. *V. n.* 31. and *c.* 10. *p.* 2. *n.* 12.

In *Libra* Dandelion, Heath, Iuie, &c.

In *Scorpio* Dandelion, Iuie, Arch-angell, &c.

And in this great varietie this is strange, that where they beginne they will make an end: and not meddle with any flowre of other sort, vntill they haue their load. *Mos apibus ne florum plura genera petant uno eodemq́, profectu, sed singulis singula.* Insomuch that those which beginne with the flower of the Vetch will not once touch the rich spotted leafe of the same, before they haue beene at home. Although when they come to a flower that yeeldeth both *Nectar* and

Ambrosia,

44 The time when they fall.

Nat. Hist. li. 11. c. 12.

45 What Leo yeeldeth.

46 Virgo.

47. Libra.

48. Scorpio.

49. The Bees gather but of one kinde of flower in one voyage.

H. st. an. l. 9. c. 40.

Ambrosia, they will vse sometime the Tongue, and sometime the Fangs, and gather them both.

But this may seeme more strange and wonderfull, that out of the most stinking and poisonfull weeds, as Redweed, * Margs, Henbane, and the like, they gather most sweet and holesome Honie: and yet regard not some of the best and sweetest Hearbs and Flowers, as the Rose, the Prim-rose, Cloue-Giliflowers, Wheat, Barley, Pease, &c.

What store of Wax and Honie a stall may gather, is vncertaine: some hauing more, some lesse, according to the number of the Bees, the greatnesse of the Hiue, and the plentifulnesse of the yeares. With vs it is counted a good stall that yeeldeth two or three gawnes of Pulse: although in a tree there haue beene found more than seuen or eight. But in other Northerne Countries we reade of farre greater quantities. *Plinie* affirmeth, that there was seene in *Germany* a Honie-comb eight foot long. And *Paulus Iovius*, that in *Moscovia* there are found in the Woods and Wildernesses great Lakes of Honie, which the Bees haue forsaken, in the hollow trunkes of maruellous huge trees. In so much that Honie and Wax are the most certaine commodities of that Countrey. Where, by that occasion, he setteth downe this Storie, reported by *Demetrius* a *Moscovite* Ambassadour sent to *Rome*. A neighbour of mine (saith he) searching in the woods for Honie, slipt downe into a great hollow tree, and there sunke into a Lake of Honie vp to the breast: where when he had stucke fast two daies, calling and crying out in vaine for helpe, because no bodie in the meane while came nigh that solitarie place; at length when he was out of all hope of life, he was strangely deliuered by the meanes of a great Beare: which comming thither about the same businesse that he did, and smelling the Honie stirred with his striuing, clambered vp to the top of the tree, and thence began to let himselfe downe backward into it. The man bethinking himselfe, and knowing that the worst was but death, which in that place he was sure of, beclipt the Beare fast with both his hands about the loines, and withall made an out-cry, as lowd as he could. The Beare being thus suddainly

---

Marginalia:

50
They gather Honie out of poison.
Mathers or May-weed, Cotula foetida.

51.
What store of Honie a stall may haue.

Nat. hist. li. 11. c. 24.
De legatione Moscovitaru, & Munsterus de Moscovia.

Of the Bees Worke.

dainely affrighted, what with the handling, and what with the noise, made vp againe with all speed possible: the man held, and the Beare pulled, vntill with maine force he had drawne *Dun out of the mire*: and then, being let goe, away he trots, *more afeard then hurt*, leauing the smeared Swaine in a ioyfull feare.

THE Bees earnest and hot Labour, and the drought of the Aire, together with their cholerike Complexion, which their very hue bewrayeth, doth cause them much to desire cold Water. Some thinke it serueth onely to feed their Schadons: (*Aquam tum portant, cum prolem nutriunt*) v: and that not without reason, seeing that *Ambrosia* their daily food is hot and dry: and indeed when the Drones are done away, and breeding is ended, the Bees are nothing so frequent at the watring-places. But *Columella* thinketh the vse thereof to be more generall, *Sine qua neq; favi, neq; mella, nec pulli deniq; figurari queunt*. Vnto whom the Poet, in the place first cited in this Chapter, seemeth to assent; making water and flowers the common matter of their three workes.

The Watring-place should a not be farre from your Garden, b in the next side of a Pond or Brooke, c made sheluing, not very steepe, in manner of a Foord, and d defended from Beasts, Geese, Duckes, and such like: and especially young Ducklings, *v. q 3. in n. 59.*

 a For they will neuer goe farre for water, if any be to be had neere hand. *Sub menibus urbis aquantur*. And therefore when you see Bees watring in woods or other places, not neere any Hiues; bee sure those are wilde Bees, which are not farre from their neast. Watch them therefore which way they flie: for they will thence directly to it. Which if it be not within view, take a Reede or Kex, or some like hollow thing open at one end, with a chinke cut in the other to let in light: and taking vp a Bee by the wings put her into the Cane, and shut her in with your thumb: while she goeth downe to the light, put in an other, and so as many as you thinke good. And then where you last see the Bees flying homeward from the water, goe to that place, and there let out one of the Bees in the box: which, when she hath cast a Ring to know where she is, will fly as directly home as the other: likewise where you see her last, let out another: and so the rest, vntill they haue brought you to the stall.

---

52. *Bees haue necessarie vse of water.*

53. *Chiefly for their breed.*
Hist. an. l.9.c.40
V.6.7. n. 24.

De re rust. l 9.
c. 5.

54. *The making of the Watering place.*

Virg. Geor.
55. *How to finde wilde Bees.*

b Lest the Bees, flying ouer the water vnto it, bee throwne downe by tempestuous winds, and so drowned: for which cause it is good to lay lugs ouerthwart the water, and other staies; that recouering them they may dry themselues againe, and so escape.

Virg. Geor.

*In medium, seu stabit iners seu profluet humor,
Transuersas salices & grandia conijce saxa,
Pontibus ut crebris possint consistere, & alas
Pandere ad æstiuum solem, si forte morantes
Sparserit, aut præceps Neptuno immerserit Eurus.*

c That they may safely settle vpon it, and that it may alwaies be kept moist by the neerenesse of the water. For they choose rather to draw their drinke out of moist earth, than from the water it selfe, though it be neuer so cleare: peraduenture that the earth hauing receiued his earthinesse, which before was insensibly mixt with the water, their triple searching tongue might the better trie out the pure element of water.

d Which otherwise will be the death of many: for they are so earnest in their businesse, that though you offer to tread vpon them, they will not moue.

*56.
Bee-troughes in Gardens profitable.
V. n. 53.*

But because in the cold windie weather of the Spring, (at which time of the yeare the Bees haue most vse of water, *v.*) these watering places of Ponds and Brookes are dangerous; (where you may then see many throwne downe and drowned, and others, that scape drowning, to be so chilled, when they haue filled themselues with cold water; that they are not able to endure the wind, but faile and fall by the way) therefore it is behoueful to haue Troughes in your gardens, made for the nonce: whence the Bees may both sooner and safer fetch their water.

*57.
The forme and size of a Bee-trough.*

For the forme and size of a Trough, let his hollownesse be two foot in length, seuen or eight inches in breadth, and foure in depth; the bottome foure inches thicke; the ends six or seuen; and the sides halfe so much. Moreouer, let the hollownesse be diuided into foure equall parts, by one partition of inch-board, in the middle from side to side; and by two partitions of halfe-inch-board, from each end vnto the middle partition: after this fashion.

Of the Bee Workes.   C. 6.

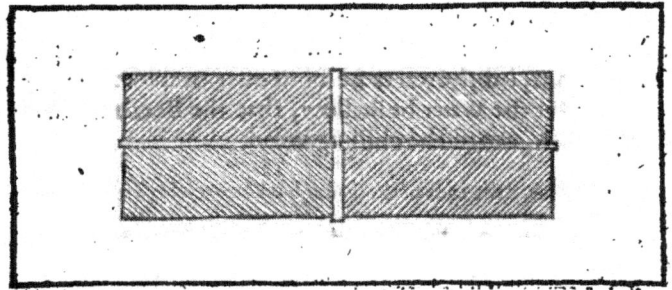

And to keepe the Bees from danger of drowning, vnto which they are very obnoxious, (for if they but touch the water with their wings, they cannot rise from it) let each Quarter of the Trough haue his Couer, in thicknesse about halfe an inch, in breadth and length fitting to his Quarter; but so, that without let it may rise and fall with the water.

The matter of this Couer must be corke, which must as well haue open spaces for the water to take aire; as places for the Bees to light on: lest it being couered too close, doe corrupt and become vnsauourie. It is best to diuide each couer into two equall parts: and in the edges on both sides to cut little nickes. And so this may be the forme of it.

58. The trough-couer, and the vse of it.

Other fashions both of their Troughes, and of their Couers, may be deuised: but these haue seemed to me in all respects most fitting.

A new Trough thus framed and fitted, is to be seasoned before it be vsed, by often scalding it, and changing the foule water; vntill, hauing stood a day or two, it remaineth cleare, and without a glistering slime: afterward the older and more earthie it is, the better they like it.

The Trough being seasoned, set in some conuenient place, about a pearch from the Bees; hauing a moueable plancke,

59. The seasoning and ordering of the Bee-trough.

Of the Bees Worke.

or the like, to defend it from cold rough winds in the spring, and from the Sunne when it is hot. At which time keepe the Trough full, lest the water be soone ouer-heated: and in cold weather let the water be shallow, that the Bees may drinke safely below, out of the chilling wind.

¶ 1 Bespread the ends of the Trough with cow-cloome, to keep them from chapping.

¶ 2 In frostie nights couer all the Trough, to keepe the water from freezing.

¶ 3 Keepe all Poultrie, and specially Ducklings, and Hens with chicken, out of your Garden: for, drinking at the Troughes, they will trouble, and tread vpon the Bees. And the brood-hens will kill them, for feare of stinging their chicken: and so will Ducklings also at the first, taking them for flies; which when they haue tasted, they will afterwards let alone.

60. Bee-troughes of stone.

You may also make good Troughes of Free-stone, with woodden partitions let into the stone: but they are more apt to chill the Bees in cold weather, vntill they be mossie.

61. Sometime they water in the streets.

Sometime they will lie sucking at the neere plashes, puddles, and mire in the streets: where many are trod vnder foot of men and beasts. See therefore that such places be kept cleane and drie.

62. And after a showre, all about the garden.

V. c. 4. n. 13.

After a showre they water for the most part in your Garden vpon the bare earth, the grasse, and wheresoeuer they finde it wet from aboue. In the chiefe breeding months *Aries, Taurus* and *Gemini, v.* when the cold raine or wind hath kept them in some part of the day, they will lie so thick vpon the ground, if you haue any store; that you can scarce tread beside them. At such time therefore let no heedlesse stranger come among them.

CHAP.

Chap. VII.
Of the Bees Enemies.

He good Bee, as other good things, hath many Enemies, from which shee needeth your helpe to defend her: namely, 1. the Mouse, 2. the Wood-pecker, 3. the Tit-mouse, 4. the Swalow, 5. the Hornet, 6. the Waspe, 7. the Moth, 8. the Snaile, 9. the Emet, 10. the Spider, 11. the Toad, 12. the Frog, 13. the Bee, and 14. the Weather.

1. The Bees Enemies are many.

The Mouse, whether he be of the field or of the house, is a dangerous Enemie. For if he get into a Hiue, he teareth downe the Combes, makes hauocke of the Honie, and so starues the Bees. Some enter by the doore, or by some open place in the skirts of the Hiue: some gnaw a hole thorow in the top of the Hiue, where they know the Honie lieth: some keepe their old homes, and come to the Hiue onely for their baits: some make their nests betweene the Hackle and the Hiue, that they may the sooner and the safer come to the Honie at their pleasure.

2. The Mouse.

For remedie, first you must looke that your Hiues, whether they be of straw or wicker, be close and fast wrought. For if the straw be loose and soft, they will more easily gnaw their way thorow: and if the wicker be thinne, when they haue torne downe the cloome, they will creepe in betweene the twigs. Next see that the Hiues be daubed close round about the skirts, that there be no entring but by the Doore: which in *Taurus*, when the Bees come downe to watch, and thenceforth all the Summer, they will keepe well enough both day and night: but all the Winter, at which time the Mise make most spoile, it must be made so narrow, that they cannot get in. *v.* Also it behoueth you to remoue all things about your Hiues, that may hide and harbour them, *v.* for they will feare to

3. Remedies against the Mouse.

1

2

v. c. 3. n. 31.

3

v. c. 2. n. 8.

Of the Bees Enemies.

to come and goe in sight, lest the Cat meet with them by the way. Moreouer, it is good now and then, in drie and warme daies, to take off the hackles, as well for this as for other causes. *v.* Those that neastle vpon the top of the Hiue, when the hackle is taken off, will sit still amazed so long, that you may be sure to crush them against the Hiue with your hand. Lastly, you shall doe well to set baited * traps in their way, that so they may come short.

4

V.c. 5. *n.* 23.

5

A Samsons post.

* There is none better than a Samsons Post: which is a flat Couer or Roofe supported by a triangular Pillar or Prop, whose three sides doe so hold one by another, through the weight of the Roofe, that the loosing of one is the loosing of all: and so the Prop failing the Roofe falleth.

The Roofe.

The Roofe may bee a Plankes or Boords end, or the like, twelue inches long and ten broad: which of it selfe, or with some aduantage weigheth foure or fiue pound.

The parts of the Prop.

The three sides or parts of the Prop (namely, the Post, the Sweeke, and the Brace) are three sticks, all almost halfe an inch broad, and halfe a quarter of an inch thicke.

The Post.

The Post is moreouer three inches and a halfe long, and sharpned at one end.

The Brace.

The Brace likewise three inches and a halfe long, and sharpe at one end; with a nicke on the broad side halfe an inch within the other end.

The Sweeke.

And the Sweeke eight inches long, with a nicke on the vpper broad side a little within the out-end; and another on the left edge, two inches and the thicknesse of the Post within the broad nicke.

The framing of the Prop.

The parts of the Prop being thus formed apart, are to be framed together in a triangle, after this manner. First, take the Brace in your left hand and beare vp the fore-side of the Roofe with the blunt end, the nicke being inward: then set vp the Post somewhat leaning toward you, with his sharpe end in the nicke of the Brace: then hooke the edge-nicke of the Sweeke to the Post: and make all fast with the sharpe edge of the Brace fixed in the broad nicke of the Sweeke.

The baiting of the Sweeke.

But first bait the Sweeke with a thinne peece of good Cheese, or Bacon, or Suet, eyed with a thread vpon the inner end. And bee sure that the Prop doe stand so fickle that it may easily be loosed: and that the Roofe when it falleth, lie flat and euen with the Floore, lest the poore Mouse lose hir labour.

Sed instar omnium erit hoc unum. ℞. Farinæ 1. auenaceæ noue aridæ dulcis Drachmas IV. tere: 2. Arsenicæ albæ 3. semidrachmam, in puluerem quam queas 4. minimum per se pertere: 5. sacchari puri semi-drachmam cum arsenica contere; saccharatam arsenicam farinæ permisceto. 6. Compositum hunc puluerem latercalis superimpositum, juxta murium caua, & in locis

Of the Bees Enemies.

ab ijsdem frequentatis (cæteris amotis esculentis) dispone. Sed nocte prima simplicem expone farinam: cui verate farinam saccharatam substituas secunda: tertia triplex hic pulvis succedat: qui jam audaces satis & nihil suspicantes, duarum vel trium spatio noctium, & mures & sorices pariter, ædes tuas infestantes una omnes perdet. Si vero adversus luxuriantes sorices certius velis remedium; cum pertrita arsenica drachma una contere sacchari drachmam unam: saccharatam arsenicam bynes dulcis molita uncia uni permisceto, & tribus quatuorve locis frequentatis dispone. Aut etiam ibidem passas arsenica mera pertrita intus modicè aspersas. Sed diligenter cura, ne Canes, Gallinæ, aliæve innocua animalia istud degustent: quod facies, si noctu tantum expositum interdiu recondas.

1. *Vel triticeæ.*   2. *Vera.*
3. *Vt arsenica sit tantum decima compositionis portio: nam si prædominetur, mures, & magis sorices, virus odorantes recusant escam, quam rite compositam avidè vorant: sed modicum sufficit.*
4. *Ne mandentes durities offendat.*
5. *Et quod dulcedine oblectat, & quod, vt arsenica bene trita, inter dentes stridet: hoc enim secunda nocte tuto vorantes, tertia arsenicam, quam stridore & colore refert, minus metuent.*
6. *Quantitas nucis avellanæ singulis sufficit laterculis.*
7. *Nam si alia suppetant cibaria, fucatas escas devitant: nec vbi fraus semel subluxerit, vllis postea decipulis facilè decipientur.*

 The Wood-pecker or Yippingale, if hee finde any hoale in the Hiue against the Honie, doth with his long round tongue draw it out: but he doth more harme to Wood-Bees then Garden-Bees.

 Of Titmise, there are three sorts. The great Titmouse (which of his colly head and breast some call a Colemouse) is a very harmefull Bird. For although sometime hee seeme content with dead Bees, yet is hee a great deuourer of the quicke also. In winter hee taketh them at the Hiue as they come forth: when the cold makes them keepe in, hee will stand at the doore, and there neuer leaue knocking till one come to see who is there: and then suddenly catching her, away he flies with her: and when he hath eaten her, he comes againe for more: eight or nine will scarce serue his turne at once. If the doore be shut that none can come forth, hee labours to remoue the Barre: if that be too heauie, he falls to

      moining

4.
2. The Wood-pecker.

5.
3. The Titmouse.

6.
The subtill practice of the Titmouse.

moining about the doore for a new way: and when these deuices cannot get them out; some haue the skill to breake the wals of the daubed Hiues aboue, ouer against the place where they lie: and there they are sure to haue their purpose. But in the spring, when the Bees come to the palme, hee standeth there watching for them; and while they are busie at their worke hee devoureth many. The little Russet one in the Winter feedeth only on dead Bees; but in the Spring he will take part with the great one. The little greene Titmouse I cannot accuse: except it be only for eating a few dead Bees, and that but seldome in some hungrie time.

The Swallow taketh them as they flie, *Populatur hirundo,* & *alibi. Ea demum sola avium non nisi in volatu pascitur.* But I am perswaded shee doth much lesse harme than the Titmouse, although she haue a worse name. The Long-winged Hauke makes the fairer flight; but the Short-winged is the Kitchen-hauke. These birds therefore are not to be suffered.

--- *Absint meropesq́; aliaq́; volucres,
Et manibus Progne pectus signata cruentis.*

Let boyes destroy their neasts in Summer, and catch the Titmouse in Winter, with * Traps baited with dead Bees, Oats, or Tallow. *Aristotle* ioyneth the Waspe, the little Titmouse, the Swallow, and the great Titmouse together. *Inferunt injuriam apibus maximè vespa, & avicula quas paros vocant, atque etiam hirundo, & merops qui apiaster est. Quamobrem apiary vesparam latibula, & hirundinum ac meropum nidos propinquos alveis tollunt.*

* As Cage traps, Pit-falls, and Samsons-Posts (v. * in n. 3) But then set a Lath before the Prop, leaning from the Floore to the Roofe, lest the busie Bird throw it downe for nothing.

The Hornet also devoureth Bees: being so much too strong for them, that they can make no resistance. Which the Poet meant where he said,

Aut asper crabro imparibus se immiscuit armis.

Hir manner is to fly about before the hiue, till she haue spied hir prey settled at the doore: and then suddenly she taketh it in hir feet, and flieth away with it as a Kite with a Chicke.

In

In destroying the Hornets you must bee warie: for one stinging doth oftimes cause a Feuer, and lesse than thirtie, as some say, will kill a man, *Ictus crabronum haud temerè sine febri est. Auctores sunt ter novenis punctis interfici hominem.*

10. The Hornets sting is dangerous.
Nat. hist. li. 11. c. 21.

The Waspe doth much more hurt than the Hornet. For the Hornet now and then killeth a Bee: but the Waspe wasteth the Honie, whereby many whole Stalls doe perish. For, besides the harme that she doth hir selfe, she doth oftimes set the Robber *v.* on worke: who, when the Waspe hath begun, will be readie to take part with her, and then all goes to wracke. A Waspe is by nature harder and stronger than a Bee, specially in *Libra*: insomuch that oftimes she breaketh from two or three of them, though they haue all hold of her at once: and perhaps killeth one of them out of hand. At *Cancer*, or, the Spring being hot and drie, in the later part of the former moneth, the Waspe beginneth to bee bred: *v.* within a moneth after shee first appeareth: and in a while she beginneth to feed vpon dead and weake Bees: which shee quickly cutting off in the middle with hir Fangs, first carrieth away the neather-part; and anon fetcheth the other, when she hath bitten off the wings (for easier carriage) not farre from the place where she tooke it vp.

11. 6. The Waspe.
V. n. 25.
V. c. 4. n. 8.
12. When she feedeth vpon Bees.

Within a moneth after hir comming abroad, shee waxeth bold, and aduentureth into the Hiues for honie: but, by reason of the strangenesse of hir voice and habit, shee is descried before shee come neere. And at the first (while the weather is warme, and the Bees both early and late keepe watch and ward at the Hiues doore) comming single against many, she is commonly repulsed, and sent backe againe with a Flea in hir eare: and if by chance shee slip in, shee doth not alwaies escape. Sometime shee is killed in the Hiue, and brought forth dead: sometime without the doore, when she hath got hir prey. But afterwards, the weather waxing cold, and specially in mornings and euenings, and the Bees therefore retiring from the doore higher into the Hiue; the Waspes make great spoile, specially among them that are weake. And this they continue vntill *Scorpio*: after which time they begin to weare. Neuerthelesse while they liue, that is vntill

13. When she stealeth Honie.

14. When they weare away.

Q 2 *Sagittarius*

Of the Bees Enemies.

Sagittarius (if abundance of cold and wet rid them not a little rather) they will be filching: and one Waspe will carrie out as much as two Bees bring in.

15.
In what yere the Waspes are few.
V. c. 4. n. 8.

The Winter wet and cold, killeth many of the Mother-Waspes *v.* as they lie in their sleepe. The Spring wet and cold hindereth their breeding: for being by that meanes kept in, when their time is come to flie abroad and feed; they pine and faint, so that either they breed not at all, or verie late. And when a warme fit in the beginning of *Aries* hauing let them abroad, cold and stormie weather commeth suddenly vpon them; they are shut vp againe, and so starue for the most part with hunger and cold: that your Bees shall not be much troubled with them in such a yeere. Yea continuance of wet, though without cold, is such an enemy to the Waspes; that in the yeere 1613, though, the former Summer being exceeding dry, the Waspes were multiplied, and the Winter being milde, the Mother-Waspes were many at first; yet the Rainie Spring and Summer, did so spill their nests, that there were no small Waspes seene till *Libra*, and then verie few.

16.
In what yeere they abound.

But the Winter being milde, and the Spring and Summer continuing warme and dry, they liue and breed in euerie place: that, without continuall and diligent attendance, you shall be sure of great losse among your Bees, though the former yeere there were but few: For one nest yeeldeth breeders enough, if they should all liue, to store a whole countrey.

For these causes, *Ann.* 1611. there were euery where such multitudes, that the like I thinke was not knowne before in our memorie: insomuch that within two or three Furlongs of my Garden, were killed that Summer aboue fiftie great nests: (and yet, by the resort to our Bees, wee knew we had not all) besides 22. Mother-Waspes killed in the Spring at our Bee-trough, which would haue made so many nests. And 1620. for the same causes the number was as great or greater: and yet the exceeding wet Summer following I saw not one small Waspe.

17.
Remedies against the Waspes.

Wherefore, if you loue your Bees, suffer not a Waspes nest about you.

The ready way to rid them, is, If they be in a Tree aboue the

Of the Bees Enemies.

the hoal, to smother them with Brimstone or Bunt, as you kil Bees. If in the Thatch of an house, (when you haue made way to the Combes) to scald them. If in the ground (as most commonly they are) you may likewise scald them, and so take the Combes out whole, and giue the Grubs to your Chicken: although the Boyes make better sport in burning them. But if you be in haste, and care onely to dispatch them quickly and quietly, thus doe. First, stop their way close; that they within breake not out vpon you (for those that are abroad comming home wearie and loaded are more gentle.) Then presently with a * Waspe-spade search for the Nest: which, if it be shallow, is quickly found. When you haue found it (which you shall know by the easie entrance of the Spade) then dig downe round about it: and hauing thus rounded the Nest, stamp the earth downe vpon the Combes, and so haue you done. If you finde not the Nest because it lyeth † deepe; then dig vp the ground a foot about the hoale; and hauing found their way, stop it fast with earth, and tread in that you digged out, and let them alone. If this be done in the day when many are abroad; the euening or morning following you may kill them with your foot: but in the euening you may take them all together.

* Which is a thin Iron one, whose Padle is not aboue foure inches broad next the Socket, and thence taperd vnto three inches at the steeled point, and eight or nine inches long. If it bee broader it is not so apt to enter, and so to finde and round the Nest: and a thicker one is apt to let out the fresh Waspes, that will trouble your worke: but you may make a shift with any ordinarie Spade or Padle-staffe.

† In Corne-ground the Nest is begunne vnder a Furrow, and therefore is alwaies shallow: in old laine it is begunne in a Want-hole, and therefore it is sometime shallow, and sometime deepe.

And to destroy those that resort to your Hiues, set by them Sider, Vertjuice, sowre Drinke, or Grounds, in a short necked Violl open, or other Glasse couered with a Paper that hath a hoale in the middle: and so you shall catch many. Also you may take of sweet Apples, or Peares, or beasts Liuer, or other flesh, or any thing that they loue, soure or fiue slices or more, and lay them in so many seuerall places among your Bees:

upon which you shall haue sometime as many as will couer the Bait, which you may kill at once, as Butchers kill Flies.

Hist.l.9.c.40.

Aristotle teacheth you an other way: *Impugnantur* (saith he) *Apes à vespis: quamobrem Apiarij eas venantur constitutâ ollâ, & carne in ea positâ. Vbi enim multæ ad carnem accesserint, apposito operculo super ignem ollam ponunt.* You may also vse other meanes to kill them your selfe. How to helpe and defend your Bees against them, see *c.3.n.*46,47,54,55.

18.
7. *The Moth.*

The flying Moth lyeth betweene the Hackle and the Hiue, and breedeth little Wormes, or crawling Moths, some in the skirts of the Hiue, some within vpon the Stoole, wrapt in the drosse or scouring of the Combes, and some without vpon the Hiue, specially in the cracks of the dawbed Hiues.

Nat.hist.l.11. c.19.

Plinie speaketh thus of them: *Papilio etiam ignauus luminibus accensis advolitans pestifer, nec uno modo: nam & ipse ceras depascit, & relinquit excrementa quibus teredines gignuntur.*

19.
8. *The Snaile.*

They offend the Bees also with their mealinesse, as the Snailes doe with their sliminesse. Wherefore rid your Hiues of these guests. The Moths are easily crusht before or vpon the Hiue: and the Snailes, though you kill them not, will not long abide, if there be no harbour of long Grasse, Weeds, or other things about the Hiues. But as for the Moth, if you suffer her, your selfe shall haue more cause than your Bees to bee offended. For albeit in the cold Spring shee breed about the Hiues, hatching hir young by the heat of the Bees; yet when the heat of the aire will suffice for that purpose, shee chooseth rather to lay her blotes in woollen, their naturall nest and nourishment: especially if it bee nappie, that there she may safely hide them. In which place, till they be growne to their bignesse, they lie fretting and eating the Cloth: and then after a while they creepe out of their skins flying Moths. The Maides that sunne their clothes to rid the Fleas, let them take heed how they doe it neere the Bee-fold, lest they bring in worse enemies than they carried out. If the Woollen bee oylie or greasie they like it the better: and for that cause good Huswiues Yarne lyeth not long vnwouen.

20.
What harme the Moth doth.

21.
9. *The Emet.*

If Emets bee neere your Bees, they will much trouble them, biting them and hanging vpon them: although the
Bees,

Of the Bees Enemies.

Bees, if they be lustie, will kill many of them that come to the Hiue. But if it be a poore Stall, they will in time possesse the Hiue, and eat vp the Honie. The best remedie against them is to scald them.

The Spider, as the Moth, doth vse to harbour betweene the Hackle and the Hiue: where commonly she hath a Bee or twaine in store to feed on, an vnfit messe for such a mouth: Sometime she hangeth hir Nets vnder the Stoole; which easily intangle a wearie Bee, when shee commeth laden home, and missing of the lighting place falleth into them: yea, and sometime where the Bees are few, chiefly in the winter, they will bee bold to enter the Hiue, and there weaue their small Webbes. *In foribus laxos suspendit aranea casses. Aranei quoq, vel maxime hostiles: cum prævaluere vt intexant, enectant alueos.*

  10. *The Spider.*
  Virg.
  Nat. Hist. l. 11. c. 19.

The Toad is by nature so noysome to the Bees, that while he is about the Hiue, though he lie but vnder the Stoole, the Bees will not prosper. He is said also to deuoure them at the Hiue, as the Frog at the Watring-place. *Ranæ Apes, vbi ad aquam accesserint, rapiunt: quamobrem eas Apiarij per paludes, & stagna, vnde Apes aquantur, venari solent. Rubeta etiam Apes interimit: subiens enim aditus aluei afflat, & obseruans rapit euolantes. Nullo hæc affici malo ab Apibus potest; sed ab Apiario facile interimitur.* Item, *Insidiantur aquantibus Ranæ: quæ maxima earum est operatio, tum cum sobolem faciunt.* v. *Nec hæ tantum quæ stagna riuosq, obsident, verum & rubeta veniunt vltro, adrepentesq, foribus per eas sufflant: ad hoc prouolant, confestimq, abripiuntur.*

  11. *The Toad.*
  12. *The Frog.*
  Hist. an. l. 9. c. 40.
  Ibidem.
  Nat. Hist. l. 11. c. 18.
  v. A. 6. n. 53.

BVt not any one of these, nor all these together, doe halfe so much harme to the Bees, as the Bees. *Apes api,* as *homo homini, Lupus.* They make the greatest spoile both of Bees and Honie. For as they of the same Hiue liue in inuiolable peace one with another; so haue they no entercourse, no friendship or societie with others, but are rather at perpetuall defiance, and deadly feud with them. In fight they are fierce, and in victorie mercilesse: within the space of a day or twaine, yea, of an after-noone sometime, if the Hiue bee open

  13. *The Bee the Bees greatest enemie.*

open that they may haue easie passage to and fro, they will haue rid him cleane. And therefore all Bees, of all their enemies, doe most dread strange Bees; knowing well in what danger they are to bee robbed by them both of goods and life.

26
Robbing or fighting of Bees in winter and summer but little.

This robbing is practised all the yeere. In winter, as oft as the weather is faire and warme, some will bee prowling abroad. And some are so theeuishly disposed, that all the summer long, when abundance of Honie is euery where to bee had for a little labour, they will yet be filching though they die for it. In the Spring they are more earnest, finding now fit time to fetch after that which they left behinde at Haruest, *v.* and to repaire their decayed store, both of Honie and Bees. *v.* And therefore now haue an eie vnto them: and defend the weaker swarmes from their violent irruptions. *v.* Those Stalls that haue lost their Queene, or too many of their companie, or are offended with the corruptnesse of their Combes, or doe dislike their standing for coldnesse, moistnesse, mustinesse, bleetnesse, or vnsauorinesse; as taking no pleasure in their liues, doe now easily suffer themselues to be robbed. And if none will come to rob them, then on some faire day they will away together, sometime leauing both Honie and young ones behinde them.

27.
In the spring more earnest.
V. n. 28. & 31.
V. n. 43.
V. c. 3. n. 65.

28.
The most spoile is made in Haruest.

29.
What Stalls are most subiect to robbing.

But in *Virgo* is the most dangerous time of all. Then shall all the Stalls in your Garden bee tryed of what mettle they are made. And *Libra* would not bee much better, but that the most spoile is done before. Little and poore swarmes are now subiect to robbing. Likewise those Bees that are offended with the blacknesse and rottennesse of their Combes, caused through age, or wet, or with abundance of noisome stopping; will most of them goe forth in the swarmes, leauing a very few, sometime not past a handfull, in the stocke: which yet in robbing-time will keepe the doore, as though the Hiue were full: but the Robbers finding their weaknesse, will surely spoile them, if they bee not preuented. How to know such weake Bees, and what to doe to them, see further *c. 3. n. 46.*

30.
What Bees are the Robbers.

The Robbers are thought to bee poore swarmes and stocks

Of the Bees Enemies.

stocks, which haue not sufficiently prouided themselues for winter. Of which opinion was *Plinie* where hee said: *Quod si defecerit alicuius aluei cibus, impetum in proximas faciunt rapinæ proposito.* But indeed such are fitter to bee robbed, as before is said, than to be robbers. There is no theefe to the rich theefe: who, although he haue enough, and more than enough; yet by hooke or by crooke hee will haue more, though the poore starue for it.

Nat. Hist. l. 11. c. 17.

At the beginning of Wheat-harvest, the state of flowers decaying, which is alwaies about *Virgo*, the maine robbing beginneth. Then doe they send forth some of their stoutest yonkers to spie and giue the onset: which, going about from Hiue to Hiue so farre as their walke extendeth, doe proue all. Where they haue once sped, at their returne they bring more of their companie; vntill in the end that whole Stall be made acquainted with it. Sometime it happeneth, that though there bee an hundred Stalls within a walke; yet the robberie is done altogether by one: sometime by two or three, all the rest being quiet. And this one thing is strange, that whereas no Bees will abide strangers in their Hiues with them; yet theeues will suffer one another, and agree all in stealing, though they be of diuers Hiues.

31. *How they begin the fray.*

32. *Theeues of diuers Hiues ioyne together in robbing.*

When the theeues, hauing first made an onset, begin to come thicke, and the true Bees perceiue themselues to bee assaulted by many; they suddenly make an out-crie: and issuing out of their holds by troopes, presently prepare themselues to battell. Some keepe the gates: some as Scowt-watches fly about: some runne in againe to see what is done there; some beginne to grapple with the Enemie: and that with such a noise and dinne, as if the Drum did sound an all-arme. Besides which base sound, you shall eftsoones, in the heat of the battell, heare a more shrill and sharpe note, as it were of a Flute.

33. *The description of the Bees battell.*

34. *In the battell is heard a sound like a Drum and a Flute.*

———— *& vox*
Auditur fractos sonitus imitata tubarum.

Which I am out of doubt is raised by their generall Commander, encouraging them to fight for their Prince, their liues, and their goods. Then shall you see the enemies be-stir

Virg.

35. *The assault of the enemie.*

R

stir themselues most venterously: some violently through the thickest thrusting in at the gates, others scaling the walls, and tearing them downe. If they once make a breach, without present succour, you shall quickly haue an end of that fight. On the other side, the defendants will behaue themselues as brauely, not giuing any rest to the enemie: part encountring with them that are without, part with them that haue broken in: whom in a while they draw out by the heeles, some dead, and some aliue. Likewise without you may see some slaine forthright with the thrust of the Speare: some so deadly wounded, that they are not able to goe three foot from the place: and some more lightly strooken presently to lose the vse of their wings, and for a while to leape vp and downe, forward and backward, like mad things.

How long they liue after they are hurt, see c. 8, n. 23.

So loth are these couragious warriours to yeeld on either side, vntill there bee no remedie.

Ingentes animos angusto in pectore versant,
Vsq; adeo obnixi non cedere, donec grauis aut hos,
Aut hos versa fuga victor dare terga coegit.

In their fight they are so furious sometime, and so thicke about the Garden; that, vnlesse you haue on your complete harnesse, v. you may not dare to come nigh them.

This also I haue noted, that when the robbers are so few, that small resistance will serue; yet being called forth they will not bee idle: for you shall see some of them running vp and downe about the Hiue, to seeke and search if any more come: others, like trained Souldiers, practising to fight: here one wrestling with an other in single combat: there two, or three, or foure setting against one; as their vsuall manner is to deale with the theeues. If you would know whether this fight bee in jest or earnest, with fellowes or with foes; the manner, and the end thereof will shew you. For if they bee fellowes, their fight is not so fierce, and they will part quietly as friends: whereas if they be foes, though they scape, it shall bee with much adoe. For if the true men cannot kill the theeues; yet will they hold them by the legs or by the wings so long as they can, in hope to haue helpe, though they

they be drawne after. Moreouer the young Souldiers, which haue scarce beene abroad before, you shall see the elder sort goe round about them, smoothing and trimming them in euery place, as if they did addresse, and hearten them to fight.

During the time of this battaile, as afterward, the Waspes like Vultures prey vpon the dead carkasses, carrying them away peece-meale. *v. n. 1 z.* 39. *The Waspes like Vultures.*

The battaile being ended by repulse of the enemy, those corpses, which the Waspes haue leaft, they honestly burie as farre from the Hiues as they can beare them. 40. *The battaile ended they bury their dead.* Virg. Æneid.

——— *Tum corpora luce carentum*
Exportant tectis, & tristia funera ducunt.

And then they draw together at the Citie-gates: and there they buzze one to another, as if in their language they did talke of the fight, and commend one an other for their fortitude.

The Robbers, preuailing not that day, will vp the next day so soone as it is light, an houre before the Bees vse to come abroad: and then doe they make a fresh assault. The Bees finding the enemy among them, are presently vp in armes: and so beginnes the second skirmish, which, without the taking of the Citie or the ouerthrow of the assailants, (which seldome hapneth) continueth, vntill very darknesse part them. 41. *The second assault of the enemy.*

When the true Bees, finding themselues ouermatcht with multitude, see there is no remedie, and that no resistance will serue; at length they yeeld, and suffer the Conquerours quietly to spoile their goods. And after a while, when, by being together in the same Hiue, and sucking the same Honie, all smell alike; they will ioyne with their enemies, and help carrie away their owne goods, and so become friends and liue together. At night they lodge with them: but in the day-time they returne, with their new fellowes to fetch that is least behinde. By this meanes some venterous stalls are suddainly much increased both in Bees and Honie: although when a Swarme not ouer-stored conquereth a poore stall, and so getteth, by the victorie, more eaters than meat; it turneth 42. *When the true Bees yeeld, they goe with the Conquerors.*

Of the Bees Enemies.

turneth to their owne ouerthrow: for when their food faileth they dye all together.

Seeing therefore in so cruell and continuing a fight, oft-times the enemies are Conquerours, and then all is lost; and if they be vanquisht, yet this victorie is not without losse of men and goods, which the enemy euer now and then shifteth away; I know your desire is to know how to succour the true men, either by preuenting this dangerous conflict, or by rescuing them in the same. For the first reade C. 3. n. 45. 46. 47. For the other many practises haue beene tried: some cast dust, some drinke among them: the one whereof doth no good, the other harme. For drinke maketh them to smell all alike, so that the true men cannot know the Theeues from their fellowes: and therefore some vse to doe so, when two swarmes are put together, that they may seeme to be of one companie. If these vsuall helps be no helps, what help is there then? If you perceiue their fighting in time before any great harme be done, then this must you doe. First stop them vp close, that none can passe either in or out, leauing onely a breathing place. Then shall you haue a double conflict; one within, an other without. The theeues that are within, hauing no way to escape with their preyes, first or last will be slaine all. They that are without, after a little wrestling, seeing nothing to be had but blowes, will not long abide this bootlesse danger. When you perceiue the siege to be raised, and that there is little or no fighting without; (which will be about an houre after) then may you let out your Bees, making the doore halfe an inch high, and scarce halfe an inch wide. Those few that were within will they bring forth to buriall, some then, some on the morrow. In the euening, when the Bees are all in, shut them vp as before. The next day betimes, before the Bees would be abroad, must you looke for some of them againe. When they are come, beat them away with a bough, but kill them not: for so may you doe your neighbour a shrewd turne, and your selfe too.

But let not the Bees out before noone: and then make the doore so narrow, that but one Bee may passe at once. So

43. Remedies.

44. To preuent robbing.

45. And to stay it, if you finde it in time.

will

Of the Bees Enemies.

will they keepe the Robbers out, and follow their businesse neuerthelesse. The next day you may let them out rather: and if the doore be so narrow that it hinder their passage, you may make it wider. If this doe not suffice, but still the strange Bees will striue to get in; assure your selfe that stall will yeeld. And therefore if you bee loth to take it now, because of the Schadons that may corrupt the Honie; *v.* then must you looke vnto him carefully, lest by little and little it come to little or nothing.

V.c. 10. §. 1. n. 2

46.
When it is too late, and what is then to be done

But if the Bees haue yeelded before you are aware of it, so that the theeues rob quietly without resistance; or haue broken the Honie-cels; (which you may perceiue by the crumblets of Wax vpon the stoole) then, hauing shut the Hiue close assoone as you can, the next euening or morning take that is left: otherwise in the end you shall lose all. For the Bees there-about smelling the Honie when the Combes are broken, will haue it or die for it.

This fierce and cruell robbing being alwaies in Harueft, when people are busie in the fields; many Hiues are left Honie-lesse, and they neuer the wiser. Wherefore it is good to leaue some body at home, as well to watch these, as the two legged Robbers.

Neither is this robbing hurtfull onely to those that are robbed, but to the Robbers also. For many of them are daily cut off in the assault: (you may see them lye sprawling at euerie Hiue-doore) whereby their whole stall sometime is so weakned; that, while they seeke to prey vpon others, they become a prey themselues.

47.
Robbing hurtfull also to the Theeues.

After a moist Spring, when Swarmes are most plentifull, *v.* is robbing most rife: otherwise there is lesse danger.

48.
In what yeares robbing is most rife.
V.c. 5. n. 5.

Besides those Bees that are thus spoiled in robbing, many also are killed by other stalls when they come to them for succour. For in the Spring those Swarmes that were lateward, or haue beene halfe-robbed; when they haue spent all their store, the next warme day after, away they flye: some to a tree where they hang till they be dead: some aduenture into other Hiues: where if they haue large entrance, that they may throng in suddainely; sometime they scape with the

49.
Bees kill poore swarmes that wander in the spring.

the death of some few, and being mingled together continue with them as one stall: but for the most part they die euery each one. *v. c. 1. n. 22.*

50
To preuent the death of poore Swarmes.
V. c. 10. p. 1. n. 18.

To preuent this losse, (1) when you perceiue them to wax light and weake; driue them into a stall that hath prouision enough, *v.* (2) If it be your hap to see them entring a stall that is well stored, lift vp the Hiue and let them in together, and so perhaps they may scape: and (3) if you finde any hanging abroad, you may put them into what stall you list; by rearing the stall before a handfull from the stoole,

V. c. 10. p. 1. n. 25.

and laying the Bees vpon the Table, *v.* close to the doore.

51.
Many killed in swarming.

Lastly, the Bees doe much destroy one an other in swarming-time. *v. c. 5. n. 64, 65, 66, 68, 75, 76, 77, 80, & 81.*

52.
14. *The weather.*

Next vnto Bees, the greatest Enemy that the Bees haue is vnkinde Weather: whereby at all times of the yeare both they and their fruits are much empaired.

53.
In Summer heat hurteth the Bees.

In Summer extreme heat melteth the Combes (specially of Swarmes) and so sheddeth the Honie; if the Hiues be not shaded, and well hackled. It also causeth the Bees to lye out, and so hindereth their swarming. *v. c. 5. n. 20.*

54.
In Winter the Sun-shine in frost and snow.

At Winter, the Sunne shining in frostie or snowie weather, is dangerous to the Bees. For the shine tilleth them abroad, and the Frost chilleth them: many as they flye, that they cannot returne: and many that returne, while they rest on the ground before the Hiue. But the Snow amazeth them, and dazeling their eyes causeth them presently to fall, and with his vehement cold to rise no more: and most of all then, when, to shun the wind, they light in the shade. And

55.
The remedie.

therefore if, the Snow lying, the mildnesse of the weather draw them abroad; it is good to strew the Snow with straw, not onely in your Garden, but also without the fences, specially in the Lee-sides, if conueniently you may: and so shall you saue a number; which else you might see lying about, like slaine men in a foughten field.

56.
Also the Easterne winds and great frosts.
V. c. 3. n. 61.

Also the freezing Easterne winds, and all great Frosts kill many in the Hiues that be open, or vncouered: and therefore at such times it is good to shut them vp close, *v.* and to

Of the Bees Enemies.

see them well hackled, *v. c. 3. n. 5.*

And if the cold continuing keepe them long in, it maketh them so sicke, heauy, and chilly; that many dye assoone as they come abroad into the aire, vnlesse it be very pleasant. *v. 6. 3. n. 62.*

Also the raine doth oft-times soake into the Hiues, and so corrupteth the Combes, and killeth the Bees: specially where the company is small, not hauing heat enough to drie them againe. Wherefore prouide that alwaies your hackles be good. And for remedie (if any such chance happen) pull off the hackles in warme daies, that the Sunne may dry the Hiues againe.

But the greatest losse is in the Spring. For the Bees, specially the young frie (being laded and wearie with their labour) some at their worke, some in the way home, some at the Hiue-doore are beaten downe; not onely through suddaine stormes, but also through cold rough winds: and then, vnlesse the Sunne shine or the wind lye, they neuer come home againe: insomuch that sometime you may see the Lanes *vt* strewed with them.

And therefore, when being a field they see a stormie or rainie Cloud arising, presently they hie them home for life: tumbling to the Hiue as thicke as Haile, thronging, and throwing downe one another before the doore for haste. Where, if the cold raine catch them before they can recouer the Hiue, they are in no better case than those that the storme beat downe by the way: although, when they are fresh and light, they will flye abroad in the midst of a warme shower, not caring for it.

They which are thus taken abroad, must take their chance: but if you defend your Bee-garden as you ought, *v.* you shall preuent the fall of many at home. And those that you finde chilled with cold (though they be quite dead, without sense, motion, and breath, yea and haue lien so all the day) you may, if you be disposed, reuiue with the warmth of your hand; so that it will seeme a miracle vnto you. For presently (their spirit returning) you shall see them begin to pant and breath againe: and anone they will flye away as lustie as the best.

57. And the cold continued maketh them sicke.

58. The raine rotteth the Hiues.

59. The remedy.

60. The greatest losse by weather is in the spring: for then infinite multitudes are beaten downe, laden and wearie, with stormes, and wind. V. 6. 1. n. 49.

61. At the rising of a Cloud they post home.

62. Yet will they goe a field in the midst of a warme shower.

V. 6. 2. n. 2. 3. 4. & 5.

63. How to restore Bees to life.

Of the Bees Enemies.

best. But if you spie any store of such dead or halfe-dead Bees, then your way is to put them in a Glasse, and couering it, to some it wound against the fire, till you see them ready to flye.

Also where Palme-withies, or other trees whereon they gather, doe hang ouer the water; the rough winds throw downe and drowne a number of them, while they bee at worke. Many also, where there are no such trees, when they come but to drinke.

For remedie of the first, cut downe the trees: and for the other, see c. 6. n. 56.

Tot hostibus, tot casibus, tam munificum
animal expositum est.

¶ There remaineth yet another Enemie worse than all these. For these all doe wrong the Bees but by little and little; some in their goods, some in their persons: and there is remedie shewed, if industrie be not wanting, against them all. But this, when he commeth, playeth sweep-stake with them; carrying away both Honie, and Wax, and Bees, and Hiue, and all at once: and there is no sufficient remedie found, either in the Bee-master, or in the Bees themselues against him: neither shall I, with all my skill, be euer able to deuise any; vnlesse the wisest of the Land, when they meet together, will ioyne with me in the inuention. For first the Bees are least destitute of their Keepers helpe, seeing at the times of greatest danger, he cannot alwaies be *sub Dio* with them, nor they conueniently *sub Lare* with him: although some haue, for their safetie, put this in practise, housing them and shutting them vp close all the Winter: but not without much inconuenience. For by this meanes they are debarred of their necessarie recreation: in a warme houre, when it happeneth: and if by chance they breake forth, they lose their way in againe, and their liues withall. And as they want herein their Keepers helpe, so haue they no meanes to saue themselues, no not so much as the silly sheepe, which happily may runne away. For their resistance, which against some Enemies doth often preuaile, against the violence of this flie *Tenebrio* auaileth nothing at all: who stealing vpon them

Of the Bees Enemies.

them, while they be at rest, & suddainly surprising them, carrieth the poore Captiues (alasse) they wote not whither. Although I haue read a Storie of a Stalk, that being stolne did sharply punish the Malefactor, making him to submit himselfe vnto their Master, and to aske him forgiuenesse. Indeed I will not be bound for the truth of it, for it is no childe of mine: but if any man desire to take it as it is, he shall haue it as good cheape as I. *Cum nostu latro apes S. Medardi subripuisset, apes ipsæ in sancti viri ultionem, relictis vasis suis, in malefactorem illum vitcunq; ac, diffugientem: acerrima earūm insinuatione persecutæ sunt, quousq; ad Sanctum vellet nollet, regrederetur, & ejus prouolutus vestigijs suppliciter pro commisso crimine veniam precaretur. Cui mox ut Sanctus manum extendit benedictionis, apes, tanquam obedientes, ab ejus insecutione cessauerunt, & antiquo Domini sui dominio euidenter sese reddiderunt.* Laur. Surius in vita S. Medardi. Tom. 3.   When a Theefe by night had stollen S. Medards Bees, the Bees in their Masters quarrell, leauing their Hiue, set vpon the Malefactor, and eagerly pursuing him which way soeuer he ranne, would not cease stinging of him, vntill they had made him, whether he would or no, to go backe againe to their Masters house, and there falling prostrate at his feete, submisly to crie him mercie for the crime committed.   Which being done, so soone as the Saint extended vnto him the hand of benediction; the Bees, like obedient Seruants, did forthwith stay from persecuting him, and euidently yeelded themselues to the ancient possession and custodie of their Master.

It were to be wished that *Pares culpâ* might be *Pares pœnâ*; that all like offendors might haue like punishment. But sith our Bees are not of S. *Medards* kinde, thus to rescue themselues from this mischieuous Enemie; it is meet their merit procure them a protection: and as they prouide for the health and safetie of men, v. so men should prouide for the safetie and secure being of them. That such as delight in things for their Country so profitable, might not by idle and theeuish Varlets, vnprofitable members of the Common-wealth, be discouraged in their honest courses. Where-

V. c. 1. n. 1: & C. 10. p. 3. n. 1. & 2.

S   fore

fore I humbly and heartily entreate all those, whether they be high or low, which shall reape either profit or pleasure by these my paines, that they would endeuour, as much as in them lyeth, by themselues and by their friends, that against this odious rapine it may be enacted, as a Law of the *Medes* and *Persians* which altereth not, that they which feloniously breake open these true labourers houses, shall, like other House-breakers, bee deemed and iudged as guiltie of Burglairie, and so haue no benefit or fauour by the *Muses*, that thus violate the *Muses* sacred Fauorites. And heere, now my hand is in (though it may seeme a hard digression) let me begge the like boone for those other necessarie creatures, which, for their like certaine and generall profit, the Prouerbe hath ioyned with them in speciall commendation to the world.

Who so keepe well Sheepe and Been,
Sleepe or wake, their thrift comes in.

They serue for mans vse both without and within, not only to feed the belly, but also to cloath the back: for which necessarie vses, they deserue especially to be beloued and defended of all. And yet I thinke that in any thing, nay in all things else, there is not so much wrong and spoile done to the Countrey, as in them alone: Sheepe-stealing, through foolish pittie, is now growne so common and so continuall. Whereby, besides the infinite losses which true Subiects daily suffer in that kinde, the Commonwealth sustaineth an other great damage in Corne; the Husbandmen oft-times fearing and forbearing to fold their Land, lest their losse should be greater than their gaine. Surely, in my opinion, the very Boot-halers, or High-way-Robbers are more worthy fauour than such. For they are men of more generous spirits, both apt for seruice themselues, and to breed bold Souldiers for their Prince and Country, who, by good admonition, better imploiments, or conscience of the sinne, are oft-times reclaimed: Whereas these Night-Rauens, for the most part, are base cowardly Knaues, neither fit for seruice, nor labour; a meere burthen to the Commonwealth,

Of the Feeding of Bees.

weakth: and as incorrigible as sheep-biting Curres, which being once flesh't, doe seldome desist; vntill the bones or somewhat else doe happily choake them.

Chap. VIII.

Of the Feeding of Bees.

Hree moneths of the twelue are rich and plentifull (in which the Bees gather abundantly, and store themselues for all the yeere) *Gemini, Cancer, Leo;* but *Cancer* is better than both the other. In *Virgo* and *Libra* they liue of their daily labour from hand to mouth: little increasing or diminishing their store; vnlesse they fall into the hands of Robbers, and then, without reskue, they lose all. But in the other seuen, either wholly or partly they feed vpō that store, which the three rich moneths did afford them. For *Scorpio* hath but the poore gleanings of decaying plants: the three still moneths nothing at all. *Pisces* beginneth to put forth fresh plants, which in *Aries* and *Taurus* are well increased: but this breeding time the mouths are multiplied more than the meat, which * vnkinde weather oftentimes suffereth them not to fetch in. So that all this while, they, more or lesse, spend vpon the stocke: yea the weaker stalls somewhat longer, being not so well able to indure the sharpe aire: and therefore, for want of some store to feed on betweene whiles at home, I haue knowne some die after Mid-*Gemini*.

For which seuen spending moneths, some swarmes are sufficiently prouided: which you may reckon as Iewels, the verie *Spes gregis*; whose increase the next yeere is certaine, if they be not ouer-hiued. Some are not prouided for halfe the time: and these, as desperately poore, are not worth the feeding.

1. *In seuen moneths the Bees spend of the Stocke.*

* *Rainie, cold, and windie.*

2. *Three sorts of swarmes diuersly prouided.*

Of the Feeding of Bees

feeding. Others are prouided for six, or fiue, or foure moneths: which, by the helpe of feeding, may liue and doe well.

3. The first sort.

V. c. 5. n. 11.

Of the first sort are timely prime swarmes vnbroken: also faire Castlings not ouer hiued, before *Cancer*; yea and in kinde or backward Summers before *Mid-Cancer*: when the black-bery-blossomes are not yet come, *v.* nor the hony-deawes gone: For such haue sufficient both company and time, to make sufficient prouision.

4. The second.

V.c. 5. n. 68.

Of the second sort are the ouer-little and late swarmes, whose paucitie and pouertie makes them vnlustie to trauell for more, and ynable to keepe what is gotten or giuen them. Such are sure to bee put before winter be past, by cold and hunger, out of hunger and cold. And therefore if you haue omitted to saue such by *Vnion* ; *v*. yet omit not to saue that little which they haue, and your vaine labour and cost in feeding them. *v.c. 10. p. 1. n. 3. in III.*

5. The third onely are to be fed.

Of the third sort are the midling and indifferent swarmes, which by their earnest labour haue gotten well, and gathered good store of wealth together: but yet, for some want of number or time, the summer leaueth them in some want of prouision.

6. Stockes out of proofe neuer to be fed.

As for Stockes that haue stood two yeeres, and yet haue not sufficient stocke for these seuen moneths; (whether they be such as haue not gotten it, or hauing gotten it haue lost it againe) they are out of proofe: and therefore fit to be taken, not fed. *v.c. 10 p. 1. n. 3. in III.*

7. Trie your swarmes in Virgo.

V.s. 10. p. 1. n. 2.

But because vnkinde summers may make good swarmes but poore, as contrarily a plentifull summer may much mend the worst; after *Mid-Virgo*, when Bees are to be taken, *v.* it behoueth you to trie all your swarmes, by knocking and poising them: for the noise will tell you the greatnesse of the company, and the weight, their wealth. They that are vsed to poise them by hand, will resolue you readily in this point by aime: which till you know to doe, the Scales may direct you. For hauing taken the iust weight of the Hiue and all together, if, the fore-knowne weight of the leere spleeted Hiue being deducted, there remaine not fifteene pound in all, to

8. What quantitie of Hony is requisite.

wit,

Of ... Feeding of ... C. 3.

wit, for fiue pound ʋ. in Bees, the double weight in honie and wax; that swarme is desperately poore, ʋ. and fitter to be taken than fed *. If the swarme with his store doe weigh betweene fifteene and twentie, due feeding ʋ. may saue him. If betweene twentie and fiue and twentie, hee is able to shift for himselfe, and liue without helpe. If betweene fiue and twentie and thirtie, esteeme him as right good, plentifully prouided euen for a hard winter, and fitted to be forward the next spring †. And aboue that the greater the store is, the better increase it promiseth. Vnlesse, in some extraordinarie yeere, the Hiue be cloyed with too much: ʋ. for too much, as well to Bees as men, doth ofttimes more harme than good.

V. † *Ins. c. 5. n. 45.*
V. n. 2.

V. n. 14, &c.

V. c. 10. p. 1. n. 3. in VII. & VIII.

* Yet they that haue but a small Bee-fold, and are content to be often troubled (specially at the second feeding-time) may try those that lacke a pound or two of this weight.

† And yet such though neuer so good, will perish neuerthelesse, if they chance to lose their Queene: ʋ. which sometime happeneth to those that are much troubled in the hiuing. ʋ. c. 5. n. 51.

V. c. 1. n. 6.

Moreouer, because a long winter and a rough spring following, with some other accidents, may waste them that were good, as, on the other side, a short winter and a milde spring may helpe those that were scantily prouided; it shall not be amisse to try againe in *Pisces* or *Aries*, those that you suspect; and to feed them if you see cause. *ʋ. n.* 15. & 16.

9.
Trie againe in Pisces or Aries.

THE naturall food of Bees is Honie: for want, or for sparing whereof, many other things haue beene deuised. *Aristotle* mentioneth Figs, and all such sweet things. *Apiariis ficus ac reliqua id genus dulcia in cibum apponunt.* And *Plinie,* speaking more particularly, commendeth Raysings, and Figs, and teased Wooll, wet in sweet Wine made of Raisings, or new Wine boiled, or Hony-water. *Si cibus dresse censeatur apibus, uvas passas siccas ve, ficosq; tusas ad fores earum possuisse conveniet, item lanas tractas madentes passo aut defruto, aut aqua mulsa.* And some of our Country-men haue practised to giue them Bay-salt, Bean-flower, Groundmault, rosted Wardens, and Apples, and sweet Wort. All which

10.
The Bees food.

Hist. l. 9. c. 40.

Nat. hist. li. 21. c. 14.

Of the Feeding of Bees.

which things, though they will spend; yet cannot they be preserued by them without Honie.

P. n. 11.

Touching the counsell of *Plinie*, this is to be noted, that if you place their food *ad fores* before the doore, it will draw strange Bees vnto them; whereby the liues of the one, and the goods of the other will be indangered: if you place it abroad from your Hiue, then will it be common: and if within vpon the stoole, which is best, then must you remoue it in time, or keepe it close: *v.* otherwise it will be no better for them, than if it were set *ad fores*. And as for the deuice of teased Wooll, it is a fitter meanes to catch Bees, than to feed them. For if the liquor be aboue the Wooll, it will lime the wings of many; if not, many will be intangled in the small haires, as Birds in a grin. Couer it therefore with a linnen cloth, so that the Bees may not creep betweene.

11. *Priuate feeding.*

The manner of feeding Bees in their Hiues is diuers. Some giue them Honie in a spoone: but that way many of them be-smeare their wings: and if their fellowes licke them not cleane presently, before the cold chill them, they die. Others, to auoid this inconuenience, giue it them in a warme Toste: but this way wasteth the hony, & doth not altogether auoid the former inconuenience. Others haue other deuices. But indeed the only good way to feed Bees is with a combe, after this manner. First, take a fresh Combe of Liue-honie out of a Hiue, & lay it vpon some Prop or stay, that the Bees may worke, as well vnder as vpon. This Prop may be a woodden grate seuen or eight inches square, made of two sides halfe an inch deepe, and three ribs fastened into them with Douetailes, or with small nailes. For a need two seuerall square stickes may serue: but then you cannot so quickly either set it in, or take it out.

Then in a faire calme euening (when the heat of the day, and the Bees worke is past) place this vpon the stoole: so that the Feeding-combe be reared as neere the Hiue-combes as may be, not touching them, lest the Bees fasten this and them together. Then see that the Hiue, set downe in his place, be close euerie where: and at the doore but roome enough for a Bee or two to passe. Then will these Bees to worke afresh, not ceasing day nor night vntill they haue rid the Combe cleane: which within eight and fortie houres will be effected. If they need any more, the next euening doe likewise.

Of the Feeding of Bees.   C. 8.

likewise. But alwaies when it waxeth darke, and the Bees are all in, barre vp the doore: and let them not out till the next euening, when other Bees are quiet. Or if you doe it in the morning, be sure also to take out the Combe, whether he be rid or no. And still leaue the Hiue close, with a narrow passage.

If your poore Bees should not be thus defended from strangers, the feeding of them would proue a staruing of them. For the Borderers smelling the bootie will be sure to haue part of it, if they can come at it: and when that is done, they will set vpon the other, and so spoile all: as often it falleth out through this carelesnesse. Which causeth some to condemne all feeding of Bees, as painfull and fruitlesse: saying, If you feed them not, they can but die: and so will they doe when you haue bestowed your labour and cost. But this is disproued by experience: for those, which being fit to be fed v. are thus fed, do seldome miscarrie. That summer they prouide sufficiently for winter, and the next they are as likely to swarme and be fat as an other.

12.
Carelesse feeding is staruing.

V. n. 5.

You may also feed your poore swarmes together, (if you haue no neighbour-Bees to beguile them) by setting any refuse-honie or leauings abroad in your Garden, hauing first barred vp those that need it not. This feeding-Hony, as that which is stolne, when they haue first taken their refection, they conuey into their void Cells: which, because they cannot now shut them vp, as before Virgo, for want of wax yet, they doe but halfe-fill. And therefore they first spend of this late gotten hony, reseruing that, which was more safely laid vp, vnto the last.

13.
Publike feeding.

V. c. 6. n. 15.

It is good to feed Bees before they need: (that they may saue their store, which they haue shut vp in their Cells, vntill the spring) namely, in the later part of Virgo, when the Combes are taken, v. or in Libra. For those that haue spent their owne store, and haue little or nothing leaft in the end of Winter, are so discouraged and so feeble with fasting; that knowing their thin bodies can beare out no cold, they wil not come abroad, but when they are fed: vnlesse the weather be exceeding warme and calme: and the more they keepe in, the
weaker

14.
The first time of feeding.

V. c. 10. p. 1. n. 2.

Of the Feeding of Bees.

weaker still they are, and lesse apt to breed. But those whose rashe feeding hath caused them to spare their store till the Spring, will be as cheerefull as the best: in any reasonable weather they will abroad, and fetch in that fruitfull *Ambrosia*, which causeth them presently to increase and multiply. *v. c. 4. n. 12.*

At this first time therefore first finish the publike feeding: and then begin the private, specially of those that are vnder eighteene pound: to which if you giue now the better part of their * due allowance, you may supply the defects of them, as also of the rest, at the second feeding-time, when their need will better appeare.

* Their due allowance, first and last to be giuen them, is so much at least, as the swarme with his store lacketh of twentie pound. *v. n. 8.*

15. The second time of feeding.

In *Pisces* or *Aries*, as soone as the weather is warme (not before, lest the cold chill them in their worke) if you feare they will lacke (which you may perceiue by their lightnesse & vnwillingnesse to come abroad) supply their want againe, and againe, if need be. But in this second feeding, for lacke of a Hony-combe, take a drie Combe, reserued for the purpose, and poure thereon so much Honie as it may receiue. If you thinke it be not liquid enough; then either warme it first ouer the fire, or else spread it all ouer the Combe with your finger, that it may sinke into the Cells: (for which purpose Liue hony is best) then vse this honied combe as the Hony-combe. *v. n. 11.*

16. The third time of feeding.

If either these fed Bees, or any other, chance afterward to lacke (namely in *Taurus*, or somwhat before or after) then feed them daily vntill mid-*Gemini*, giuing them, euerie euening or morning betimes, a spoonefull of Honie; and taking away the Combe againe before other Bees be at worke. But this is to be done without intermission: for the Bees will duly looke for it, and languish, if once or twice they lacke it.

If you vse to knocke the Hiue, when you put in the Honie; they will come downe together, like sheepe to a call, when they are to be soccred.

By this meanes I haue saued swarmes that forsooke their Hiues for hunger, hiuing them againe in their owne Hiues: which proued good the same yeere.

CHAP.

Chap. IX.
Of the remouing of Bees.

N remouing of Bees be carefull to auoid these fiue euills: 1. hindering of their swarming: 2. and of their Hony-gathering: 3. breaking of their Combes: 4. robbing: 5. and losse of Bees.

Fiue things to be auoided in remouing Bees.

Remoue alwaies in a faire day, and, as neere as you can guesse, in setled weather. For when they are moued to another place, if it be within their circuit or walke; they will flie to their old standing as soone as they are let goe, and hanker about it three or foure daies, and sometime longer: where if the cold wet catch them, many lose their liues. And if you remoue them out of their knowledge, then, as amazed in an vncouth place, they flie about for a while viewing the countrie, and searching for their old home: when they are wearie, they rest wheresoeuer: and if foule weather come vpon them, they are in like danger.

2. Remoue alwaies in faire weather.

For the time of the yeere, remoue not in the three still moneths, or in a fortnight afore or after, for losing the Bees. For if foule weather fall not, the very still cold will kill many, while they are straying abroad: and of those that returne, being not yet acquainted with the Hiue doore, some will fall short, some vpon the Hiue: where, while they rest panting, the cold chilleth them.

3. Not in Winter.

Taurus, *Gemini*, and especially *Cancer*, are naught, for hindering the swarming, as well as their hony-gathering: and *Cancer* for danger also of breaking their soft Combes.

4. Nor in Summer.

In *Leo* though the swarming time be past, and robbing time not yet come; yet there remaineth some honie-gathe-

T   ring,

ring, and the Combes being then most weightie and most weake, the danger of breaking them is greatest.

V.c.7.n.31.

To remoue in *Virgo* (when the Bees doe euer vse to be trying of masteries) *v.* is dangerous for robbing. For the *Indigene* or old inhabitants of the Garden (as they goe about prying for booties) finding new neighbours come among them, will be sure to visit them: and while the chiefe of their strength is stragling abroad, seeking for their old dwelling; they will bring the rest such cheere to their housewarming, as shall haply make the house too hot for them, And then they must be faine to goe along with them, and helpe to carrie their owne goods after them. *v.c. 7. n. 42.*

5.
The Autumne and Spring are fit times for remouing.

The fittest time is either in *Libra*, and the fore-part of *Scorpio*, that they may throughly know their new standing before the weather be too cold; or in *Aries*, and the later part of *Pisces*, that they may be acquainted with it before much gathering of Honie.

Neuerthelesse, if you haue Bees in other mens keeping, whose care and skill you mistrust; you were better to remoue them vnseasonably with some losse, than to hazard all by their ignorance and negligence.

6.
Libra, the best month in all the yeere.

But if you may choose, remoue in *Libra* onely: which is simply the best.

7.
When to remoue a swarme.

And for the remouing of a Swarme into an other Garden, (whether it be neere or far off) the only time is the euening or night next after the hiuing: that he may be at his new standing, readie to worke, in the morning; and so lose no time, nor breake his first Combe in the carriage.

8.
The time of the day, and manner of remouing.

IN the euening, when you mean to remoue, an houre before sun-set prop vp the Hiue from the Stoole, with three Bolsters two or three inches thicke, that the Bees may ascend from the stoole. About halfe an houre after, hauing prepared an other stoole of the same height, and couered it with your Mantle, so, that the middle of the mantle be ouer the middle of the stoole; moue the stall with his stoole, if you may, a little aside; and set this couered stoole in his place: or if it cannot well be moued, then set the couered stoole close

to

Of the Remouing of Bees. C. 9.

to the old stoole, either beside it, or before it. This done, lift vp the stall from his old stoole, and set it vpon the new: and then wiping the Bees from the old stoole (if any remaine) with your Brush; either take the stoole away, or couer it with a cloth. And then if your new stoole be onely a planke without legs, borne vp by some other meanes; it is good to set it vpon the old. Within a while when the Bees are all in, knit the mantle at the foure corners ouer the top of the Hiue, so as the knots may not slip: and presently binde it to the Hiue about the middle slackly with a small line, and wrest it fast with a little sticke. And so is the stall readie to be remoued.

They vse commonly to make no more adoe, but after sun-set when the Bees are at rest, to lift vp the stall, and set it vpon a mantle spread on the ground, and so to binde it vp, leauing the Bees vpon the stoole (which in a good stall are not a few) behinde them. Which way, for such stalls as haue all their Bees vp in the Hiue, may serue well enough.

The best way to carrie your * Stall is vpon a Cowl-staffe betweene two.

* If you haue many to remooue; two lustie fellowes may beare two or three of them at once: but let them be all fast bound together.

If it be light, one may carrie it in his hand. But, howsoeuer, be sure it hang perpendicularly for feare of breaking the Combes; specially if you chance to remoue before *Libra*, when the wax is soft, and the lower parts of the Combes are heauie with Schadons, as well as the vpper with Honie.

When you haue brought the Stall home, you may let it stand bound as it is, all night in the house. The morrow, when the weather serueth, set him on his seat: but if it be foule all the next day, keepe him still bound vntill it be faire. And then hauing loosed the line, and taken away the Mantle, cloome him vp presently: leauing, for three or foure faire daies, a verie narrow entrance, for feare of robbing. For their new neighbours, euen now also (though not so eagerly as in *Virgo*) will proue them: and they will not so stoutly resist, vntill they be acquainted in the place.

T 2 CHAP.

---

9. *The vsuall manner of remouing.*

10. *Which is fit for poore stalles.*

11. *How a good stall is to be carried.*

12. *How a bad.*

13. *What to do when they are brought home.*

14. *And what when they are seated.*

Chap. X.

Of the fruit and profit of Bees.

Wherein is shewed first the *Vindemiation* or taking of Combes: secondly, the trying of the *Wax* and *Honie*, with the making of *Meth* or *Hydromel*: and thirdly, the singular vertues of them, for the vse and comfort of man.

The first part of this Chapter sheweth the taking of the Combes.

1.
The first kind of Vindemiation.

2.
The best time for killing Bees.

1.

Col.l.9.c.15.
2.

3.
What Stalls are to be taken.

V.c.4.n.31.&
32.
I.

He most vsuall, and generally most vsefull manner of taking the Combes, is by killing the Bees. For which the naturall and seasonable time is the latter part of *Virgo*, from the end of the *Dog-daies* vnto *Libra*: because till then the Combes are full of Schadons, which deceiue the Honi-men, making the Hiue heauier and the Honie worse: (for the young Bees as well as the Coome corrupt the same, *Pulli & rubræ sordes sunt mali saporis, & succo suo mella corrumpunt.*) and after that time, the weather waxeth colder, not so fit for the running and working of the Honie: and the Honie is likely to decrease, either by their owne spending or by the spoiling of Robbers. Except in the heath-countries, where their gathering lasteth longer: for there they defer their taking vntill Mid-*Libra*.

At this time therefore consider with your selfe what Stalls you will kill. Swarmes that may liue, yeerlings and two yeerlings that are in proofe, keepe for store. Likewise those that rid their Drones betimes, and specially those that draw out their young Cephens *v*. Those of three or foure yeeres, which, by reason of their not swarming this last summer, are

ful

Of the fruit and profit of Bees.

full of Bees, lightly are fat, and therefore worth the taking: but they are also good for store, vnlesse the frequent Honi-dewes haue made them ouer fat. But those of that age which haue cast twice (except they were very forward and had beat away their Drones betimes) are not likely to * continue: and therefore are to be taken.

If you would haue any such to stand an other yeere, and not to bee weakened by his late castling; put it backe into the stocke againe. v.c.5.n.11.

II.

Likewise all poore swarmes vnworthy to be fed, v. and all light stocks whose stocks are decayed: v. For they will surely die. Neither is it safe to trust any after they haue stood fiue yeeres: vnlesse it be some speciall kinde of Bees, which cast often, and yet beating away their Drones betimes, doe still keepe themselues in heart. For such I haue kept nine or ten yeeres: and I haue heard of some of a greater age. Moreouer, all stalls of three yeeres old and vpward, that haue mist swar-ming two yeeres together: and especially those, that hauing lyen forth the summer before, did not cast this last summer: for such doe seldom after prosper. It is therefore better to take them now while they are good, than in a vaine hope of increase, to keepe them till they perish. Likewise if you haue any that are very fat and full of Honie, (as some yeeres some will be, euen downe to the Stoole) those are ripe and ready to yeeld their fruit. One such is worth three or foure. Take them therefore in their season: For wanting roome to breed in (their Cells being full of Honie) they will decay by little and little, and consume to nothing. And therefore, as in a wet hungry yeere you must keepe the best, so in a drie yeere, rich and plentifull in Honie-dewes, the worst are like to proue best for store.

V.c.8.n.4. III.
V.c.8.n.6. IV.
V.

VI.

VII.

VIII.

But generally take the best, and the worst. *In medio virtus.* And euer suspect those that rid not their Drones in time, v. Also those which the Robbers doe eagerly assault, v. and if their Combes bee once broken, v. delay not their taking.

IX.
V.c.4.n.30. X.
V.c.3.n.50. XI.
V.c.7.n.46.

Hauing made choice of your Stall to be taken, some two or three houres before † Sun-set: dig a hole in the ground, as neere the Stoole as may bee, about eight or nine inches deepe,

4.
The manner of killing Bees.

T 3

deepe, and almost as wide as the Hiue-skirts: laying the small earth round about the brims. Then hauing a little sticke slit in one end, & shript at the other, take a † Brimstone-match 5. or 6. inches long, and about the bignesse of your little finger, and making it fast in the slit, sticke the sticke in the middle or side of the hoale; so that the top of the Match may stand euen with the brim of the pit: and then set another by him drest after the same manner, if that bee not sufficient. When you haue fired these Matches at the vpper ends, set ouer the Hiue: and presently shut it so close at the Skirts, that none of the smoake may come forth. So shall you haue the Bees dead and downe in lesse than a quarter of an houre.

* That you may haue the euening and morning to finish your workes while the store-Bees be at rest: which otherwise will trouble you in handling the Honie, if by any meanes they may come at you. But if the weather be cold enough to keepe them in, or the house bee close enough to keepe them out; you may take what time of the day you please.

† Matches are made of linnen rags and Brimstone, after the manner that maids make Sluts. First, melt pounded Brimstone: then take a linnen rag a foot long, and holding both the ends in one hand, dip the rest in the melted Brimstone, turning it vp and downe with a sticke: then taking one of the ends in the other hand, winde it a little; for hard winding makes it burne the worse. This cut in the middle maketh twaine.

5.
Sundry meanes to kill Bees.

Next vnto Brimstone is the smoake of Bunt or great Puc-fists, Tuchwood, or Mushrums, vsed in like manner: but they are neither so quicke, nor so sweet. And for a need, some smother them with danke Straw, or Hay: but then the Honie will smell of the smoake. And therefore some drowne them in a Tub of water: but that hurteth the Honie, and doth the Hiue no good: and, besides that, many of the Bees being not quite dead, will sting them that handle the Honie.

6.
The Bees being dead; house the Hiue.

The Bees being dead, carrie the Hiue into the house, &c. See Part 2. If any Bees escape, they will die that night: but if you feare they will doe any harme, you may kill them presently vpon the Stoole.

7.
The second kinde of Condemnation.

ANother way to take the Combes is by Driuing the Bees. The manner of it is this. At Mid-summer, or within two or three daies after, in a faire morning an houre before Sun-rising,

rising, lift the Stall from the Stoole, and set it vpright and fast on the ground in a Brake *v.* with the bottome vpward: and quickly couer it with an emptie Hiue, hauing first laid two spleets vpon the full Hiues bottome, that the emptie Hiue may stand the faster. Then wrapping a Mantle *v.* round about the Chincke or meeting of both the Hiues, and binding it fast with a small cord aboue and beneath, that a Bee may not get forth, clap the full Hiue or *Remouer* round about a good many times, pawsing now and then a little betweene, that the Bees may ascend into the void Hiue. And when you thinke that most of them are driuen vp (which will bee about halfe an houre after) set the vpper Hiue or *Receiuer* vpon the old stoole: B V T bee sure &c. *as it followeth note 15.*

Prouided alwaies, before you goe about this businesse, that all the Stalls in your Garden be first shut vp, lest they trouble you and your poore Bees.

This kinde of taking is much applauded at the first, because men thinke thereby to saue both Bees and Honie: but it falleth out with them as it is in the Prouerbe, *All couet, all lose.* For the Honie is neither so good, as being not yet in season, and to bee corrupted with the Schadons, *v.* which can hardly be cleane taken from it; neither so much by almost the one halfe, sith there remaine yet six or seuen weekes of Honie-gathering.

And the Bees, as men forcibly driuen from their goods and children, are so discouraged, that they seldom thriue after it: specially those that haue swarmed; seeing their companie is least but small, and the after-brood is destroyed, which should haue supplyed the roomes of them that are gone. And as for those that haue not cast, they might after that time yeeld a swarme; which would be better than the whole stall being driuen: and if they did not swarme at all, they would bee so much the better, either to take for Honie, or keepe for store. *v. c. 5. n. 28.*

This Driuing of Bees into keere Hiues being nothing so profitable as it seemeth, I doe rather commend vnto you the Driuing of one stall into another: whereby the fruit of one is

---

8.
The time and manner of Driuing Bees.
V. c. 5. n. 24.
V. c. 5. n. 48.

9.
This driuing of Bees vnprofitable.

10.
The Honie taken is little and naught.
V. n. 2.

11.
And the Bees driuen, few and poore.

12.
Another kinde of driuing.

is taken; and the liues of both are saued together.

And thus some are to be driuen in the latter part of *Virgo*, when they haue done breeding; *v.* and some in *Aquarius*, or *Pisces*, before they begin to breed againe. *v.c.4.n.12.*

In *Virgo* such stalls onely are to be driuen, as are fit to bee killed: *v.* and that into yeerlings or two-yeerlings, which that yeere haue cast twice, and therefore haue few Bees left in them; but yet haue Honie enough. The manner of it is this. Hauing first placed these two stalls, the *Remouer* that is driuen and the *Receiuer*, as neere as may be one to another, and so let them stand together six or seuen daies, till they be well acquainted with their standings; when you see the weather faire and constant, late in an euening, about ten a clocke, set the *Remouer* fast on the ground in a Brake, *v.* with his bottome vpward, and the *Receiuer* vpon: and binde them close together, as in the former driuing. And then, by often clapping the *Remouer* betweene your hands about the space of a quarter of an houre (now and then pawsing betweene) hauing driuen most of the Bees into the *Receiuer*, and so mingled them all together; let them so stand til the morning. In the morning about Sun-rising, if the weather bee faire, (otherwise you must stay * longer) doe the like: hauing first shut and couered the other stalls. *v.c.5.n.25.*

* If the weather fit not the next day, you may safely stay till it doe fit, so that no Bees get forth in the meane space.

This done, set the *Receiuer* vpon the *Remouers* stoole: BVT, be sure to bolster him vp with three Tile-shards, that the driuen Bees may easily get into the Hiue on euery side. And then knocke the *Remouer* downe vpon a Table two or three foot square, set close to the forepart of the stoole: and, by clapping of the Hiue, presently get as many of the Bees forth as you can. And forthwith carry the *Remouer* about a Pearch from the stoole; and there laying him downe, so that the Combes may lie edgelong, after a little while clap him twice or thrice, which will make many of the Bees to fly forth. Then remoue him to another place about the former distance, and there doe likewise: and so to an other, and an other, vntill few or no Bees will come forth; by this meanes

And

Sidenotes:

13.
At two times.
V. n. 2.

14.
1. *Driuing in Virgo.*
V. n. 3.

15.
The manner of driuing in Virgo.

V.c.5.n.24.

Of the fruit and profit of Bees.

And euer when you be come to a new place, and there haue got out some Bees; leaue there the *Remouer*, and goe directly to the *Receiuer*, and a little beyond: for the Bees will follow you, and thereby the sooner recouer the Hiue.

After this, hauing remoued the *Receiuer* againe, and laid him with the Combes edglong as before; stay till you see the Bees ascended to the highest part of the Combes in the Skirt of the Hiue: and then resting it on the edge of a Kiuer, and turning the Bees toward your readiest hand; with two or three claps force them out into the Kiuer: and then suddenly carry the Hiue to an other place: and when you see more Bees ascended, haue it backe againe to the Kiuer, and there clap them out as before. This iterate as often as you see any store arise vnto the vpmost part of the Hiue-skirt. Which when they cease to doe, the Hiue is well nigh rid of his Bees. Betweene whiles, carrie the Kiuer to the stall, and knocke out the Bees vpon the Table. Then, hauing first loosed the spleets ends, take out the Combes, beginning at one side: and euer when you haue taken out a Combe, wipe off the Bees with a fether of a Goose wing into the Kiuer, and send it in, out of their sight. When the Combes are all gone, set the Hiue and Kiuer before the *Receiuer*, that the Bees may take vp your leauings. As soone as they begin to bee quiet, take away the Bolsters, and cloome vp the Hiue very close, leauing the doore no wider than must needs bee. And when all is done, set open your other stalls: and carry the Hiue and Kiuer from among the Bees.

If you thinke there be not sufficient prouision for this double Stall in that single Hiue, bestow a full Combe or twaine, *v*: as need requireth, of the *Remouers* vpon them: and thus will your Bees delight and prosper in new Wax, which in old corrupt Combes would decay.

In *Aquarius* or *Pisces*, when you haue poised your Hiues, those that you finde by their lightnesse, vnlikely to indure the Spring for lacke of food, you may in like manner driue into such prouided Stalls, as haue fewest Bees: and so will those *Receiuers* be much the better, and cast both the rather, and greater Swarmes. And if by chance, at any time after, you

16. *How to helpe those driuen Bees that want.* V. c. 8. n. 11.

17. *Driuing in Pisces.*

18.
How to reuiue those that are chilled in driuing
V. c. 7. n. 63.

you finde a Stall decayed, thus may you saue them. Otherwise, if he be fit to be fed (*v. c. 8. n. 5.*) feed him, *v. c. 8. n. 15.* and 16.

If, the weather being not warme, you finde some Bees chilled about the Hiue; fill your warme hands full of them, and anone they will flie away to their fellowes. *v:* And if haply any chance to pricke you, (which they will seldom doe) your hand will haue the more vertue to reuiue the rest.

This driuing will not bee so troublesom as the former, because the poore Bees will easily change their hungry home for a place of plentie.

19.
A third kind of Vindemiation.

20.
Exsection vsed at two times.

EXsection or Castration, is a third kinde of taking: which is the cutting out of part of the Combes, part being least for the Bees prouision. And this was to be done at two times in the yeare, *In ortu, & occasu Vergiliarum.*

* *Vergiliarum ortus* after *Columella*, l. 9. c. 14. is the eight and fortieth day from *Æquinoctium vernum:* after *Var.* the foure and fortieth: but then you must vnderstand that they accounted the *Æquinoctium* to bee in the eight degree of *Aries*: (although *Hipparchus*, as *Columella* saith, had then found it to be in the first.) With vs the Cosmicall rising of *Vergiliæ* or *Pleiades*, being seuen starres in the necke of *Taurus* and in the foure and twentieth degree of that signe, is knowne to be in the third of May, the fiue and fiftieth day after the true *Æquinoctium:* which iumpeth with the account of *Columella*. And *Vergiliarum occasus*, being in the same degree of the opposite signe, is vpon the fift day of Nouember.

21.
What part to be exsected is vncertaine.
l. 9. c. 15.

But what part is to be taken, and what least, I finde it not determined. *Priore messe* (saith *Columella*) *dum adhuc rura pastionibus abundant, quinta pars fauorum; posteriore, cum jam metuitur hyems, tertia relinquenda est.* But *Varro* then requireth for their store two third parts; *Vt ne plus tertia pars eximatur mellis, reliquum hyemationi relinquatur.* And *Aristotle* because (as *Columella* granteth) *hic modus non est in omnibus regionibus certus*; doth not prescribe any certaine part, but leauing it to the discretion of the Bee-master, saith,

Hist. an. l. 9. c. 40.

Cum fauos apiary eximunt, cibi tantum relinquant, quantum per hyemem sufficiat: quod si satis sit, seruatur examen; sin minus, vel moritur ibidem, (sine discedat hyemis obstet) vel deserit sedem, si serenum nanciscitur.

This.

This way of taking, as appeareth, was anciently vsed in plentifull Countries, as *Greece, Sicily, Italy,* &c. But the former exsection, to wit, in the Spring, *Aristotle* no where mentioneth: and surely it must needs doe more harme than good, seeing the Hiues are then full of Schadons, which being spild, spill their swarming; and the store of Honie, which they seeke for, is then well spent.

And that also in the Autumne (which yet is the fitter time) seemeth no lesse vnprofitable than troublesom: because the Bees, in the Spring following, if they lacke not Honie to liue on, yet shall they lacke Cells to lay their young in, whereby their breed will bee hindered. And at neither time can it be done without much spoile of Bees.

But howsoeuer it faied with them, for our Country I take it to be verie vnfitting. And therefore I say the lesse of it: referring the curious Reader vnto the fifteenth Chapter of the ninth Booke of *Columella,* and vnto *Georgius Pictorius,* who in his foureteenth Chapter writeth thereof at large.

22. Exsection ancient, but not profitable.

23. Neither first.

24. Nor second.

25. Specially for our Country.

The second part of this Chapter sheweth the trying of (1) Honie and (3) Wax, with the (2) making of Meth or Hydromel.

THE Hiue being housed, *v:* squat it softly against the ground, vpon the sides, not the edges of the Combes: and loosing the ends of the Spleets with your fingers, and the edges of the Combes, where they sticke to the sides of the Hiue, with a woodden Slice; take them out one after an other. Then hauing wiped off the halfe-dead Bees with the Feather of a Goose-wing, breake the Combes presently, while they are warme, into three parts: the first sheere Honie and Wax, the second Honie and Wax with Sandarach, the third dry Wax without Honie. And that they may breake right where you would haue them, marke the places deeply with the edge of your knife. But first prouide necessarie Instruments, as Panns, Kiuers, Tongs, wide Sieues, or Wheat-ridders, a Slice, Kniues, Straining-bagges, a Tub or Kieue, with a Tap, and Tap-waze,

V. p. 1. n. 6.

1 The Combes to be diuided into three parts.

2. Necessarie Instruments being first prouided.

Tap-waze, a hairen Clenſieue, * Honie-pots, Wax-moulds, Meth-barrels, &c.

* Treene veſſels, if they leake not, are better than earthen: which if they breake not by ſome miſchance, the verie force of the Honie is able to cracke.

Theſe things prouided, take out the firſt Combe: and ſetting the Honie-end in a Ridder, reſting vpon Tongs ouer a cleane Pan or Kiuer that will not leake; marke and breake off the firſt part for Honie, and leaue it there: then going to the Kieue fitted with a Tap and Tap-waze, marke and break off the ſecond part for Meth or Hydromel, and leaue it there: and lay the third part aſide for Wax. Then taking out another Combe doe the like, &c. till the Ridder be full.

3. The dreſſing of the firſt part for Honie in two ſhoots

If you meane to make two ſhoots, and ſo two ſorts of Honie; let your aſſiſtant preſently cut the firſt part into thin ſlices, and, without any more adoe, let the Honie runne his firſt ſhoot. But this is to be vnderſtood of the darker part of the Combes: for the pure white Cells in the vpper part (which containe nothing but pure white, or yellowiſh Liue-Honie) you may as well cruſh betweene your hands: and this will be fine ordinarie Honie.

4. The firſt ſhoot for fine ordinary Honie.

5. Or for Virgin-Honie, which is moſt fine.

But if, for ſome ſpeciall vſe, you would haue ſome Honie yet more fine and pure; then onely ſlice the purer part of the Combes, being yet warme with the temperate heat of the Bees, and ſo let the pure Liue-honie runne through a cleane Clen-ſieue. For, *In omni melle quod per ſe fluit, (ut muſtum oleum q,) appellaturq, acœton, maxime laudabile eſt.* Of all Honie that which runneth of it ſelfe, (as new Wine and Oile) and is called * *Acœton*, is moſt commendable.

Nat. hiſt. l. 11. c. 15.

This *Acœton* or fineſt *Nectar*, for his incorrupted puritie, is called Virgin-Honie. *Quod è fauis ſponte primum deſluit, virgineum mel vulgo appellatur.* Plantius in Fernel. l. 7. de Meth. Med.

6. Two ſorts of virgin-honie.

V. c. 6. n. 23.

V. c. 6. n. 14.

Whereof there are two ſorts. The right Virgin-honie is of a Swarme: *v.* that which is of an old Stall, though it runne firſt and of it ſelfe, and were gathered the ſame yeare; yet being partly mixt with other, and laid vp in corrupter veſſels, not in the pure Virgin-Cells, *v.* is but a ſecond or baſtard

bastard Virgin-honie, rather to be called the finest ordinary *v: c. 6. n. 30.*

* *Acates* without drosse or dregges. For χοῖνος doth properly signifie *Cubile* a Bed, and is here vsed for Dregges, because the Dregges of Wine and Oyle and such liquors, are as a Bed or *Ground* whereon they *lye*: in which respect we also call them *Lees* or *Grounds*. But this *Metaphor* to the Dregs of Honie is somewhat Catachrestical: because the Honie beareth his Drosse, and not the Drosse the Honie.

But the hard Corne-honie *v:* in the top of the Combes, specially if there be any store, because it will not runne, you must either wash into the warme Meth-liquor; or melt it with the Cells on a soft fire, or in a hot ouen, or in *Balneo Marie, v:* and so shall you haue the Honie by it selfe, and the Wax swimming aboue it: which you may take away when it is cold. But so this good Honie will become but course: and therefore put it to the second shoot.

    7. Corne-honie got out by water or fire. V. c. 6. n. 27. & 28. V. p. 3. n. 7.

Hauing now taken so many Stalls as you can dresse this euening, *v:* take the rest as soone after as you may, *v:* and let the Honie be all tryed out, before you soake the second part.

    V. * in p. 1. n. 4. V. Ibidem.

The Hiues being rid, carrie them into your Garden (a Pearch at least from any Stall) for the Bees to take vp your leauings : *v:* And haue still by you a paile of faire water to wash your hands in : which water must be for the Meth.

    V. c. 8. n. 13.

When the Honie hath runne what it will ; put this first shoot, whether it be ordinarie or Virgin-honie, into a picked bag, to straine it into his pot by it selfe. And let the remainder bee crusht with warme hands that it may runne againe for a second sort, which is likewise to be strained. That which is left at the last, in the Bags, Ridders, and else-where, wash into the second shoot of the Must *v:* to giue it his iust strength.

    8. The second shoot for course Honie. V. n. 17.

The weather being not warme, set the Honie by the fire to helpe the running.

Otherwise if you be in haste, and meane to make but one sort of Honie ; first slice off the vpper part of the Combe (euen as much as you finde void of Sandarach) for Honie : and presently let your assistant worke all together with warme hands, and so make but one shoot, which afterward

    9. The dressing of the first part in one shoot.

V. n. 7.

is to be strained. *v:* Then going to the Kiue, slice off the second part (euen all that hath Honie) for Meth. And set aside the drie part for Wax. And thus will your Honie be good enough: and such as, compared with the vulgar Honie, may well goe for fine.

10.
The vulgar Honie grosly handled.

For the Honie-men (because thus to cut each Combe into diuers parts, and diuersly to dresse each part, would be too tedious to them that haue much to doe) doe vse to make but one worke of all; with a thin light shouell pounding and compounding the Honie, and Wax, and Bees, and Schadons, and Sandarach all together. And then putting this confused stuffe into a strong hairen Bag, doe with a Presse or Wrenge violently wring out all that will runne. And this, hauing first his season of heat ouer the fire, they put vp into barrels or other vessels to worke: whereby though it bee much purged, yet can it not choose but participate the nature and taste of those things wherewith it was so throughly infected. This done, the Pulse remaining in the Bagge they slice with a shredding-knife into a Trough or other vessel, and all to-wash it and mash it in faire water for Mede: which, when the sweetnesse is all washt out, being crushed dry, the balls they try for Wax.

11.
The working of Honie, and how to helpe it.

Honie: being put vp warme into pots, will in two or three daies worke vp a skum of Wax, Honie, and Drosse together: which being taken off with a spoone, put to the second part. In cold weather the Honie will not worke well without the heat of the fire. The best way is to put it into an ouen after the batch is forth, but not before you can abide to hold your hand vpon the bottom, for feare of ouer-heating the Honie. The next way is to stirre it in *Balneo Mariæ,* v: till it be all warme.

V. p. 3. n. 7.
12.
Diuers Countries yeeld diuers kinds of Honie.

V. c. 6. n. 31.

The differences and degrees of Honie in goodnesse, are as well naturall as artificiall. For as it is made better or worse by the ordering and handling of it; so is it in it selfe better or worse, according to the different condition of the soile where it is gathered. *v.* The Champian-honie is accounted almost twice as good as the Heath-honie, although they bee ordered both alike. For when the vulgar champian is sold

for

for nine pound the Barrell, the like Heath-honie will scarce yeeld fiue. And generally the finer the Wheat and the Wooll is, the finer is the Honie of the same Region: *v.* and therefore no maruaile that the course Heath, hath as course Honie as Wooll.

V. p. 3. n. 4. & c. 6. n. 31.

Good Honie, when it hath wrought, hath these properties whereby it is knowne: It is cleere, odoriferous, yelow like pale gold (but right Virgin-honie is more crystalline at the first, *v.*) sharpe, sweet, and pleasant to the taste, of a meane consistence betweene thicke and thinne, so clammie, that being taken vp vpon your fingers end, in falling it will not part, but hang together like a long string, as that vseth to doe which is clarified. So doth *Iacobus Sylvius* describe the best honie. *Mel optimum sit purum adeo ut totum perluceat, odorum, flavum, acerrimum, dulcissimumq́, gustanti, & iucundissimum, consistentiâ nec crassa nec liquida, sed tam sibi cohaerens ut continuitatem suam, quasi linea longissima, non intercisam servet, si digito attollatur: idem coquendo paucam spumam emittit.* And *Guil. Plantius. Mel probum est quod inter crassissimum & tenuissimum, sit mediocre, sapore dulcissimum, & acerrimum, simulq́, dulcedinis sensum inferens & vellicatu pungens linguam, colore pallidum aut subrutilum, & pellucidum, odoratissimum & recentissimum, quodq́, sublatum non facile ob sequacem lentorem abrumpatur, pondere grave, & inter coquendum spumae parum emittens.* In Fern. l. 7. de Oxymel.

13.
How to know good Honie.
V. c. 6. n. 29.

This good Honie, specially that part which is in the bottom, will in time grow (like vnto Corne-honie, *v.* in the vppermost part of the Combes) hard and white: such as is the Honie of * *Spaine* and *Narbona* in *France*, which is accounted the chiefest, and compared with that of † *Hymettus* and *Hybla*. But this is to be vnderstood of ordinarie Honie: for the pure Virgin Honie will bee neither hard nor white, but changeth his liquiditie and crystalline cleernesse *v.* into a thicke softnesse, and bright yelow colour.

14.
Good Honie with standing waxeth hard and white
V. c. 6. n. 27. & 28.

V. c. 6. n. 29.

* *Quin Hispani & Narbonenses mittunt albissimum & longè praestantissimum, idemq́ praedurum.* Sylu. l. 1. med.

† *Nec Attico aut Hyblae inferius, cum regionis temperatura, & thymi larga luxuries vtrobiq́, consentiant.* Idem l. 2.

And

15.
The best of the Honie is in the bottome.

And alwaies the best part of all Honie is that which is lowest in the vessell. * For as the best oyle is in the top, and the best wine in the middle; so the best Honie is in the bottom. *Mellis exilior pars fluitat, quæ eximenda est : pura vero & valida subsidit*, Arist. Hist. ani. l. 9. c. 40. *In imo vase quod sidit, supernatante pretiosius*. Plan. in Fern. l. 7. de Oxymel.

* As among liquors Oyle excelleth in lightnesse, and Honie in heauinesse; so in both that part is best, which excelleth in his excelling qualitie: and Wine being of a midling weight, is best in the middle.

The weight of these three, one to an other, hath this proportion. Oile is not so heauie as Wine by one tenth part: for if you fill a measure with Wine, and diuide it into ten parts; the same measure of Oile is no heauier than nine of them. And Honie is heauier than Wine by the halfe : for if you fill a measure with Wine, the same measure of Honie will weigh that and halfe so much more. *Quoniam Oleum levius est Vino parte * nona, Mel vero grauius Vino parte dimidia; quæcunq, mensura capit Mellis uncias quindecim, capit Vini uncias decem, & Olei novem*. Fern. Meth. l. 4. c. 6.

* *Ceu potius decima*.

16.
The dressing of the second part for Meth.

The second part of the Combes, appointed for Hydromel or Meth, you must first rid of the sandarach as neere as you can : cutting off that which is by it selfe, and * picking out that which is among the Honie : all which refuse, because of the wax that is with it, cast to the third part.

* If thus to part the Honie and the drosse shall seeme but a tedious piece of worke; you may leaue it vnto them that are expert in it. V. c. 8. n. 13. And make your Meth of more meere Honie.

17.
How to make the Meth-liquor in two sboots.

And then, when the Honie is all strained, and put vp; lay this second part a soake in milk-warme faire water, (that which commeth from heauen is counted best) in the Kiue or Tub with his Tap and Tap-waze. But first wash the drie Combs therein, if any Honie chance to sticke vnto them in the handling : then scrape and wash the Spleets, and lay them aside out of the way : and lastly, crush all the Pulse well betweene your hands, specially that which lieth lowest, and stirring it about all-to-wash it: and so let it steepe all that night.

In

Of the fruit and profit of Bees.

In the morning let this first shoot of the Must or Woort, being made of his iust strength, *v:* runne through the Tap-waze. The Pulse which remaineth, when you haue squeezed out the liquor, breake and wash in fresh warme water in the Kiue, for a second shoot. When it hath lien a while in soake, first take those parcels that swim, and squeezing out the liquor * betweene your hands, lay the balls aside to the third part: (but let your Bees haue the perusing of them) then take vp those that lie in the bottome, and doe likewise: which because they haue most Honie, you must take most paines in washing and crushing them. And while this is doing, let this small liquor runne into a vessell by it selfe. When it is out, wash into it all the remainders of Honie *v:* adding some course Honie, if need be, to make it of his iust strength: *v:* and then let both shoots run together through a † Clensieue into the Kiue againe. And thus shall you lose none of your Honie.

The first shoot.
V. n. 19. & 24.

The second shoot.
V. n. 8.

V. n. 19. & 24.

* If there be much Pulse, vse a presse, when the liquor hath runne what it will.

† The Clensieue is vnto the Tap-waze for Methe, as the Strainer to the Ridder for Honie. *v: n. 7.*

Meth or *Hydromel* is of two sorts: the weaker and the stronger, *Mede* and *Methaglen.*

For the making of *Mede*, if the Must, when it is all together, be not strong enough to beare an Egge the bredth of a two-pence aboue it, then put so much of your course Homie into it as will giue it that strength: which is sufficient for ordinary *Mede.* And afterward vntill night, euer now and then stirre it well about the Kiue.

If you would make a greater quantitie, then must you adde a proportionable measure of water and Honie: namely six of that for one of this. The learned Physitian *Mathias de Lobel* requireth this proportion of six to one to be boiled to foure. His receipt of Spices is Cinamom, Ginger, Pepper, Graines, Cloues, *Ana* two drammes. The second morning put to the Must the scum of the Honie, stirre all together, and stoope the Kiue a little backward. When it hath

18.
Two sorts of Hydromel, Mede and Methaglen.

19.
When the liquor is strong enough for Mede.

20.
What proportion of water to honie.

Of the fruit and profit of Bees.

hath setled an houre or two, draw it ouer to be boiled. And when you see the grounds beginne to come, stay; and let the rest (saue the very thicke grounds, which cast to your Bees) runne into some vessell by it selfe: which, when it is setled, peere out into the boiling vessell through the Clensieue, and cast out these grounds also into your Garden.

21. How, and how long the Must must be boyled.

This Must being set ouer a gentle fire, when you see the Scum gathered thicke all ouer, and the bubbles at the side begin to breake it; hauing slacked the fire, to cease the boyling, skim it cleane. Then presently make a fresh fire to it: and when you see the second skum ready, hauing * slacked the fire againe, take it quickly away: then make to it the third fire, and let it boyle to the wasting of a fourth part, if it bee made of the washing of Combes; and to the wasting of one fift or sixt part, if it be made of cleane Honie: not ceasing in the meane space to take off the Scum as cleane as you can. One houres boyling may suffice: but if the Meth bee of albane Honie, it may as well be done in halfe the time.

* Insteed of twice slacking the fire, you may twice coole the boyling Must with cold Must reserued: or else be sure that it doe boyle still the while onely at one side, and not all ouer.

22. The recipe of Spices.

After all this, put in the spices, viz. to a dozen gallons of the skimmed Must Ginger one ounce, Cinamom halfe an ounce, Cloues and Mace Ana two drams, Pepper and Graines Ana one dramme, all grosse beaten, the one halfe of each being sowed in a bag, the other loose; and so let it boile a quarter of an houre more.

The end of boiling is throughly to incorporate the Boorne and the Honie, and to purge out the drosse: which being once done, any longer boiling is vnprofitable; as diminishing more the quantitie, than increasing the strength and goodnesse of the Hydromel.

23. How the Must is to be vsed when it is boyled.

As soone as it is boiled enough, take it from the fire, and let it a cooling: the next day, when it is setled, poure it out through a Haire-siue or linnen bag, into the Kiue: (reseruing still the Lees for the Bees) and there let it stand couered three or foure daies till it worke; and let it worke two daies.

Then

Then draw it through the Tapwaze, and tun it into a Barrell scalded with Bay-leaues, making the Spice-bag fast at the tap. If there remain much grounds, you may purifie them by boiling and skimming againe as before: but this will neuer be so good as the first: and therefore you may put it by it selfe, or with some remainder of the best, into a small vessell to spend first, before it be soure. If the *Meth* be not much, you may tun it the next day, and let it worke in the Barrell. Being tunned, it will in time be couered with a mother; which, if, by iogging the vessell, or by other meanes, it be broken, the *Meth* will turne soure. But so will it make excellent Vineger, and the sooner, if it be set in the Sun: which the longer you keepe, the better it will be.

Metheglen is the more generous or stronger *Hydromel*: being vnto *Mede* as *Vinum* to *Lora*. For it beareth an Egge the breadth of a groat or six pence: and is vsually made of finer hony, with a lesse proportion of water; namely, foure measures for one: receiuing also in the composition as well certaine sweet and holsome hearbs, as also a larger quantitie of spices: namely, to euerie halfe Barrell or sixteene Gallons of the skimmed Must, Eglantine, Majoram, Rose-marie, Time, Winter-sauourie, *ana* halfe an ounce; and Ginger two ounces, Cinamom one ounce, Cloues and Mace *ana* halfe an ounce, Pepper, Graines, *ana* two drams, the one halfe of each being bag'd, the other boiled loose. So that whereas the ordinarie *Mede* will scarce last halfe a yeere; good *Metheglen* the longer it is kept, the more delicate and holsome it will be: and withall the cleerer and brighter, according to the *Etymon* of the name. v.* in p. 3. n. 23.

He that listeth to know the many and sundry makings of this holsome drinke, must learne it of the ancient *Britaines*: who therein doe passe all other people. One excellent receit I will here recite: and it is of that which our renowmed Queene of happie memorie did so well like, that she would euerie yeere haue a vessell of it.

First, gather a bushell of Sweet-briar-leaues, and a bushell of Tyme, halfe a bushell of Rose-marie, and a pecke of Bay-leaues. Seeth all these, being well washed in a Furnace of faire

24. The making of Metheglen.

25. The Queenes Metheglen.

faire water: let them boile the space of halfe an houre, or better: and then poure out all the water and herbes into a Vate and let it stand till it be but milk-warme: then straine the water from the herbes, and take to euerie * six Gallons of water one Gallon of the finest Honie, and put it into the Boorne, and labour it together halfe an houre: then let it stand two daies, stirring it well twice or thrice each day. Then take the liquor and boile it anew: and when it doth seeth, skim it as long as there remaineth any drosse. When it is † cleere put it into the Vate as before, and there let it be cooled: You must then haue in a readinesse a Kieue of new Ale or Beere, which as soone as you haue emptied, suddenly whelme it vpside downe, and set it vp againe, and presently put in the *Metheglen*, and let it stand three daies a working. And then tun it vp in Barrels, tying at euerie Tap-hole, by a Pack-thread, a little bag of Cloues and Mace, to the value of an ounce. It must stand halfe a yeere before it be drunke.

* If you maruell that so great a quantitie of water is required; it is partly because of the goodnesse of the Honie, which being pure and fine goeth further than ordinarie: and pardy that it may haue the longer time in boiling, before it come to his strength. And therefore some will haue eight parts of water to one of Honie: but then they boile it so much the longer.

† The third part at least being wasted.

26.
The dressing of the third part for Wax.

27.
First boile it with water.

28.
Then straine it by pressing.

THE third Part consisting of wax and drosse, set ouer the fire in a Kettle or Caldron that may easily containe it: and poure into it so much water as will make the wax to swim, that it may boile without burning: and for this cause, while it is seething with a soft fire, stir it often. When it hath sod a while and is throughly melted, take it off the fire, and presently poure it out of the Kettle into a Strainer of thin strong Linnen, or of Twisted-haire, readie placed vpon a Wrenge or Presse: and then winding and doubling the necke of the Bag, lay on the Couer and presse out the liquor as long as any Wax commeth into a Kiuer of cold water, but first wet therewith both the Bag and the Presse, to keepe the Wax from sticking. At the first commeth forth most water, at the last most drosse, in the middle most Wax.

The

Of the fruit and profit of Bees.

The Wax waxing hard, make into Bals, squeesing out the water with your hands. When you haue thus done, presently while they are warme breake all the Balls in (2.) small Crumlets into a Skillet or Kettle set ouer a (3.) soft fire. While it is melting, stir it and skim it with a spoone (4.) wet in cold water: and as (5.) soone as it is melted and skimmed cleane, take it off. And hauing prouided the (6.) mould, first (7.) warme the bottome, specially if the cake be small, and (8.) besmeare the sides with Honie, and then instantly poure in the wax (9) (being as coole as it may run) through a linnen straining-bag. When you come neere the bottome, peere it gently till you see the drosse comming: Which straine into some other mould by it selfe. And when it is cold, either trie againe, or hauing pared away the bottome, reserue it, as it is, for some vse.

When the Wax is in the mould, if any froth yet remaine vpon it, blow it together at one side, and skim it off lightly with a wet spoone.

This done, set not the cake abroad, or where it may coole hastily vpon, but in the warme house: and if it be great, couer the mould with a Platter, as close as you can, to keepe the top from cooling, till the (10.) inward heat be alayed: and so let it stand, not mouing the mould till the cake be cold. If it sticke, a little warming of the vessell or mould will presently loose it: so that it will slip out.

29. Next make the Wax into Balls.

30. Last of all melt it and cast it in a mould.

31. And keepe the cake from cracking.

(1.) So will they breake the smaller with lesse labour. (2.) That the wax may melt the sooner, and all together. (3.) For a rash fire will burne it, and change both colour and qualitie. (4.) That the skum sticke not. (5.) For ouer-heating will discolour the Wax, turning the bright yellow into a darke or reddish colour, not so commendable in Wax: for thereby it is knowne to haue lost of his fatnesse and sweetnesse, and to be the worse for all vses. (6.) Which may be a bason or other vessell of mettall or earth, bigger vpward than in the bottom. (7) Lest the Wax first poured in (which is the best) being presently cooled, lie beneath the drosse. (8.) To keepe the Wax from sticking to the sides of the mould, and consequently to helpe saue the Cake from cracking. For Wax shrinketh in cooling, as new walles in drying: and therefore if the Cake sticke not, it shrinketh together from the sides, and so is lesse than the mould, and whole: but if it sticke fast to the sides, then must it needs cracke, one part shrinking from another (specially if it coole hastily vpon) as it happeneth commonly in great Cakes: For small ones, whose inward heat is alayed

alayed by that time the vpper part beginneth to harden, are not so subiect to cracking. (9.) & (10.) For the great heat of the Wax doth cast vp the watrie vapours mingled with it: Which so long as the vpper part of the Cake continueth liquid, doe easily passe: but when it is hardened, and the Wax yet feruent hot beneath; the vapours being violent through the inward heat, must needs either cracke the Cake, or heaue it and make it hollow, or both, specially if it be verie great: for then will the heat be both stronger and longer: but this is helped by not sticking. v. ante num. (8.)

<small>32. How to know good Wax. Silv. de med. simpl. delectu. lib. 1.</small>

The properties or tokens of good Wax are (1) most yellow, sweet, fat, (2) fast or close, (3) light, (4) pure, and void of all other matter. *Cera sit flavissima, odorata, pinguis, coacta, levis, pura, & alienâ omni materiâ carens.*

(1) That is most light yellow, farthest from red, and neerest to white: for as in gold the deepest, so in Wax and Hony (v.n. 13.) the palest yellow is best: yea the pure Virgin-wax at the first is white. v. c. 6. n. 14. (2) not hollow as the froth is. (3) For Wax, like Oile, is best in the top, as Hony in the bottom (v.n. 15.) except the hollow froth, which is to be skimmed away. v.n. 30. (4) and therefore the bottom, vnto which the drosse doth descend, is not good.

The third part of this Chapter sheweth the singular vertues of (1) Honie, (2) Methe, and (3) Wax for the vse and comfort of man.

<small>1. The properties and vertues of Hony.</small>

Honie is (1) hot and dry in the second degree: it is of (2) subtill parts, and therefore doth pierce as Oile and (3) easily passe into the parts of the bodie: It hath (4) a power to cleanse, and some sharpnesse withall, and therefore it (5) openeth obstructions, it (6) cleereth the brest and lights of those humors, which fall from the head to those parts, it (7) looseth the belly, (8) purgeth the foulnesse of the bodie, and (9) prouoketh Vrine, it (10) cutteth and casteth vp Flegmatike matter, and therfore sharpneth the stomackes of them which, by reason thereof, haue little appetite, (11) it purgeth those things which hurt the cleerenesse of the eyes, (12) it nourisheth verie much, (13) it breedeth good bloud, (14) it stirreth vp and preserueth naturall heat, and prolongeth old age (*reade the note*) (15) it keepeth all things vncorrupt, which are put into it, and therefore (16) Physisians doe temper therewith such medicines as they meane to keepe long:

Of the fruit and profit of Bees.

long: (17.) yea the bodies of the dead, being embalmed with Hony, haue beene thereby preserued from putrefaction. (18.) It is a soueraigne medicament both for outward and inward maladies; (reade the note.) (19.) It helpeth the griefes of the jawes, (20.) the kernels growing within the mouth, (21.) and the squinancie or inflammation of the muscle of the inner gargil, for which purpose it is gargarized, and the mouth washed therewith: (22.) it is drunke against the biting of a Serpent (23.) or mad Dog: and (24.) it is good for them which haue eaten Mushromes, (25.) or drunke Popy, against which euill yet, Rosed-hony is taken warme. (26.) It is also good for the falling sicknesse, and better than Wine, because it cannot arise to the head, as the Wine doth. (27.) Lastly, it is a remedie against a surfet: for they that are skilfull in physicke, when they perceiue any mans stomacke to be ouercome, they first ease it by vomit: and then, to settle his braine, and to stay the noisome fume from ascending to his head, they giue him Honie vpon bread. In respect of which great vertues (28.) the right composition of those great Antidotes, *Treacle*, and *Mithridate* (although they consist, the one of more than fiftie, the other of more than sixtie Ingredients) requireth thrice so much Honie as of all the rest. All which premisses considered, no meruell though the wise King said, My sonne eat Hony, for it is good: *Prou. 24. 13.* that the holy Land is so often and so much commended for flowing therewith: *Exod. 3, 8. 13, 5. 33, 3. Leu. 20, 24. Num. 13, 27. Deut. 8, 8.* and that the Eternall *Immanuel* did vse it for his food. *Isa. 7. 15. Luk. 24. 43.* Yea Honie, if it be pure and fine, v. is so good in it selfe; that it must needs be good, euen for them whose queisie stomackes are against it. But indeed the vulgar hony may well be disliked, as being slutishly handled, & much corrupted with stopping, and Bees both young & old, v. & some with other mixtures also.

(x) Galen. de simpl. med. facult. lib. 9. (2.) aeruginem partium. Simeon Seth. (3.) facile distribuitur. Matthias de Lobel. (4.) detergendi vim, Galen & Seth. (5.) Lobel. (6.) Wikerus, & Freitagius. (7) Seth. & Freitag: & Plancius in Fernelium, de syrupis. (8) Seth. (9.) Seth. & Victorius. (10.) (11) Lobel. (12.) (13.) Freitagius. (14.) ———
Exempla

2.
Against both outward and inward griefes.
Synanche.
Angina.

V. p. 2. n. 4. & 6.

V. p. 2. n. 10.

Exempla citat *Franciscus Valeriola* Medicus locorum com. lib. 3. cap. 13. *Antiochus Medicus, & Telephus Grammaticus* annosi senes Attico melle ex pane alicâve excepto plurimum utebantur. Quos *Galenus* l. 5. de Sanit. tuendâ ceu exempla vitæ senum, quibus esset optimâ victus ratione illæsa senectute, proposuit. Melle itaque senibus plurimum utendum consulo, si modo suæ ipsorum valetudinis rationem habere velint. Et l.3,c.19. Mellis vim proferenda vita, senectæq; longæva agenda, authores affirmant: *Democritus Philosophus,* qui melle oblectatus assidue, in annum centesimum nonum; fati diem distulit, interrogatus, ut scribit *Athenæus,* quomodo quispiam sanus vivere possit. Si exteriora oleo, inquit, interiora melle irriget. Erat etiam Pythagoricorum cibus panis cum melle. *Aristoxenus* eos sine morbo vivere posse asserit, qui ea semper in prandijs comedunt. *Licus* multum Cyrnios vivere scribit, quia, apud Sardonem habitantes, melle semper vescuntur. Nec immerito, quum alimentum sic familiare, & naturæ amicum, dulcedine quam possidet jucundum: obstructiones insuper eximat, infarctusque liberet, ventrem molliat, corporis habitum calefaciat, urinam cieat, thoracem pulmonesq; juvet, tonsillis & uva medeatur. Qua cum tanta possit, vel *Dioscoridis & Galeni* testimonio haud immerito producendæ ætati vitæq; prorogandæ idoneum esse medicamentum asserimus. (15) Seth. & Plin. hist. l.7.c.3. (16.) Pictorius. (17.) Claudius Cæsar scribit hippocentaurum in Thessalia natum eodem die interijsse. Et nos principatu illius allatum illi ex Ægypto in melle vidimus. Pl. hist. l.7.c.3. (18) *Mel calidum siccumque ordine secundo aperit, putredini obsistit, siccat, detergit, expurgatque meatus & ulcera.* Fern. Method. lib. 6, c. 12. Item, *Mel & saccharum potionibus admista vires naturales in morbis sopitas & languentes excitant, & erigunt: nati nunque calorem qui solus morbos concoquit & mitificat, recreant: crassaque extenuando, viscosa extergendo, & obstructa expediendo purgationes quam facillimas præstant.* Plantius in Fern. de Syrupis. Item, *Mel abstergendi vim habet, ora vasorum aperit, humores evocat, qua ratione in sordida ulcera sinusque commodè infunditur, decoctum atque impositum abscedentem carnem glutinat, medetur lichenibus, impetigini coctum cum liquido alumine & illitum. Item aurium sanitati & dolori cum fossili sale trito tepidum instillatur: lendes & fœda capitis animalia illitum necat, oculorum caliginem discutit, faucibus, tonsillis, anginæ collutum gargarizatumque medetur, urinam ciet, auxiliatur tussi; contra haustum meconium cum rosaceo calidum assumitur, adversus venena fungorum & rabiosi canis morsus linctum aut potum proficit: crudum tamen alvum inflat, tussim lacessit: & ea de re despumato utendum.* Dioscorid. lib. 2, cap. 101. (19) (20) (21) (22) (23) (24) (25) Pictorius. Mellis natura talis est, ut putrescere corpora non sinat; Faucibus, tonsillis, anginæ, omnibusque oris desiderijs utilissimum, arescentique in febribus linguæ. Pl. hist. l.22.c.24. (16.) Lobel. (27) Pict. (28) Fernel. Method. l.7.

3.
For whom Hony is best.
V. (14) *in note* 2.

Hony is most fit for (1) old men, *v.* for women and children, for such as are rheumaticke and flegmaticke, and generally for all that are of a cold temperature. (2) To young men, and those that are of a hot constitution it is not so good, because it is easily turned into choller: and yet *Lobel,* faith wee know that Honie taken fasting doth much good vnto some natures,

natures, which haue hot liuers: and in this point he preferreth our English Honie. *Minus* (saith he) *speciosum ac delicatum Anglum: sed quibusdam præsertim saltibus & pascuis, ubi lana commendatior, v. lectum, biliosa excrementa inferius extergendo pellit, & aciei oculorum prodesse putatur.* So that he seemeth to say, that our honie is hurtfull to none; because it purgeth that euill humour, which other Hony, in some bodies, is thought to breed. But the Prouerb saith, *Too much of one thing is good for nothing*: and the Wis-man in his Prouerbs, *It is not good to eat much Honie.* Prou. 25, 27. and in the 16, 6. *Hast thou found Honie? eat so much as is sufficient for thee*: &c. For all Hony often and immoderately taken (3) causeth obstruction, (4) contrarie to his naturall qualitie, and so in time (5) breedeth the scab.

(1)(2) Galen.l.4.simpl.med. dist. 3.c.5. *Item* Seth. Pictorius, & Freitag. (3) Wikerus & Freitagius. (4) *vide* (8) & (18) *supra.* (5) Lobel.

Raw Hony doth (1) more loose the belly, (2) causeth the cough, and (3) filleth the entrailes with winde, specially if it be of the courser sort. Being boiled it is (4) more nourishing, (5) lighter of digestion, and (6) lesse laxatiue, also (7) lesse sharpe and abstersory: for which cause they vse it (8) to knit together hollow and crooked vlcers, and likewise (9) to close other disioined flesh. It is also good against the (10) pleurisie, against the (11) phthisis, and all other diseases of the lungs.

(1)(2)(3) Freitag. Pictor. & Wikerus. (4) Freitag. & Wiker. (5) Wikerus. (6) Pictorius. (7) Gal. & Seth, & Fernelius Methodi. lib.6. c. 12. *Crudum cocto & despumato detergentius quidem multo est & mordacius: sed eo minus agglutinat.* (8) *ad sinuum glutinationes,* Seth. *sinuosorum ulcerum,* Galen. (9)(10)(11) Pictorius.

Honie is clarified by boiling: and that either by it selfe, or else with a fourth part of water, or other liquor. But alwaies in boiling skim it, that it may be pure.

By it selfe you must boile it vntill it will yeeld no more skum, (which will be about halfe an houre) and that with a very soft fire, or in a † double vessell; lest, by ouer-heating, it get a bitter taste, and lest it suddainly run ouer and flame.

4. English Hony. V. p. 2, n. 12.

5. Too much Hony vnholsome.

6. The different operations of raw & boiled Hony.

7. Two waies to clarifie Hony.

† The

* The right skum, which is drosse, is short and brittle: which when it is cleane taken away, the force of the fire will cause the very Hony to rise vp like a skum: but that will then be tougher and more clammy than the drossie skum, and so will all the rest be, when it is cold, as being ouer-boiled: therefore be sure to take it off in time.

† i. a vessell set in a vessell of boiling water, called, *Balneum Marie*, which is best.

V. Fernel. l.4.c. 15.

With water it is to be boiled an houre at the least, euen vn-till the water be euaporated.: *v.* which thing is knowne by the bubbles that rise from the bottom: then, to make it more pure, put into euery pound of Hony the *white of one Egge, and afterward skim it againe in the boiling. The fire may be more feruent at the first; but toward the end it must be slacke: for it is then apt to be set on fire, as the meere Hony, and to become bitter with violent heat.

* *Lesse white may serue, if the Honie be good.*

The course Honie being boiled and clarified hath a pleasant taste, and is comparable for most vses to the purest bottom-honie being raw.

Which pure Honie, if you be disposed to boile it, will aske lesse time to be clarified, as yeelding little or no skum at all: and in taste and vertue it is more excellent.

When your Honie is boiled enough, take it from the fire; and rather too soone, than too late: for if there bee any drosse remaining, you shall finde it in the top, when it is cold: but ouer-much boiling consumeth the spirituous parts of the Honie, and turneth the sweet taste into bitter.

8. *The quintessence of Honie.*

And such is Honie in his owne kinde, both raw and boiled. It is also altered by distillation into a water, which *Raimundus Lullius* that excellent Chymist calleth the Quintessence of Honie. This Quintessence dissolueth Gold, and maketh it potable: likewise any sort of precious stone that is put therein. It is of such vertue, that, if any be dying, and drinke two or three drammes thereof, presently he will re-uiue. If you wash any wound there-with, or other sore; it will heale quickly. It is also good against the Cough, Catarre, and paines of the Milt, and against many other diseases. Being giuen for the space of six and fortie daies together to one that hath the Palsie, it helpeth him. Which thing

9. *The vertues of it.*

Iohn

Iohn Hester a Practicall Chymist, in his Key of Philosophie, professeth himselfe to haue proued. It helpeth also the falling sicknesse, and preserueth the body from putrefaction. Of so maruellous efficacie is this water.

The making of it is after this manner. Take two pound of perfect pure Honie, and put it into a great Glasse, that foure parts of fiue may remaine emptie : * Lute it well with a Head and Receiuer, and giue it † fire vntill there appeare certaine white Fumes : which, by laying wet clothes on the Receiuer and Head, and changing them when they are warme, will turne into a water of a red colour like blood. When it is all distilled, keepe the Receiuer close shut, and let it stand till it be cleere, and of the colour of a Rubie. Then distill it in *Balneo Mariæ* seuen times; and so it will lose this reddish colour, and become yellow as Gold, hauing a great smell and exceeding pleasant.

10. *The making of it.*

* The Lute may be made of Clay, Flockes, and Salt-water, tempered together; or of Meale and whites of Egges.
† The Lute being first dried in the Sunne or by the fire.

Now as Honie is good by it selfe, either altered or in his owne kinde; so is it also being mixt with many other Simples : which here to declare would seeme but tedious and impertinent. Notwithstanding it shall not be amisse, in two or three instances, to giue you a taste of such Confections; and first of those that are inwardly, then of those that are outwardly receiued.

11. *The vertue of Honie in Confections.*

Of the first sort are Marmalade, and Marchpane, preserued Fruits, as Plums, and Cherries, &c. Conserues of Roses, Violets, &c. with Syrups of the like matter.

Marmalade is thus made. First boile your Quinces in their skins till they be soft : then, hauing pared and strained them, mix therewith the like quantitie of clarified Honie : and boile this together till it be so thicke, that in stirring (for you must continually stirre it for feare of burning) you may see the bottom; or, being cooled on a Trencher, it be thicke enough to slice : then take it vp and box it speedily. You may also adde a quantitie of Almonds, and Nut-kernels : also Cinamom, Ginger, Cloues and Mace, of each a like quantitie,

12. *Marmalade made of Honie.*

titie, pounded small and put into the Honie with the Quinces, and in boiling to be stirred together. This is very good to comfort and strengthen the stomack. For want of Quinces you may take Wardens, Peares, or Apples, and specially the Peare-maine, Giliflower, Pipin, and Roiall.

13. Marchpane.

Marchpane may be made after this manner. Boile and clarifie by it selfe, so much Honie as you thinke meet: when it is cold, take to euery pound of Honie the white of an Egge, and beat them together in a Bason, till they bee incorporat together and wax white, and when you haue boiled it againe two or three walmes vpon a fire of coles, continually stirring it, then put to it such quantitie of * blanched Almonds or Nut-kernels stamped, as shall make it of a iust consistence: and after a warme or two more, when it is well mixt, powre it out vpon a Table, and make vp your Marchpane. Afterward you may ice it with Rose-water and Sugar. This is good for the Consumption.

* Steepe them a night in cold water, and the peeles will come off.

14. Preserues.

Preserue Fruits after this manner.

The Damascens, or other Fruit, being gathered fresh from the tree, faire, and in their prime, neither greene or sower, nor ouer-ripe or sweet, with their stalks, but cut short, weigh them, and take their weight in raw fine Honie: and putting to the Honie the like quantitie of faire water, boile it some halfe quarter of an houre, or till it will yeeld no skum: then hauing slit the Damascens in the dented side for feare of breaking, boile them in this liquor with a soft fire, continually skimming and turning them till the meat commeth cleane from the stone, and then take them vp. If the liquor be then too thinne, boile it more: if in the boiling it be too thick, put in more faire water, or Rose-water if you like it. The liquor being of a fit consistence, lay vp and preserue therein your Fruits.

If they be greater Fruits, as Quinces, Pipins, or the like; then shall it bee expedient, when you haue bored them through the middle, or haue otherwise coared them, to put them in as soone as the liquor is first skimmed: and then to let them boile till they be as tender as Quodlings.

Conserues

Conserues of Roses is thus to be made. Take of the juice of fresh Red Roses one ounce, of fine Honie *clarified tenne ounces, boile this together: when it beginneth to boile, adde of the leaues of fresh Red Roses clipt with Scissors in little pieces foure ounces, boile them to the consumption of the juice, and presently put vp the Conserues into some earthen vessell. Keepe it long therein: for in time it waxeth better and better. *Sylv. l. 3. de med. simp. mist.*

After the same manner is made Conserues of Violets. Syrup of Roses make thus. Steepe fresh Roses in hot water ouer the Embers, (the vessell being couered) vntill the Roses wax pale: then straine out the Roses, and put fresh in their places, vntill they also are pale: this doe ten times, or vntill the water be red. And this being purged with Whites of Egges, (to euery pinte of liquor one) boile it gently with like quantitie of fine Honie, vntill it be of conuenient thicknesse. If you prepare it for present vses, the lesse boiling will serue: if you meane to keepe it, it requireth more, for which purpose the sunning of it is good. This purgeth a little, specially being new. *Sylv. Med. S. Mist. l. 3.*

Or thus. Steep one pound of Red Rose leaues in foure pound of water foure and twentie houres. When the water is strained, put vnto it two pound of fine Honie, and boile it to the thicknesse of a Syrup, taking off the skumme as it riseth. It tempereth the hot affections of the braine, it quencheth thirst, it strengthneth the stomacke, it procureth sleepe, and stayeth thin rheumes. *Fern. Meth. lib. 7.*

The Syrup of Violets is made, after the same manner, of fragrant Violets, and steeped vntill the liquor be blew. Being well boiled, it may be kept a yeare without vinewing or corruption. It tempereth and purgeth hot and sharp humours; and therefore is good in a Pleurisie: it expelleth Melancholie, and the effects thereof, as head-ach, waking, dreaming, and heauinesse of heart: it is fit to be vsed before, and after purging. *Plantius in Fernel. meth. l. 7.*

If any man like better to make these Confections with Sugar, let them take the like quantitie of Honie: for Sugar also

---

15.
Conserues.
Mel rosatum.
* Cum vncijs aquæ tribus mediocriter despumetur.
v. n. 7.

Mel violatum.
16.
Syrupi.
Syrup of Roses.

Syrup of Violets.

Of the fruit and profit of Bees.

also hath with his sweetnesse a power to * preserue, as being a † kinde of Honie.

* Condiuntur fructus aut melle, aut Saccharo. *Fernel. Meth. l.4. c.17 & Sylv. simpl. med. mist. l. 3.*
† Saccharum quod ex India & fælici Arabia convehitur, concrescit in calamis: estque mellis species, nostrate certè minus dulce, sedissimilis ei vires obtinens, quod ad abstergendum, desiccandum, & digerendum pertinet. *Galen. de simpl. med. facult. lib. 7.* Item, *Est & quoddam mellis concreti genus quod Saccharum nominant: quodque in India & fælici Arabia in arundinibus reperitur.* Saccharum est mel in arundinibus collectum. *Plin. l. 42. c. 8.* Saccharum mellis species cum sit, siccat quoque & abstergit. *Fern. Meth. l. 6. c. 12.*

17.
Honie to be preferred before Sugar.
V. p. 2. n. 4 & 6.
V. n. 1. & 2.

But in respect of the maruellous efficacie, which fine v. and pure Honie hath in preseruing health, v. that grosse and earthy stuffe is no whit comparable to this Celestiall Nectar. Although some queint and Ladilike palats (whom nothing but that which is farre saught and deare bought can please) vnhappily neglect it. In preseruing Fruits it hath more power through the viscositie thereof. Also Conserues, and Syrups being made with Honie* continue longer, and doe more kindly worke their effects. So that wee may conclude with *Ecclesiasticus, cap. 11. 3. The Bee is little among such as flye: but hir Fruit is the chiefe of sweet things.*

* Ex melle confectus syrupus diutius asseruatur; is quoque magis incidit, ac detergit. Ex Saccharo suavior, sed non æque efficax. *Fern. Meth. l. 4. c. 12.*

18.
Honie good in outward medicines.

Honie is vsed in outward medicines for diuers purposes: * not onely to conteine the other ingredients in forme of a Plaister; but also to open, to cleanse, to dry, to digest, and to resist putrefaction. And therefore it hath the predominance in that excellent Salue, called † *Vnguentum Ægyptiacum*: which serueth to cleanse and mundifie old sores, and to take away both dead and proud flesh. The receipt whereof is this. Of Verdegrece fiue ounces, of strong Vineger seuen ounces, and of Honie foureteene: boile first the Honie and Vineger, and stirre them together: after a little while put in the Verdegrece, being pounded to powder: and then, stirring all together,

19.
A salue for an old sore.

together, let them boile vntill the Ointment haue his iuſt thickneſſe and Purple colour.

* Mel panaciæ & alijs quibuſdam emplaſtris miſcetur, ut corpus præbeat emplaſticum, & præterea ſiccet, tergeat, digerat, à putredine vindicet. *Sylv. de med. ſimp. miſt. l. 3.* Mel calidum ſiccumque ordine ſecundo aperit, putredini obſiſtit, ſiccat, deterget, expurgatque meatus & ulcera; nec ut ſal, corporum ſubſtantiam coarctat. *Pern. Meth. l. 6. c. 12.*

† *Sylv. de med. ſimp. miſt. l. 3. ſect. 10. & Fern. Meth. l. 7.*

Another of like vertue, but not ſo much corroſiue.

20 Another.

Boile a quart of good Ale in a Skillet to halfe a pinte, skimming off the froth as it ariſeth: then put in a ſpoonfull of good Honie: and skimming ſtill as need is, let it boile to the halfe, or till it be ſo clammy, that being taken vp, vpon a ſtickes end it will not drop, but ſtring downe like clarified Honie.

22. The properties and vertues of Mede and Methæglen.

What are the vertues and properties of *Meth* or *Hydromel*, may partly be knowne by that which hath beene ſaid of Honie. For ſeeing Honie is the chiefe matter whereof it is made; it muſt needs, together with the ſubſtance of Honie, participate the naturall qualities thereof. The which, by the purifying in boyling, together with the acceſſe of ſundry holſome ingredients, &c. are rather confirmed and increaſed, than any way extenuated or diminiſhed. Therefore ſaith Lobel, *Mulſum, ubi aqua plurimum mellis non multum, diuturnâ inteſtinâq; mellis ebullitione in vinum longè utiliſſimum abit.* And Pictorius, *Hydromel longâ vetuſtate tranſit in vinum ſtomacho convenientiſſimum.* Meth, when it is old, is a Wine moſt agreeable to the ſtomack: it recouereth (1) the appetite being loſt, it (2) openeth the paſſage of the Spirit or breath, it (3) ſoftneth the belly, it (4) is good for them that haue the cough. (5) If a man take it, not as his ordinarie drinke, but, as Phyſick, now and then; he ſhall receiue much benefit by it againſt Quartan Agues, againſt Cacexies, and againſt the diſeaſes of the braine, as the *Epilepſie*, or the falling Euill: for which Wine is pernicious: it (6) cureth the Yellow Iaundiſe: it (7) is alſo good againſt Hennebane with Milke, and againſt the

V. p. 2. n. 21. 22. & 24.

Winter-

Winter-cherrie, it (8) nouriſheth the bodie. (9) So that many haue attained to long old age, onely by the vſe thereof. And therefore no maruaile that *Pollio Romulus*, who was an hundred yeares old, imputed the greateſt cauſe of his long continued health to this Soueraigne drinke. (10) For being asked of *Auguſtus* the Emperour, by what meanes eſpecially he had ſo long preſerued that vigor both of minde and body, his anſwer was, *Intus mulſo, foris oleo.*

(1.2.3.4.) *Piſterius, & Plin. hiſt. l. 22. c. 24.* (5) *Lobel.* (6.7.8.9.10.) *Plin. hiſt. l. 22. c. 24.*

22. Meth *much vſed of the ancient Britaines.*

The ſame thing is more manifeſted by the generall example of the ancient *Britaines*: who, aboue all other Nations, haue euer beene addicted to *Meth* and *Metheglen*. For vnder Heauen there is no fairer people of complexion, nor of more ſound and healthfull bodies. Of whoſe *Metheglen Lobel* writeth thus; *Cambricus ille potus Methagla, non patrio, uti putant illi, sed* Græco nomine dictus, eſt altera liquida & limpida Septentrionis theriaca.*

23. *Whence Meth and Metheglen haue their name.*

* *Hydromel* borealibus, quibus vineta deſunt, pro vino eſt. Ideoque Cambris à μέϑυ *Meth* dicitur. Pro qua voce Germani (quibus Teutonico idiomate ſolenne eſt D pro Th vſurpare, ut in *De, Diſ, Dat, Dander*; pro *The, This, That, Thunder*) adeoque Angli etiam, alijque populi boreales à Germanis oriundi, corruptè dicunt *Mede*. Medonis plurimum bibunt Poloni & Lituani, quod Melle abundent, inquit Andreas Matthiolus. *Metheglen* vero, quod *Hydromel* eſt præſtantius, à μέϑυ αιγλήες ſiue contractè αιγλᾶν, id eſt, vinum ſplendidum denominatur: quod (modò vetus ſit & ritè confectum) non minus colore ſuccino, quam ſapore & virtute præ vinis vinaceis ſplendeat. De hoc Mercator in *Transylvania. Ex melle incolæ delicatum potum conficiant: qui etiam rerum peritis, vinum Creticum ceu Malvaticum opinantibus, facile imponat.* Et Vlyſſes Aldrovander de mulſo. *Fit præterea ex melle potus genus toti nunc Sarmatiæ, viciniſque Moſcovitis familiare. Unde etiam per totam Europam fere, præcipuè per Germaniam devehitur. Decoquitur multipliciter aromate addito,* (Medonem vocant) *tam * nobile ſæpe ut lautiorum tantum menſarum ſit, & primates ſolùm bibant.* Item Mercator in *Bohemia* de civitate *Egra. Tota ornatiſſima, ſita pulcherrimis eſt. Intus pulchris ædificijs, civili vrbanoque populo, magnifico & eximia virtute præſtantibus viris illuſtris: foris vero amæniſſimis ac fæcundiſſimis hortis & agris varijſque pomorum ac fructuum generibus luxuriat. Claret hodie hæc civitas ob Medonem* (potionem ex melle) *qui nullâ paratur quam in hac civitate excellentior.*

* Methæglen.

And as good and old *Metheglen* excelleth all Wines, as well

well for pleasantnesse in taste, as for health; so being burnt it is better than any burnt Wine, for comforting and setling of a weake and sicke stomach, and for recreating the naturall heat.

The manner of burning it (if you know not) may be this. First set on the fire a * deepe Skillet or Kettle, almost full of water: when it boileth, put in a Pewter pot full of *Methaglen*: before that beginneth to boile, skimme it and put in two or three bruised Cloues, and a branch of Rose-marie: then beat the yolke of an Egge in a dish, put vnto it a spoonefull of the *Meth* cold, and stirre them together to keep the yolke from curdling; then put to that a spoonfull of the hot *Meth*: and after that an other, and an other, alwaies beating them together: and then, some and some, put all into the pot, still stirring it about. Then as soone as it boileth, take vp the pot, and, sauing your hands harmeleffe, powre it into another warme pot of like capacitie, firing it as it runneth: and so brue it till it will burne no more. A *Methaglen*-posset is of the like vertue.

* The deeper the pot standeth, the sooner it boileth. You may, for a need, set the pot on the Harth in the midst of hot Embers: but take heed the flame melt not the Pewter.

WAx hath no certaine elementar qualitie, but is a meane betweene (1) hot and cold, and betweene dry and moist. It (2) mollifieth the sinewes, it (3) ripeneth and resolueth Vlcers. (4) The quantitie of a Pease in Wax, being swallowed downe of Nurces, doth dissolue the Milke curded in the paps, and (5) ten round peeces of Wax, of the bignesse of so many graines of Millet or Hempseed, will not suffer the Milke to curdle in the stomach.

Moreouer, it maketh the most excellent; light fit for the vses of the most excellent; for cleernesse, sweetnesse, neatnesse, to be preferred before all other: Which *Staliger* in his *Ænigmata*, giuing it the precedence, doth intimate;

24. *The properties and vertues of naturall Wax.*

Aut Apis, aut Hircus, vel pinguia viscera Piri
Ostendere diem, post simul ante diem.

(1) *Galen*

(1) *Galen de simp. med. facul. l. 7.* (2, 3, 4, 5.) *Georgius Pictorius. Cera flava magis emollit, relaxat, dolorem soluit: eoque illa utimur ad abscessus calefaciendos, emolliendos, concoquendos, & maturandos. Iohannes Guintherius Andernacus. Omnis cera mollit, calefacit, explet corpora: recens melior. Datur in sorbitione dysentericis, favique ipsi in pulte aliæ prius tostæ: adversatur lactis naturæ; ac milij magnitudine decem grana ceræ hausta, non patiuntur coagulari lac in stomacho. Si inguen tumeat, albam ceram in pube fixisse remedio est. Nec hujus usus, quos mixta alijs præstat, enumerare medicina potest. Pli. nat. hist. li. 22. cap. 24.*

25. Artificiall Wax.

This naturall yellow Wax is by Art, for certaine purposes, made white, red, and greene.

26. To make white Wax.

Wax is whited after this manner. Take the whitest and purest Wax: which, being cut into small peeces, put into an earthen vessell, and poure Sea-water or Brine into it, as much as may suffice to boile it. And cast in also a little Niter: all this set ouer a soft fire. When it hath boiled vp twice or thrice, lift the vessell from the fire, and, the wax being presently cooled with cold water, take it out: and when you haue scraped off the drosse, if any such hang on, and put it into other Salt water, seeth it againe. And hauing boiled vp twice or thrice, as before, lift it from the fire againe. And then take the bottom of an other earthen pot, or a little round board with a handle in the middle like a Churn-staffe, but without holes: and hauing first wetted the bottom of it in cold water, dip it into the hot vessell, and assoone as this wet bottom toucheth the wax, pull it out againe, and you shall haue sticking to the bottom a thin cake: which when you haue taken off, wet the bottom againe, and dip it as before: and thus doe till you haue taken vp all the wax in cakes. These cakes hang in the open aire vpon a line drawne through them, so that they may not touch one an other, besprinkling them with water in the Sun-shine vntill they be white. If any man would haue wax whiter, let him boile it oftner, and doe all other things in like manner as before.

Hanc dealbandæ ceræ rationem docuit Dioscorides, l. 2. c. 105.

27. To make red Wax.

To make Wax red, Take to one pound of Wax, in Summer three ounces of cleere Turpentine, in Winter foure. These

These dissolue ouer a soft fire, and by and by take it off to coole a little. Afterward mix therewith the red Root of *Anchusa* or *Vermilion*, well ground on a Marble or Glasse, and sweet Oile, of each one ounce: stirre all those and mix them well together. For want of *Vermilion*, they take three times so much red Lead, but that is not so good.

*Cinabrium.

Minium.

28. *To make greene Wax.*

To make greene Wax, take in stead of *Vermilion*, the like quantitie of *Vert-degreete*.

29. *Oile of Wax.*

And such is Wax in his kinde, both Naturall and Artificiall. Naturall Wax is altered by distillation into an Oile of maruellous vertue. *Raymund Lully* greatly commendeth it, prouing it to be rather a Cœlestiall or Diuine medicine than humane; because in wounds it worketh miraculously: which therefore is not so well allowed of the common Chirurgians. For it healeth a wound, be the same neuer so wide and big, being afore wide-stitched vp, in the space of eleuen daies or 12. at the most. But those that are small, this Oile healeth in three or foure daies, by annointing onely the wound therewith, and laying on a cloth wet in the same. It stayeth the shedding of the haire, either on the head or beard, by annointing the place therewith.

30. *The vertues of it.*

Also for inward diseases, this Oile worketh miracles; if you giue one drachme at a time to drinke with white Wine: for it is excellent in prouoking vrine which is stopped, it helpeth stitches and paines in the loines, it helpeth the cold Gout, or Sciatica, and all other griefes comming of cold.

31. *The making of Oile of Wax.*

The making or drawing of this Oile is on this wise. Take of pure new yellow Wax so much as will halfe fill your Retort or Body of Glasse: melt it on the fire, and then powre it into sweet Wine, wherein let it soake: wash it often, and wring it between your hands: then melt it againe and powre it into fresh Wine, wherein soake it, wash it, and wring it as before: and this doe seuen times, euery time putting it into fresh Wine. When thus you haue purified the Wax,

V. n. 10.

to euery pound thereof adding foure ounces of the powder of red Bricke finely bruised; put it all together into your Retort of Glasse well luted: *v.* then set the Retort into an Earthen pot, filling it round about and beneath with fine sifted Ashes or Sand; and set the pot with the Bodie in it on a Furnace, and so distill it with a soft fire. And there will come forth a faire yellow Oile, the which will congeale in the receiuer like Pap when it is cold. If you should rectifie this oile or distill it often, vntill it will congeale no more, then shall you make it ouer hot to take inwardly, and so quicke in the mouth, that you cannot drinke it downe. In the comming forth of this Oile, shall appeare in the Receiuer the foure Elements, the Fire, the Aire, the Water, and the Earth, right maruellous to see.

32.
The vertue of Wax in compound medicines.

So vertuous is Wax by it selfe, both in his owne kinde, and altered by distillation. It is moreouer of great vse mixed with others, and is the ground and foundation of *Cere-clothes* and *Salues*: whereof to set downe two or three examples shall not be amisse.

33.
A Cere-cloth.

A *Cere-cloth* or *Ceratum*, so called of *Cera*, doth consist chiefly of Wax and Oile mixed in such proportion, as may make the ointment of iust consistence: and therefore (*s*) being made in Summer, or compounded with Turpentine, Lard, Gum, Marrow, or any liquid thing, a greater quantity of Wax is required: and being made in Winter, or compounded with Rozin, Pitch, Metals, dried Hearbs, Powders, or any dry thing, a lesse quantity of Wax than Oile is conuenient.

V. n. 7.

The Ingredients being prepared, first melt the Wax, and whatsoeuer else of like nature, as Pitch, Suet, &c. in the Oile ouer a gentle fire, or in a double vessell, *v.* for feare of burning: when they are melted together, put in the Powders and other like Ingredients, if there be any; and assoone as you haue stirred them well together, (before the liquor be very hot) set it a cooling, and make your *Cere-cloth*.

A *Cere-*

A *Cere-cloth* to refresh the wearied Sinewes and tired Muscles is thus to be made. Take (1) Oile and Wax *ana* two ounces, Turpentine two drams, & Hony halfe an ounce.

To comfort the stomacke and helpe concoction, make a *Cerat* thus. Take (2) Oile of Masticke, of Mint, of Wormwood, of Nutmeg, and *Speeke, or any of these, and a convenient quantitie of Wax.

For the wormes in the belly of a childe or other, Take Wax and Rozin *Ana* one ounce, Treacle one spoonfull, Aloes two drams. Melt & mingle the Wax & Rozin together in a Pewter-dish, vpon a Chafing-dish and Coales: being melted, skimme it cleane: then taking it off, put in the Treacle, and stirre it among: then hauing pounded the Aloes to powder, strew it vpon, and stirre it in, so that it may not clod. And if, by this time, it be too cold to come from the dish; warme it a little vpon the Chafing-dish againe: then hauing wet the Table with Butter, poure it thereon, and worke it together with your knife: and so make it vp in a Roule. To make the Dish cleane, warme it, and wipe it with a woollen cloth.

This *Cerat* is to be applied to the Brest, and to the Nauell. For the Nauell, spread it vpon a round peece of Leather three inches ouer, with a hoale in the middle; that, the Nauell comming through, the plaister may lie both closer and faster: and for the Brest, spread it vpon a square peece three inches broad, and twice so long: and lay it athurt the Brest, betweene, or close vnder the Paps.

This doe twice together, and let the Plaisters remaine each time vpon the place, vntill the heat of the stomacke haue dried them, and made them loose: which, in some that are much troubled with the wormes, will be within foure and twentie houres; although in some they will sticke a whole weeke together.

(1) Fern. Meth. lib. 4. c. 19. & 20. (2) Fern. Meth. l. 4. c. 19. (3) Fern. Meth. l. 5. c. 22.

For example of a Salue, take *Emplastrum de janua*, maruellous effectuall in curing greene wounds and new vlcers.

34. *A Cere-cloth to refresh the Sinewes and Muscles.*

35. *A Cere-cloth to comfort the stomacke.*

*Nardinum.

36. *A Cere-cloth for the Wormes.*

37. *A Salue for a greene wound.*

It aſſwageth inflammation, it cleanſeth, it cloſeth, and filleth with fleſh, and maketh whole. It is thus made: * Take the juice of Parſley, Plantan, and Betonie, *ana* one pound: Wax, Pitch, Rozin, and Turpentine, *ana* halfe a pound: boile the Wax, Pitch, and Rozin in the Iuices, ſoftly ſtirring all together, vntill the quantitie of the Iuices be waſted: and then taking them off the fire, put in the Turpentine, and mix it with the reſt.

Another of like effect.

An other.

Take Deere or Mutton-Suet, Wax, Rozin, *ana* two ounces: Turpentine one ounce: boile theſe together, and skim them: then take this liquor from the fire, and, when it is ſomewhat cooled, put in two handfulls of the Tops of vnſet Hyſop, and ſtirre it about, and ſetting it ouer the fire againe, boile it ſoftly about a quarter of an houre, till it be greene: and then ſtraine it, and let it coole. This is chiefly to bee made in *May*, becauſe then the Hyſop is in his prime.

* Sylvius de medicam. ſimpl. miſt. lib. 3. & Fern. Meth. lib.

PSAL. III. V. 2.

CPSIA information can be obtained
at www.ICGtesting.com
Printed in the USA
BVOW08s0435170317
478573BV00007B/228/P